ROUTLEDGE LIBRARY EDITIONS: COLONIALISM AND IMPERIALISM

Volume 39

PARLIAMENT AS AN EXPORT

PARLIAMENT AS AN EXPORT

Edited by
SIR ALAN BURNS

LONDON AND NEW YORK

First published in 1966 by George Allen & Unwin Ltd.

This edition first published in 2023
by Routledge
4 Park Square, Milton Park, Abingdon, Oxon OX14 4RN

and by Routledge
605 Third Avenue, New York, NY 10158

Routledge is an imprint of the Taylor & Francis Group, an informa business

© 1966 George Allen & Unwin Ltd.

All rights reserved. No part of this book may be reprinted or reproduced or utilised in any form or by any electronic, mechanical, or other means, now known or hereafter invented, including photocopying and recording, or in any information storage or retrieval system, without permission in writing from the publishers.

Trademark notice: Product or corporate names may be trademarks or registered trademarks, and are used only for identification and explanation without intent to infringe.

British Library Cataloguing in Publication Data
A catalogue record for this book is available from the British Library

ISBN: 978-1-032-41054-8 (Set)
ISBN: 978-1-032-43684-5 (Volume 39) (hbk)
ISBN: 978-1-032-43686-9 (Volume 39) (pbk)
ISBN: 978-1-003-36842-7 (Volume 39) (ebk)

DOI: 10.4324/9781003368427

Publisher's Note
The publisher has gone to great lengths to ensure the quality of this reprint but points out that some imperfections in the original copies may be apparent.

Disclaimer
The publisher has made every effort to trace copyright holders and would welcome correspondence from those they have been unable to trace.

PARLIAMENT AS AN EXPORT

―――――

SIR HILARY BLOOD SIR DENIS BROGAN
IVOR BULMER-THOMAS SIR ALAN BURNS
SIR CECIL CARR S. A. DE SMITH
SIR JOHN FLETCHER-COOKE C. A. S. S. GORDON
SIR JOHN CRAIK HENDERSON SIR FRANCIS LASCELLES
E. C. S. WADE

EDITED BY SIR ALAN BURNS

London
GEORGE ALLEN & UNWIN LTD
RUSKIN HOUSE MUSEUM STREET

FIRST PUBLISHED IN 1966

This book is copyright under the Berne Convention. Apart from any fair dealing for the purposes of private study, research, criticism or review, as permitted under the Copyright Act, 1956, no portion may be reproduced by any process without written permission. Inquiries should be made to the publishers.

© *George Allen & Unwin Ltd.* 1966

PRINTED IN GREAT BRITAIN
in 11 *point Bell type*
BY UNWIN BROTHERS LTD
WOKING AND LONDON

PREFACE

In the Preface to *Parliament: A Survey*, I explained the origin of the Group which was formed to study Parliamentary Government in Britain, and which in 1915 under the Editorship of Lord Campion, the distinguished Clerk of the House of Commons, published *Parliament: A Survey*, which has apparently proved useful and has been repeatedly reprinted.

It was later decided by the Group to publish another book dealing with the adoption by overseas countries and particularly the Commonwealth countries of our Parliamentary system, and this book is the result. Unfortunately in the interval four of the original contributors have died—Lord Campion, Mr Amery, Mr Dale and Mr G. M. Young, and of the remaining eight original contributors, all have contributed to the new volume with the exception of Lord Salter and Mr Arthur Goodhart, who, though sympathetic to the project, were prevented by pressure of other work from contributing. The Group has, however, been fortunate in being able to obtain the services as editor of Sir Alan Burns, who has wide experience of the Commonwealth countries including the Governorship of the Gold Coast, Acting Governor of Nigeria, and permanent United Kingdom representative on the Trusteeship Council of the United Nations. The Group has also been fortunate in obtaining as new members and as contributors, Sir Hilary Blood, Sir John Fletcher-Cooke, Professor de Smith, and Mr C. A. S. S. Gordon, all of whom have intimate experience or knowledge of the Commonwealth countries.

J. J. CRAIK HENDERSON
27th January, 1966

N.B.
This volume was passed for press before the coup d'état in Ghana and the suspension of the Uganda constitution in February, 1966. References to Ghana and Uganda must therefore be understood as relating to conditions in those countries before these events.

CONTRIBUTORS

SIR HILARY BLOOD, G.B.E., K.C.M.G., M.A.

Colonial Civil Service, 1920–42; Governor of the Gambia, 1942–47; of Barbados, 1947–49; and of Mauritius, 1949–54. Constitutional Commissioner, British Honduras, 1959; and Zanzibar, 1960. Chairman of Constitutional Commission, Malta, 1960.

PROFESSOR SIR DENIS BROGAN, LL.D., M.A., F.B.A.

Professor of Political Science, Cambridge, and Fellow of Peterhouse. Author of books and articles on American and French political problems. (Contributor to *Parliament: A Survey*.)

IVOR BULMER-THOMAS, M.A.

Writer. Member of Parliament for Keighley, 1942–50. Parliamentary Secretary to Ministry of Aviation, 1945–46; Parliamentary Under Secretary of State for the Colonies, 1946–47. Served with United Kingdom Delegation to the United Nations, 1946–47. (Contributor to *Parliament: A Survey*.)

SIR ALAN BURNS, G.C.M.G.

Colonial Civil Service, 1905–34. Governor of British Honduras, 1934–39; and of the Gold Coast, 1941–47. Under Secretary of State for the Colonies, 1940–41. Served with United Kingdom Delegation to the United Nations, 1947–56.

SIR CECIL CARR, K.C.B., Q.C.

Counsel to the Speaker of the House of Commons, 1943–55. Chairman of Statute Law Committee, 1943–47. Author of books and articles on Administrative Law in England and delegated legislation. (Contributor to *Parliament: A Survey*.)

PROFESSOR S. A. DE SMITH, M.A., PH.D.

Professor of Public Law in the University of London since 1959. Author of *The New Commonwealth and its Constitutions* and other works on constitutional and administrative law. Constitutional Commissioner for Mauritius, 1961–.

SIR JOHN FLETCHER-COOKE, C.M.G., M.A., M.P.

Member of Parliament for Southampton (Test) since 1964. Served in Colonial Office and Colonial Civil Service, 1934–61. Constitutional Commissioner, Malta, 1946. Served with United Kingdom Delegation to the United Nations, 1948–51. Minister for Constitutional Affairs and subsequently Deputy Governor of Tanganyika, 1956–61. Visiting Professor (African Affairs), University of Colorado, 1961–62.

C. A. S. S. GORDON, M.A.

Fourth Clerk at the Table in the House of Commons since 1962. Author of articles on parliamentary matters.

SIR JOHN CRAIK HENDERSON, KT.

Formerly Professor of Mercantile Law, University of Glasgow, and a Member of Parliament. (Chairman of Group responsible for *Parliament: A Survey*.)

SIR FRANCIS LASCELLES, K.C.B., M.C., M.A.

Clerk of the Parliaments, 1953–58. (Contributor to *Parliament: A Survey*.)

PROFESSOR E. C. S. WADE, Q.C., LL.D., F.B.A.

Emeritus Downing Professor of the Laws of England, Cambridge University, and Fellow of Gonville and Caius College. Member of Law Reform Committee, 1952–63. Author of a text-book and articles on constitutional law. (Contributor to *Parliament: A Survey*.)

CONTENTS

	Page
PREFACE	7
THE CONTRIBUTORS	9

CHAPTER

 I. *The History of Commonwealth Parliaments*   13
  BY SIR ALAN BURNS

 II. *The Drafting of Laws*   38
  BY SIR CECIL CARR

 III. *Procedural Links between Commonwealth Parliaments*   59
  BY C. A. S. S. GORDON

 IV. *The Position of Members of Parliament*   80
  BY SIR JOHN CRAIK HENDERSON

 V. *The Party System*   103
  BY IVOR BULMER-THOMAS

 VI. *Parliament, the Executive and the Civil Service*   142
  BY SIR JOHN FLETCHER-COOKE

 VII. *The Second Chamber in Parliaments of the Commonwealth*   166
  BY SIR FRANCIS LASCELLES

 VIII. *The Possibilities of the Presidential System in Africa*   190
  BY PROFESSOR SIR DENIS BROGAN

 IX. *Legislatures under Written Constitutions*   208
  BY PROFESSOR S. A. DE SMITH

 X. *Parliament and the Courts*   229
  BY PROFESSOR E. C. S. WADE

 XI. *Parliaments in Small Territories*   246
  BY SIR HILARY BLOOD

INDEX   264

Chapter I

THE HISTORY OF COMMONWEALTH PARLIAMENTS

BY ALAN BURNS

I

It is obviously impossible to compress within the limits of a single chapter separate histories of the various Commonwealth parliaments. It is, however, practical to consider the units in groups, bearing in mind the infinite variations within each group. For convenience, therefore, the history of Commonwealth parliaments will be dealt with under four heads, the original colonies, the 'old' Dominions, the Indian sub-continent, and the newer colonial territories.

A few definitions at this stage may be useful. The constitutions of the first English colonies of settlement in North America, the North Atlantic and the West Indies, under what became known as the 'old colonial system', provided for 'representative government'. These constitutions were modelled on that of England *of that period*, with a governor representing the sovereign, a nominated Council as the Upper House of the legislature, and an elected House of Assembly. The franchise was very limited (as in England at that date) and excluded all the slaves and most of the free coloured population as well as the poorer whites; hence the Houses of Assembly could hardly be regarded as truly representative. Nor was the Executive (the governor and his advisers) in any way responsible to the local legislature as the governor could only be removed from office by the sovereign, acting on the advice of his ministers in the United Kingdom. The governor could veto Bills passed by the Houses of the legislature but could not compel the House of Assembly to pass a Bill against its will. The sovereign could also disallow a Bill even after the governor had given it his assent. This, then, is what was curiously called representative government.

In 'responsible government' the elements were the same except that a Cabinet replaced the Executive Council which had previously advised the governor. The Cabinet, as in the United Kingdom today, was responsible to the local legislature, and the governor was bound to accept the advice of the Cabinet except on certain 'reserved' subjects such as defence. As the local legislature was precluded from legislating on external affairs, which were still dealt with by the metropolitan government, this could properly be described as 'internal self-government' or 'home rule'.

In Crown Colony government there is only one legislative House, generally called the Legislative Council. In the beginning all the members of this Council were appointed (nominated) by the Crown and a majority of these nominated members were civil servants, usually styled 'official members', bound to support the policy of the governor (as representing the Crown) who was thus able to control the legislature as well as the executive. As time passed the composition of the Legislative Council was altered in various ways. Sometimes the number of official members was reduced so that they were outnumbered by the nominated non-officials, and sometimes a few elected members were admitted, while at a later date the number of elected members often exceeded that of the official and nominated unofficial members together. In all such cases, however, Crown control was preserved, for use in emergencies, by investing the governor with 'reserve powers' which allowed him to over-ride the Council and to enact legislation without the consent of its members. This was a positive power, additional to the negative power he possessed to veto legislation.

'Dominion status' is the expression used in referring to the final stage through which former colonies passed on their way to independence, but the expression has never been formally defined. The Westminster Statute of 1931 declared that **Canada, Newfoundland, Australia, New Zealand, South Africa**

HISTORY OF COMMONWEALTH PARLIAMENTS 15

and the Irish Free State were Dominions (which they had been informally called since the beginning of the century) but nowhere was there any legal definition of Dominion Status. Newfoundland, which reverted to Crown Colony status in 1934, is now part of the Dominion of Canada.

While the above definitions are sufficient for general guidance, it must be emphasized that no one of them has the same precise meaning in connection with every territory. 'Crown Colony' obviously has its different shades of meaning, and even 'responsible government' could be variously interpreted in individual Dominions.

II

The constitutional progress of the different groups has varied considerably. In the original colonies of settlement the first stage was representative government. There was then, in most cases (as regards those remaining in the empire), a constitutional retrogression to Crown Colony rule, and this gradually changed to a form of more genuine representative government followed by responsible government. In the 'old' Dominions, after a very brief period of rule by the governors, representative government was introduced followed by limited responsible government which led to virtual independence even before this was legally recognized. No part of the Indian sub-continent was ever considered to be a colony, but a form of Crown Colony rule existed in effect until recent times. In the newer colonial territories Crown Colony rule was practised from the beginning of British administration until after the second world war, when representative and then responsible government followed quickly.

The independence of the 'old' Dominions had been legally recognized as a fact by the Statute of Westminster in 1931: the independence of other nations of the Commonwealth was in each case explicitly declared by a separate Act of the United Kingdom parliament.

The original West Indian (and North American) colonies, of great importance in early days, were later overshadowed by the larger territories in Asia and Africa which came under

British rule, but it should not be forgotten that it was in these small islands (and in the mainland colonies now included in the United States) that the principle of representative government in the oversea dependencies was first recognized. It has been said that the West Indies was a constitutional laboratory where representative government, as it then existed, was proved to be a failure and where Crown Colony government was developed. The so-called representative institutions failed because they were not truly representative, but the precedent established in these first English colonies was later followed more successfully in the Dominions. The Crown Colony system developed in the West Indies was afterwards applied in the new colonial territories throughout the world.

III

The Original Colonies. When the first English colonies were established in North America, Bermuda and the West Indies, it was taken for granted, and later generally asserted, that the emigrants to these countries took with them all the rights of Englishmen as established by the common law and other legislation then in force in England. In the words of Blackstone, 'It hath been held, that if an uninhabited country be discovered and planted by English subjects, all the English laws then in being, which are the birthright of every subject, are immediately there in force'.[1] The rights which were particularly valued were those of trial by jury, of *habeas corpus*, and later of a form of self-government through a local legislature constituted on lines similar to those of the English parliament.

The first charter of Virginia, granted by James the First in 1606, declared that all 'our Subjects which shall dwell and inhabit within' any English colony, and their descendants, 'shall have and enjoy all Liberties, Franchises and Immunities ... as if they had been abiding and born within this our realm of England', and the Council of Virginia was given authority 'lawfully from time to time (to) constitute, make and ordaine such constitutions, ordinances and officers, for the better order, government and peace of the people'.

[1] Sir William Blackstone, *Commentaries on the Laws of England* (1765).

Provision was thus made, in Virginia and later in other colonies, for a legislature which, in the first instance, consisted only of a nominated Council presided over by a governor. It was not long, however, before provision was made for an Assembly, the members of which were elected by the freeholders in the colony, the first Assembly being constituted in Virginia in 1619.

Jamaica, although it was a colony by conquest, having been taken from the Spaniards in 1655, was treated as though it had been settled, and the historian Edward Long, who had been a judge in Jamaica, describes the constitution of that colony, which was similar to others of the period:

'The form of government here resembles that of England almost as nearly as the condition of a dependent colony can be brought to resemble that of its mother country. . . . There is somewhat the same resemblance preserved in the forms of our legislature. It is composed of three estates, of which the governor, as representing the king, is head. Having no order of nobility here, the place of a house of peers is supplied by a council of twelve gentlemen appointed by the king, which in the system of our legislature forms the Upper House. The Lower House is composed, as in Britain, of the representatives of the people elected by the freeholders.'[1]

The similarity is obvious but must be considered with certain reservations. The governors had neither the prestige nor the powers of seventeenth and eighteenth century kings, as they took their orders from the ministers of these monarchs, and the Councils also lacked the prestige of the House of Lords. The Assemblies more closely resembled their model and, as we shall see, they quickly laid claim to all the privileges of the House of Commons.

It is, moreover, important to remember that the early colonial legislatures were modelled, not on the British parliament as we know it today with members elected to the House of Commons by universal suffrage, but on the English parliament of Stuart times. In most colonies the franchise was restricted to male freeholders, the landless whites and the

[1] Edward Long, *A History of Jamaica* (1774).

African slaves having no opportunity to elect representatives. Even as late as 1963 the right to vote for members of the Bermuda House of Assembly was accorded only to those who owned freehold property in the colony of not less than £60 in value.

Even for those who had the right to vote there was (except in South Carolina) no secret ballot. In 1754 a Jamaican 'Act for choosing the Members of the Assembly of this Island by Ballot' was disallowed by the Crown on the advice of the Law Officers who considered 'it would be dangerous and imprudent to make so great an Innovation'. South Australia was the first part of the old empire to legalize the secret ballot in 1856, a procedure which was not introduced to Britain until 1872.

Although the English parliament from time to time passed laws which were applicable to the settled colonies, the grant of a constitution to a territory, whether by charter to a company, by letters patent to a proprietor, or by the governor's commission in a 'royal' colony (supplemented by letters patent and royal instructions) was invariably, save during the period of Cromwellian rule, made under the royal prerogative. These constitutions varied in detail from time to time and in different colonies, but in all cases the constitutional right to a parliamentary system was quickly recognized. The power of colonial legislatures to make laws was established as an essential principle of English constitutional law which the settlers had taken with them to their new homes.

The governor had, and still has in some cases, the power to veto colonial laws and the Crown reserved the right to disallow colonial legislation. In the early days the power of disallowance was frequently used, especially in respect of legislation which appeared to be detrimental to the welfare of English trade or shipping. It was also used in the interests of humanity to prevent barbaric punitive legislation of local legislators against their slaves; such, for instance, was the disallowance in 1705 of an Act of the legislature of Bermuda which authorized the emasculation of slaves as a punishment for bad behaviour.

At first the two Houses of the colonial legislatures sat together, generally with the governor presiding, and no doubt the governor and his Council exercised a predominant influence in the proceedings. In 1626 Christopher Parker, of Bermuda, was charged with sedition in consequence of 'his endeavour to divide the General Assembly into an Upper and a Lower House', and was only forgiven after he had signed an apology for his outrageous proposal. Separate meetings of the two Houses, however, gradually became the practice in different colonies, though joint sessions continued to be the rule in some until 1698.

The Council was at first not only a legislative body but also, as adviser to the governor, had executive functions (besides acting in a judicial capacity as a court of appeal). Later it was divided into two separate bodies, the Executive Council advisory to the governor, and the Legislative Council (first so styled about 1774) or Upper House of the legislature. The members of the Council, selected by the governor and recommended by him for appointment by the sovereign, generally belonged to the wealthiest class in the colony, and for social and other reasons would usually be loyal to the governor and give him their support.

Notwithstanding the existence of local legislatures there were some colonials who would have preferred representation in the English parliament. In 1652 Sir Thomas Modyford, a planter in Barbados (and later governor of Jamaica) wrote to an influential member of Cromwell's government proposing, 'although it may seem immodest', that two representatives should be chosen by the island to sit and vote in the English parliament. In 1690 Christopher Codrington, governor of the Leeward Islands, made much the same suggestion. Similar proposals, not all seriously intended, were made in the North American colonies shortly before the American revolution, and Benjamin Franklin seems for a time to have favoured the plan. Even if it were possible in modern times, when aircraft have annihilated distance, such an arrangement would not have been practical in the days of sailing ships which took several weeks, or even months, to cross the Atlantic. Colonial representatives would quickly have got out of touch, and perhaps out of sympathy, with their constituents.

So the local legislatures continued to function, representing only the interests of the planters and merchants, with the Assemblies increasingly in conflict with governors and Councils. Writing of the Canadas in his famous report of 1839, Lord Durham might have been referring to almost any part of the empire. 'It may fairly be said', he wrote, 'that the natural state of government in all these colonies is that of collision between the executive and the representative body'. Both sides were probably to blame but the major responsibility must be held to rest on the intransigence of the elected Houses and the desire of their members for a power which was denied them until the principles laid down by Lord Durham were generally applied.

Soon after they were constituted the colonial Assemblies made their first major claim: full control over finance. In 1677 the Jamaica Assembly, then only thirteen years old, formally claimed all the privileges of the House of Commons, including the control of expenditure, and in Jamaica, as in other colonies, there followed an almost continual struggle between the two Houses and between the Assemblies and the governors. Even in matters other than finance the Houses were often at loggerheads as the more mature and conservative members of the Council generally supported the governors in their disputes with the hotheads of the Assemblies.

It was almost inevitable that the governors and Assemblies should disagree. It was the duty of the governor to carry out the orders of the English government, to enforce the laws for the protection of English trade, such as the Navigation Acts, and to attempt to raise taxes to defray the cost of local administration and defence. Not unnaturally, the Assembly resented restrictions which, in the interests of English merchants and ship-owners, prevented the colonists from advantageous trading with foreigners. In times of war the members of the Assembly were generally prepared to agree to taxation for local defence but were unwilling to continue to pay for the maintenance of forts and troops when peace followed. This was in spite of the fact that in some colonies the troops were the main protection of the white inhabitants against slave rebellions.

A popular governor, or one who was prepared to overlook breaches of the trade and navigation laws, might avoid friction with the Assembly, but colonial history from soon after the establishment of legislatures is a long record of struggle between the executive and the elected Houses.

In spite of his responsibilities the governor had, in fact, only a negative power in dealing with the Assembly. He could prevent the enactment of a law of which he disapproved by the exercise of his veto, but he could not compel the Assembly to pass a law which he thought desirable, even if he had the backing of the English government. If, in the last resort, he dissolved the House it was almost certain, as was proved on several occasions, that the same members would be re-elected.

Until the eighteenth century the majority of English overseas territories were colonies of settlement, in which the right of the freeholders to representative institutions was taken for granted. Although Jamaica was a conquered island, from which the handful of Spanish settlers had been expelled, in order to encourage white immigration it was deliberately treated as a colony of settlement, and another similar example was the island of Grenada, conquered in 1759. In the constitution granted to Grenada by the Crown there was provision, as in colonies of settlement, for representative institutions, but later an attempt was made, by means of the royal prerogative and without the consent of the Grenada House of Assembly, to impose a tax on exports similar to the tax in force in the old settled colonies. This was resisted by a local resident and the case was taken to the English courts where it was held that although the king did originally have the power to tax the people of this conquered colony, he had abandoned this power when he granted them a constitution and authorized the establishment of an elected Assembly.[1]

In the case of Canada (the old province of Quebec) a new model was set because here was an alien land containing people of a civilization (in European terms) equal to that of the conquerors. When the French forces capitulated to the British in 1760, following the capture of Quebec City the previous year, military rule was first established and in 1774 the Quebec Act was passed by the British parliament to safeguard French customs and laws. The Act provided for an Executive and a Legislative Council, each consisting of nominated members,

[1] This was the celebrated case of Campbell v. Hall, in 1774.

and this arrangement continued until 1791 when the colony was divided and a representative Assembly was set up in each of the two halves, Upper and Lower Canada. The Quebec Act established what was in effect 'Crown Colony' rule, and the model was followed in other colonies as they were acquired, either to avoid control by an Assembly representing a minority of the inhabitants or because it was thought that the population in general was incapable of working representative institutions. Just as the practice of Crown Colony administration originated in Canada,[1] it was similarly in Canada, through Lord Durham's report of 1839, that the idea of responsible government in the colonies first took root.

By the close of the Napoleonic wars the British empire had expanded considerably. Apart from the sub-continent of India controlled by the East India Company, Ceylon and the Cape of Good Hope had been ceded by the Netherlands; Mauritius, the Seychelles, Senegal and St Lucia had been taken from the French; and Trinidad from the Spaniards. In addition to Quebec, British rule had been established over other territories later to be joined as the Dominion of Canada. Other minor territories, such as the Falkland Islands and St Helena, had been included in the empire.

Warned by what had happened in connection with taxation in Grenada, and anxious to have the power to alleviate the conditions of slavery in response to growing humanitarian feeling in Britain (which was not shared by the slave-owners who controlled the colonial legislatures) no attempt was made to introduce the old colonial system in the newer colonies. On the contrary, these territories were treated as 'Crown Colonies', with legislative as well as executive power vested in the governors, as representing the sovereign, aided to a limited extent by nominated Councils and unhampered by any elected Assemblies.

It was in connection with the treatment of slaves, and later of their emancipation, that the contest between the legislatures of tropical colonies and the United Kingdom government

---

[1] The first Crown Colony was actually Senegambia, established in 1765, but neither here nor in Canada was this the result of deliberate policy but rather that of local difficulties.

became most intense. The successful rebellion of the thirteen North American colonies had made the British government careful, on the one hand to tighten the reins of administration in the new territories through Crown Colony rule, and on the other hand to avoid any unnecessary clash with existing local legislatures, and reluctant to irritate the sensibilities of members of the colonial Assemblies or over-ride their authority by passing laws in the United Kingdom parliament which would apply to the colonies. The zeal of the abolitionists, however, and their persistent propaganda, gradually had the effect of forcing the British government to adopt a tougher line towards colonial legislatures which resisted any change designed to improve the condition of the slave population.

In the Crown Colonies a certain amount could be done, and in Trinidad, for example, the registration of slaves (an administrative measure which allowed better control) was enforced by an Order of the King-in-Council. It was hoped that the model set in Trinidad would be followed in the other West Indian colonies, but the Houses of Assembly resisted any move in this direction. The Jamaica House of Assembly adopted a series of resolutions condemning the action of the British parliament in passing the Act of 1807 which prohibited the slave trade, asserting that parliament could not legislate for the internal affairs of the colony. Borne down by a torrent of opinion in Britain, the Emancipation Act of 1833 was, however, passed in the British parliament over the heads of the colonial legislatures, the resentment of the slave-owners (and their creditors) being ameliorated to some extent by the compensation they received (£20,000,000 in the aggregate) for the loss of their slaves.

Even more serious was the feeling aroused by the West Indies Prisons Act of 1838, which vested the management of West Indian prisons in the governors. Conditions in these prisons had long been abominable and the island Assemblies failed to pass legislation to improve matters. In these circumstances the United Kingdom government was again constrained to assert its will, reluctant as it was to interfere in the domestic affairs of the colonies.

In spite of these shocks to their prestige, the island legislatures continued to function until the second half of the nineteenth century, notwithstanding growing criticism of their unrepresentative character. The constitutions of these colonies permitted small white or near-white minorities to control the Houses of Assembly while the descendants of African slaves, by far the largest section of the population, had little or no representation. In some of the islands the system of election had become farcical. In St Kitts, for example, out of a total population of 20,741 in 1855, only 166 were entitled to vote, and in one constituency which returned two representatives to the House of Assembly there was only a single elector! In Jamaica in 1863, with a population of some 450,000, there were 1,799 electors.

Serious rioting in Jamaica in 1865 frightened the members of the local legislature into the surrender of their constitution, and for various reasons, the principal being the lack of financial viability, similar voluntary action in all but three of the original colonies led to the introduction of Crown Colony rule. The exceptions were the Bahamas, Barbados and Bermuda, where the old 'representative' system continued until the two former were given, in recent years, a form of responsible government; Bermuda still has representative government.

The Secretary of State for the Colonies, in 1868, explained in a despatch how and why the change to Crown Colony government had been made. He pointed out that the Assemblies had voted for the constitutional changes 'voluntarily and without any suggestion from Her Majesty's Government', and that the power of legislating had in the past been

'virtually exercised by Assemblies elected by a very limited number of the Colonists, and the only control over their legislation was the negative control by the veto of the Crown, or by the action of a Legislative Council, the Members of which held their seats for life. The population at large, consisting of uneducated Negroes, neither had nor could have any political powers; they were incapable of contributing to the formation of any intelligent public opinion; and the consequence was that the Assemblies performed their office of legislation under no real or effective responsibility.

'They became aware, apparently, that irresponsible legislation by small local bodies was not for the interest even of the Members of those Bodies themselves, or of the class which they represented, and still less of the inhabitants at large.'

The new constitutions provided for the abolition of the Houses of Assembly, the Legislative Councils becoming the sole Houses of the legislatures. These Councils at first consisted only of nominated members, most of these being civil servants through whom the governor could control the voting, but later the number of nominated unofficials was increased and at a still later period elected members were included. The control by the governor, either through the official majority in the Council, or through his 'reserve powers', ensured that British humanitarian and liberal principles should prevail, for the benefit of the underprivileged and often illiterate classes, against the selfish policies of the members of the old Assemblies.

IV

The Old Dominions. While the old colonial system still obtained in the West Indian islands, several British colonies had been established in North America (later to be included in the Dominion of Canada), and in Australia, New Zealand and South Africa, and in each of these representative government was quickly introduced. These colonies had been settled by people of European (and mainly British) stock and except in South Africa the native populations were sparse. In these circumstances, very similar to those which existed when the American and West Indian colonies were settled, it was natural for parliamentary systems to be taken for granted, and in the absence of a slave population or a large number of indigenous inhabitants there was nothing to hinder the development of these systems on progressively democratic lines.

Nova Scotia was given representative government as early as 1758, and the Quebec constitution of 1774 was replaced in 1791 by one which provided for an elected Assembly with limited powers for Upper and Lower Canada. In the 'fifties of last century all the Australian colonies, except Western Australia, and New Zealand also came under representative government. In all of these colonies the members of the Upper House of the legislature were nominated, but in 1853 a change was made in the constitution granted to the Cape Colony, which provided not only for an elected Assembly but also for an elected Legislative Council.

Although these constitutions followed generally the earlier West Indian models, the demands from the colonists for more complete self-government soon became insistent, and the British government was ready to accept the views of Lord Durham that 'responsible'—as opposed to 'representative'—government was essential. The old colonial system which left the Crown, as represented by the governor, in almost complete control of the administration in spite of the existence of an elected Assembly, had inevitably led to continual friction and frustration. The remedy he proposed was the introduction of partial responsible government, with an Executive Council answerable to the legislature as well as to the governor, and from this grew the ministerial system in the colonies. It was a system not dissimilar to the 'dyarchy' established in India at a later date and was clearly unworkable as a democratic institution in a modern sense, but it was an advance on the previous constitutions which had fettered and galled the elected branches of the legislatures.

The Canadian colonies were the first to benefit from this change of policy, but it was almost by chance that in 1848 the principle of responsible government was recognized in Nova Scotia and extended to Canada the same year. A vote of no confidence in the Nova Scotia government led to the resignation of the Executive Council and the appointment of a new premier. Responsible government followed in New Brunswick and Prince Edward Island and in the Australian states. In New Zealand responsible government was introduced in 1856 although for some years responsibility was limited as regards native affairs and a few other matters. Newfoundland was given responsible government in 1855 and Cape Colony in 1872. Southern Rhodesia had since 1888 been under British protection and governed by authority of a Royal Charter granted to the British South Africa Company, but in 1923 it was proclaimed a

HISTORY OF COMMONWEALTH PARLIAMENTS 27

colony and given responsible government, subject to certain reservations as to legislation dealing with native affairs and some other matters.

The next stage in constitutional development was that of federation. In Canada the provinces of Ontario, Quebec, New Brunswick and Nova Scotia were federated in 1867 to form the Dominion of Canada and by 1873 other provinces had been included (Newfoundland not until 1949). The constitution of the Dominion provides for a Senate, the members of which are appointed for life, and an elected House of Commons. There are also separate parliaments for each of the ten provinces of Canada and except in Quebec, which has a nominated Upper House, there are no second chambers.

The six Australian states were joined in 1901 as the Commonwealth of Australia, with a Senate, the members of which are elected for six years, and an elected House of Representatives. Each of the states also has its own parliament, with considerable powers, and with the exception of Queensland all are bi-cameral.

In South Africa, after the Boer War of 1899–1902, Cape Colony and Natal continued to have responsible government; the Transvaal and Orange River Colony were administered for a time as Crown Colonies but were granted responsible government in 1906 and 1907. In 1910 the four territories were joined in the Union of South Africa, with a Senate partially nominated but mainly elected, and an elected House of Assembly.

In New Zealand there was, after 1852, a quasi-federal regime with provincial councils but this proved unworkable and was abandoned in 1876, and New Zealand continues as a unitary state. Until 1951 the New Zealand parliament was bi-cameral but in that year the Upper House was abolished.[1]

By the beginning of the present century the 'old' Dominions were practically independent and their constitutional status was considerably improved as a result of their contributions to

[1] Federation has been less successful in the newer states of the Commonwealth (and in the former French colonies) than in the older nations. The West Indies Federation and the Federation of Rhodesia and Nyasaland lasted only a few years. Singapore has left the Federation of Malaysia. In India and Nigeria, however, federation has survived.

victory in the first world war. They were given separate representation on the British delegation in the negotiations which led to the signing of the Treaty of Versailles in 1919, and it was specially stipulated in the Treaty of Lausanne in 1923 that the signing of this treaty by the United Kingdom did not bind the Dominions. In the report of the Imperial Conference of 1926 the Dominions were described as

'Autonomous communities within the British Empire, equal in status, in no way subordinate one to another in any aspect of their domestic or external affairs, though united by a common allegiance to the Crown, and freely associated as members of the British Commonwealth of Nations.'

This theoretical definition was formally recognized by the Statute of Westminster in 1931. In Canada, South Africa and the Irish Free State the Act of 1931 was gladly accepted as satisfying—for the moment—nationalist aspirations, but Australia and New Zealand declined to ratify the provisions of the Statute in their own parliaments until after the beginning of the second world war.

The Irish Free State, comprising 26 of the 32 Irish counties, was established as a Dominion in 1921 and became independent as the Republic of Eire in 1949. The legislature is bi-cameral, some of the members of the Upper House being nominated, but most of the others, and all the members of the Lower House being elected. The other six Irish counties are included in Northern Ireland which continues as an integral part of the United Kingdom and elects twelve members to the House of Commons at Westminster. There is in addition a parliament of Northern Ireland with a large range of legislative powers, consisting of an elected House of Commons and a Senate of 26 members, of whom 24 are elected by the Lower House and two are *ex officio*—the lord mayor of Belfast and the mayor of Londonderry.

In 1961 the Republic of South Africa left the Commonwealth, but both Eire and South Africa have retained the parliamentary system although in the latter country only whites may vote or be members of parliament.

The model of Westminster has been followed in all the 'old' Dominions, adapted where necessary to meet local conditions. The long period of peace these Dominions enjoyed until 1914, guaranteed largely by the Royal Navy, allowed them the necessary time to overcome teething troubles and to learn the principles of the give and take of political compromise. As a result they have attained a level of stability and political maturity which few other countries have been able to achieve. Their constitutions are based on British law and precedent, and on long-standing conventions which are perhaps just as important as the written word. The medieval ritual of parliamentary procedure has been followed in these new lands and, as a Canadian political scientist has remarked, 'the British parliamentary inheritance . . . is the most significant expansion of a political way of life in the contemporary world'.[1]

The Dominions have not, however, been content to be mere imitators of British ways. They have themselves shown the constitutional way to other countries, including Britain. The secret ballot was established in four of the Australian states before 1860, and women received the parliamentary vote in New Zealand in 1893. The secret ballot was not introduced in the United Kingdom until 1872 and in the United States until 1884. Women first received the vote in Britain in 1918 and in the United States in 1920. New Zealand has been the pioneer of social legislation and was the first country of the Commonwealth to provide old age pensions. The machinery of the referendum, in order to ascertain the wishes of the electorate on specific points, has never been looked on with favour in Britain, but has been used on several occasions in Canada, Australia and New Zealand.

v

India, Pakistan and Burma. In the second half of the eighteenth century the East India Company, which had been trading in the sub-continent since it received a Charter in 1600, administered three presidencies—Bengal, Bombay and Madras, and thence gradually extended its control over much of the

[1] Professor A. Brady, *Democracy in the Dominions* (1952), p. 498.

rest of India during the first half of the nineteenth century. During Company rule there was no parliamentary system, legislative power being vested in the governors or governors-in-council.

In 1858, as a consequence of the Indian Mutiny, the Company's rule was ended and the British Crown took over the direct administration of India, with a governor-general or viceroy representing the sovereign. The governor-general's nominated Council continued as the only law-making body until 1861 when, by an Act of the United Kingdom parliament, local Legislative Councils were established in the provinces, functioning concurrently with the governor-general's central Council. In the same year nominated non-official members were brought into the Councils, the functions of which were strictly limited to legislation. Some of the non-official members in the Provincial Councils were Indians. The governor-general was given reserve powers which enabled him to over-ride decisions reached by the majority of any Council, and in 1870 the governor-general-in-(Executive) Council was empowered to pass laws without reference to the Legislative Councils.

By an Imperial Act of 1892 the functions of the Legislative Councils were enlarged to allow members to discuss financial policy and to ask questions on matters of public interest. The number of non-official members was also increased and the first approach was made to the admission of the elective principle, although the governor-general in fact nominated the members who had been elected, at his discretion. Some of the non-official members of the central Legislative Council were elected by the non-official members of the Provincial Councils, while some of the members of the Provincial Councils were themselves nominated by municipalities, universities and trading organizations. The Act still left the Indian people without any effective voice in the administration.

A further Act of 1909 enlarged the Legislative Councils and extended their functions. The central Legislative Council then consisted of 37 officials and 32 non-officials, five of whom were nominated and the rest elected. In the provincial Councils the official and nominated unofficial members together outnumbered the elected members. Elections were indirect, through electoral colleges, and there were separate electorates for Muslims. An American writer has said that 'it was perhaps inevitable in the plural society of India that party divisions generally followed communal lines instead of being based on political principle',[1] and the precedent set in this instance was increasingly followed in India. It led ultimately to the establishment of a separate Muslim State of Pakistan, and, as will be seen, it has been followed in Fiji.

The Government of India Act of 1919 set up a bi-cameral central legislature consisting of a Council of State and a Central Legislative Assembly. In both Houses the elected members outnumbered those who were nominated. About half of the elected members represented special constituencies—Muslim, Sikh, European, etc. The elected members were chosen by direct voting on a limited franchise and the governor-general retained certain over-riding powers for use in emergency. The Executive continued to be independent of the legislature.

In the provinces a system of dyarchy was introduced by the Act of 1919. Certain reserved subjects were dealt with by the governor and his Executive Council, while other subjects were handled by the governor with the help of ministers selected by him from the Legislative Council. In the provincial Legislative Councils about 70 per cent of the members were elected.

Still further material changes were envisaged by the Government of India Act of 1935 which provided for a federation of the provinces and of such of the Indian Native States as wished to join. The system of dyarchy, which had not proved a success in the provinces, was now abolished in the provinces but adopted for the central government, reserved subjects to be controlled by the governor-general, while as regards other subjects the governor-general was advised by a Council of Ministers.

It was proposed that the federal legislature should consist of a Council of State and a Federal Assembly. The members of both Houses representing the Indian States were to be nominated by the rulers of those States, while the representa-

[1] A. L. Burt, *The Evolution of the British Empire and Commonwealth* (Boston, 1956), p. 792.

tives of British India in the Council of State were to be directly elected and those in the Assembly indirectly elected. The federal legislature never came into being and, so far as the central legislature was concerned, the 1919 constitution, with some few alterations, continued to be effective.

In the provinces, however, the constitution of 1935 brought considerable changes. The reserve powers of the governors were limited and although completely responsible government was not attained the Act gave to the provinces a considerable degree of autonomy. The provincial legislatures were bicameral in six provinces, with Provincial Legislative Councils and Provincial Legislative Assemblies. In the other five provinces the single House was styled the Provincial Legislative Assembly. Some of the members of the Councils were nominated but all the Assembly members were elected, separate representation being reserved for special communities.

Soon after the outbreak of the second world war the Indian provincial ministers who were members of the Congress political party resigned their offices as they were dissatisfied with the British declaration of war aims and the failure to give a firm promise of independence for India. As a result the governors were compelled to take over the direct administration in eight of the provinces and this arrangement continued until 1946.

In 1947, by an Act of the United Kingdom parliament, the two separate independent states of India and Pakistan were established.

In 1950 India became a republic consisting of a number of States and a few 'Union Territories', with a constitution based largely on the Act of 1935. The central legislature consists of a Council of States, with twelve members nominated by the President of India and the rest elected by the State legislatures; and a House of the People elected directly by adult suffrage, with a few seats reserved for scheduled castes and tribes and Anglo-Indians. There is also a legislature in each State, the legislative powers as between the central and the provincial legislatures remaining the same as under the Act of 1935. The governor is the constitutional head of each State and acts on the advice of ministers responsible to the State legislature. In most of the States there is only a single House, the Legislative Assembly, but in some of the larger States the legislature is bi-cameral.

Pakistan. When Pakistan was separated from India and became independent in 1947, the provisions of the Government of India Act of 1935 continued to apply with suitable adaptations. A constituent assembly was set up to frame a constitution and to act temporarily as a legislature. The work of this assembly suffered many delays but an interim arrangement allowed the election by adult suffrage of Provincial Assemblies in East and West Pakistan, and a constitution was finally adopted. This constitution was abrogated in 1958 and martial law substituted. A new constitution was proclaimed in 1962 which re-instated the two Provincial Assemblies and set up a National Assembly. The National Assembly includes 75 members from each of the two provinces and six women elected by the Provincial Assemblies.

Burma. British rule began in Burma in 1826 and until 1937 Burma was regarded as a province of India. From that date it was given internal self-government. Half of the members of the Senate were nominated and half elected, and the Lower House was entirely elected. After the second world war, during which Burma was over-run by the Japanese, a constituent assembly was elected to frame a new constitution and in 1948 the Union of Burma came into being as an independent nation and left the Commonwealth. Until 1962, when the administration was taken over by a Revolutionary Council, Burma continued to be nominally a parliamentary democracy with a bi-cameral legislature consisting of a Chamber of Deputies and a Chamber of Nationalities.

VI

The Newer Colonial Territories. During the second half of the nineteenth century, while the original West Indian colonies were losing their representative institutions and the Dominions were moving steadily towards responsible government, in other parts of the world, and especially in tropical Africa, large areas were being added to the British Empire.

A representative form of government existed in Sierra Leone at the end of the eighteenth century while that country was under the control of a company, but this arrangement did not long continue and in 1808 Sierra Leone became a Crown Colony with a nominated Legislative Council. As a matter of historical interest, the first Crown Colony was that of Senegambia which existed as a British possession from 1765 to 1783, also with a nominated Council.

In those parts of Africa, as in other territories taken over later, the indigenous population was largely illiterate, with a handful of European missionaries, merchants and officials, and it was some time before effective control could be established over the whole of each territory. In such circumstances it was impractical to introduce responsible, and for a time even representative, government. There was in none of these countries any parliamentary tradition such as had existed in the older colonies and it was thought best to introduce the system of Crown Colony rule. This system had been developed in the West Indies as a substitute for the discredited form of 'representative' government which had previously obtained. In the newer colonies it was introduced as a deliberate policy.

The details of each constitution varied from territory to territory (and from time to time) but the general pattern was the same in all. In nearly every colony, and even in some protectorates, a Legislative Council was set up, the members of which were nominated by the Crown on the governor's recommendation. For a long time there was always a majority of civil servants in the Council who could be counted on to support the governor's proposals against any opposition from the unofficial members. However, although the latter were in consequence theoretically powerless, their views were generally respected and a governor would hesitate to use his majority of civil servants to over-ride strong views unanimously expressed by the minority.

The non-official minority in some territories included members of the indigenous population as well as members of the European community. The latter were appointed by the governor to represent various economic interests—banking, mining, planting, shipping or trade—sometimes on the nomination of Chambers of Commerce and similar organizations, and on account of their experience (and better knowledge of English) these Europeans were as a rule the most effective members of the minority groups. 'Native' members were not always included in the Legislative Councils. In Kenya, for example, there were no African members until 1944, although European non-officials had been nominated to the Council since 1907.

The next step was the introduction of an elected element into the Councils. For some time, in most territories, the number of elected members was small in comparison with the number of official and nominated non-official members, but was gradually increased in each colony until they were in the majority and sometimes finally the only element in the Council. At first members were elected on a limited franchise, generally to represent only the principal municipalities in each colony; thus the four Africans elected to the Legislative Council of Nigeria in 1925 (the first elected in tropical Africa) represented the towns of Lagos and Calabar.

In most cases members were elected to colonial Legislative Councils in the conventional way but in some territories special electoral procedures were adopted. In the Gold Coast, for example, from 1925 there were elected African members, some elected by ballot to represent municipalities and others chosen by the Provincial Councils of Chiefs. There were also two European elected members, one elected by the Chamber of Mines and one by the Chamber of Commerce.

Again, owing to the fact that Fiji is inhabited by three separate and distinct races—Fijian, European and Indian—it has been thought desirable to give each race separate representation in the Legislative Council, always with an official majority controlling the situation. Soon after the establishment of the colony in 1874 a few European unofficials were appointed to the Council, and from 1904 two 'Native Members' were selected by the governor from a list of six Fijians submitted by the Council of Chiefs while six Europeans were elected. In 1916 an Indian was nominated by the governor for the first time. From 1937 parity of representation has been given to the three races and at present four of each are elected by ballot, and two Indians and two Europeans are nominated, while two Fijians are chosen by the Council of Chiefs. The European population is much smaller than either the Fijian or the Indian but has a much higher economic standing. At the constitutional conference in London in 1965 the demand of the Indian representatives for a common electoral roll was opposed by the Fijian and European representatives and it is probable that separate racial representation will continue for some time.

VII

The Later Stages. The 'old' Dominions had advanced progressively along the conventional channel of constitutional development to complete independence under the Crown, a status which was legally recognized by the United Kingdom government in 1931. After the second world war most of the colonial territories followed with headlong speed and many of them are now independent sovereign states. Both in the original West Indian colonies and in the newer African and oriental colonies the progress from Crown Colony rule to independence was accomplished within a few years.

In the first instance the Crown Colony system was amended by the inauguration of a ministerial system. Elected members of the legislatures were included in the Executive Councils and made responsible for certain departments of the government, two or three officials serving with them as advisers to the governors who invariably presided over the Executive Council meetings.

The second stage was reached when the civil servants ceased to be members of the Executive Council and a Chief Minister was appointed who presided over the meetings of what now became a Cabinet. Later again, as a wider measure of self-government was achieved, the Chief Minister was styled Premier.

From this stage there was rapid movement from responsible government to independence, which was readily granted by the United Kingdom government at the request of the local legislature. Constitutions were agreed between the United Kingdom government and ministers representing the colonies concerned, generally providing for legislatures modelled on that of Westminster, consisting of the sovereign (represented by a governor-general) and one or two Houses of Parliament. Nigeria and Jamaica, for example, have bi-cameral legislatures while Ghana and Zambia have each a single House. Soon after independence several countries adopted a republican regime (while remaining in the Commonwealth), with a president instead of the sovereign (and governor-general).

The Upper House in most of the recently independent territories, if one exists, is generally called the Senate. In the Regions which form the Federation of Nigeria, each of which has its own legislature, the Upper Houses are called Houses of Chiefs, while the Upper House of the federal parliament is the Senate.[1] In most of the former colonies which have become independent the parliamentary system has continued to operate, but in some of them one party rule has been introduced. In a recent general 'election' in Ghana all the members of the legislature, nominated by the ruling party, were returned unopposed. Whether or not one party rule is the best form of government for African states,[2] the elimination of an Opposition, by whatever means, is contrary to the ideal of parliamentary democracy.

Notwithstanding the exceptions, the general tendency throughout the Commonwealth has been towards greater political maturity and the British system of parliamentary democracy is still a model which most aspire to follow. Professor Graham has written that the British Empire, 'beginning in orthodox style as an expansion of a maritime people for purposes of settlement and trade, became transformed in the late nineteenth century into a complicated laboratory where cautious experiment eventually precipitated nation after nation into active existence'.[3] The constitutional experiment has not been the least successful.

[1] The Nigerian constitution will possibly be changed as a result of the tragic events of January 1966.
[2] The distinguished West Indian economist, Sir Arthur Lewis, is certain that it is not, and that it is not natural to African culture. See *Politics in West Africa*, pp. 35, 63, 79.
[3] Article on British Empire and Commonwealth in *Chambers's Encyclopaedia*, 1950 edition.

Chapter II

THE DRAFTING OF LAWS

BY CECIL CARR

―――――

Before Parliament can enact a law, a Bill must be drafted. Before the Bill can appear, discussions and conferences will have taken place and some responsible expert will have had to express the proposals in terms which take account of the difficulties of interpretation and enforcement. His exacting duties are anonymous. More than eighty Public Acts received the Royal Assent in Britain in 1965. How many of us could name the draftsman of a single one of them? The difficulties of early draftsmen in this country, and the improvements in the arrangements for drafting here and in the United States and Canada, may provide a warning or an inspiration to draftsmen in other lands.

Among what Dr Johnson called the Anfractuosities of the Human Mind we may perhaps include the inclination to celebrate anniversaries. As time's winged chariot hurries through the nineteen-sixties there is one centenary which students of the law-making process might care to commemorate. In 1869 Henry Thring, afterwards Lord Thring, was appointed the first whole-time Parliamentary Counsel to the Treasury, with the duty of drafting all Government Bills (other than Scottish or Irish Bills) and any others which the Treasury might require. In this technical field of law-making lookers-on do not see much of the game; but, if one of them may set down some scattered thoughts and comments on the subject, the epoch of Thring makes a convenient starting-point.

The experts are unanimous that Thring, breaking away

from the traditions of old-fashioned conveyancing, standardized official drafting for the future. He laid down some 'Instructions for Draftsmen', later published under the title *Practical Legislation*. These rules governed the form of English enactments the more effectively as law-making at Westminster came more and more exclusively under the control and initiative of the Cabinet. Soon after the passing of the Reform Bill Arthur Symonds, author of an almost forgotten treatise entitled *The Mechanics of Law-Making*, had mentioned to a Select Committee the difficulty of passing Bills 'on account of the pressure of business'. In 1857 G. K. Rickards, Counsel to the Speaker, had told yet another Select Committee that the Bills of Government Departments now made up four-fifths of the Acts of a session. The proportion is no less impressive a hundred years later. The changes made in the expediting of legislative procedure in the House of Commons have been made in order that the Government of the day may carry its Bills. Laymen who scold Parliament for the tortoiselike pace of the legislative process, or who are disappointed in their demand for some 'simple little one-clause Bill' to remedy a grievance of the moment, are perhaps unaware of the number of floors in the law factory or of the congestion on the stairs.

Zeal for the improvement of statutory form was not the sole reason for Thring's appointment in 1869. The 'acute and frugal mind' of Robert Lowe, Gladstone's Chancellor of the Exchequer, had noted the heavy expense of paying fees to practising barristers who had to be compensated for being taken away from their normal professional work to draft a Bill. As much as £800 had been paid for a single Bill, 'and not too much either'. Thring, however, had not been the first salaried draftsman. William Harrison told a Select Committee on House of Commons Offices and Fees in 1833 that, 'as Counsel to the Treasury', he received £1,000 a year, with another £400 as law clerk to the War Office. He said he had drawn Bills for other departments besides the Treasury—peace treaty Bills and slave courts Bills for the Foreign Office, military Bills for the Colonial Office during the war, militia Bills for the Home Office, some Revenue Bills, the Bank Charter Bill and the General Banking Bill, but not Sir Robert Peel's criminal law Bills, 'not being specially conversant with criminal law'.

Harrison went on drafting till 1837. The Home Department's estimates for 1837–38 contained the following entry:

> Counsel employed in drawing Government Bills for Parliament under the direction of the Secretary of State (hitherto charged upon the Grant for the Expenses of the two Houses of Parliament)
> For one year and a half, at £1,500 per annum ... £2,250.

The Select Committee on Public Bills reported in 1836 that Mr Gregson, who for some years prepared the Bills for the Home Office, had been succeeded by Mr Drinkwater. In 1842 John Elliot Drinkwater (afterwards Drinkwater Bethune) was appointed by Treasury Minute at the salary named above. Giving evidence before the Select Committee on Private Bills in 1846, he said he was not aware that the office he held had any regular name. 'It did not exist before I was appointed; it should perhaps be called "Legislative Counsel to the Cabinet"; my duty is to prepare for Parliament whatever Bills are entrusted to me by any member of the Government.' Four years later Drinkwater Bethune was transferred to Calcutta as legislative member of the Supreme Council of India; this was the post originally occupied by Macaulay, the passing of whose Penal Code, by the way, Bethune, after attempting a re-draft, resisted. The *Law Magazine*, having previously complained of the haphazard drafting of our Bills 'by a horde of undisciplined law-writers without plan or concert', regretted the transfer. The *Spectator*, too, devoting much attention during that year to the state of the statute-book, was sorry to see Bethune's accumulated learning and experience go off to India where it would be 'of secondary value'; Walter Coulson, his successor at the Home Office, would 'from the want of records and of the means of tradition which an established office affords' be at a disadvantage in beginning afresh in 'an almost uncultivated field'. Coulson, the Cornishman who earlier had served as amanuensis to Jeremy Bentham himself, won the praise of Bellenden Ker, the conveyancer who was head of Lord Cranworth's Statute Law Commission and who was asked to keep an eye on all Bills which might need the Lord Chancellor's attention. Coulson's work, said Ker in 1854, had led to a great improvement in the form and language of the statutes; Lord John Russell had paid it a tribute in Parliament; if Coulson could give his attention to all Bills brought in, then none of the methods of Parliamentary supervision which reformers had been advocating would, as regards future legislation, be necessary.

Coulson died in 1860 and Thring succeeded to his post at the Home Office. Thring, who had found conveyancing 'the dullest of all earthly studies' and who had devoted briefless hours to the examination of the statute-book, had begun drafting in 1852 with the Succession Duty Acts and had to his credit the monumental Merchant Shipping Act of 1854. To move to the Treasury in 1869 was to create a new establishment. At the Home Office he had drafted all the Public Bills for which he could find time, with the help only of copying clerks; at the Treasury he had an official assistant (Henry Jenkyns) and younger men (including Courtenay Ilbert) whose training he could supervise. Jenkyns eventually succeeded Thring and Ilbert succeeded Jenkyns. It was the beginning of that 'corps of regularly selected draftsmen' (all the Bills coming from the same workshop) which Rickards had outlined to the Select Committee in 1857. Incidentally the attachment of Thring's new office to the Treasury strengthened the Government's financial control of projected legislation.

Conditions were by this time very different from those of the eighteen-thirties when Symonds could ask rhetorically 'English laws, what are they?' and could answer with Benthamite favour 'The clumsiest pieces of workmanship which the unskilled labours of men ever made'. Symonds had sought in vain for uniformity of language, style and arrangement among the Bills emanating from Government departments. The Revenue Department had one style, the Woods and Forests another, the Home Office another and the Irish Office another, and, of course, any individual M.P. who brought in a Bill had a plan of his own. Symonds had produced a formula; it was 'impossible that even the same man should draw a law in the same way unless he followed a form'—an opinion echoed long afterwards by James Fitzjames Stephen who declared that there was just as much variety of style between one draftsman and another as in writing books. Symonds, like other critics, ridiculed the verbosity of the old-fashioned conveyancers' compositions. He went through some contemporary statutes with a blue pencil and, to his own satisfaction, reduced their bulk by a half or more. He attacked the unnecessary phrases such as 'from and after the passing of this Act', and he compiled a Glossary of Proscribed Words, some two hundred pleonasms ranging from 'adulterated and mixed with', 'all and every', 'alter and vary', 'approved and confirmed', 'done or committed', 'execute and perform', 'good and sufficient', 'power and authority', 'receive and take', 'save and except', 'then and in every such case', down to 'when and so often as' and 'will and pleasure'. The attack was carried on soon afterwards in the Report of the Poor Law Commissioners for whom George Coode was working; amateurs, it was said, seemed to think that legislative language must be intricate and barbarous and must employ 'antick phrases' as though the qualification for drafting were 'a readiness in the use of "nevertheless", "provided always", "it shall and may be lawful and he is hereby authorized empowered and required to" or "anything in any Act or Acts to the contrary notwithstanding".'

Thring could look back over the many stages in the advance of English law-making. Acts of Parliament were now broken up into numbered sections and punctuation had appeared. The 1796 Report on the Promulgation of Statutes had advocated numbering; so had Bentham, who cited the precedent of the numbered verses of the Bible. The King's Printer's assumption of responsibility for inserting numbers was dismissed by Bentham as just 'the licentiousness of the press'; the manuscript Bills which received the Royal Assent had no divisions or numbers. Lord Brougham's Act of 1850 settled the matter; it required statutes to be divided into sections, each section a substantive enactment without any introductory words, though a few critics wondered if the judges would reject as invalid a statute printed in the old non-stop fashion. Statutory tidiness had been further encouraged when schedules became common. Symonds had recommended them as appropriate for supplementary matters; he praised James Deacon Hume for having employed this device when consolidating the customs laws in 1825; it had, however, been freely used many years earlier, appearing even in the previous century. The judges made no difficulty over accepting the device when, long afterwards, it was challenged; it was 'a mere question of drafting, a mere question of words; the schedule is as much a part of the statute and is as much an enactment as any other part'.[1] Another step forward was the discontinuance of long lists of particulars tiresomely repeated. Symonds had drawn attention to an Act of 1834 about the conveyance of fish. It spoke of 'any live salmon, salmon trout, turbot, large fresh cod, half fresh cod, haddock, skate, fresh ling, soles, whiting or other fish' brought in 'any fishing ship, sloop, smack or other fishing vessel or vessels'.[2] Definition (or interpretation) clauses abbreviated these reiterations, although, when the instances of this kind of 'parliamentary shorthand' first appeared, more than one conservative critic stigmatized them as devices for covering up a draftsman's mistakes. They were disfavoured by judges. Brougham himself wrote of 'the havoc made by the new and pernicious insertion of the interpretation clause which makes draftsmen careless and introduces doubts of its own'. It irked him to find that the Town Police Clauses Act defined 'cattle' as including horses, asses, mules, sheep, goats and swine but never mentioned cows. Even his own Act of 1850 'for shortening the language of statutes' sanctioned some abbreviations and, in doing so, invited challenge. It said that in future enactments 'land' would include messuages, lands, tenements and hereditaments of any tenure. The critics objected that 'hereditaments' would include advowsons, tithes and fisheries, which a reader would be surprised to find reckoned as land. Moreover words were finding their way into an interpretation clause which were in no need of explanation at all, and sometimes a word with a primary meaning was, by what Blackstone called 'parliamentary magic', given an arbitrary meaning. In an old Trustee Act, it was said, 'land' had been defined as including ships; Lord Cottenham had a case before him which went on

[1] Per Brett L.J., A. G. v. Lamplough (1878) 3 Exch. Div. 229.
[2] 4 & 5 Will. IV c.20. An earlier Act (33 Geo. II c.27) repeated the list of vessels nearly thirty times.

for many days before this material fact was discovered. One Act, said Thring later, defined 'stock' as including land; 'I would sooner use more words than have a non-natural definition'.

In the general crusade against verbosity one simple step was to direct that singular words should include plural and masculine words should include feminine. When Peel introduced his Bills in 1827 for re-writing the criminal law, he confessed that 'the endless repetition of words, the confusion of the singular and plural number and the frequent use of the words "party or parties", "defendant or defendants" and "corporations or persons" had always puzzled him beyond measure'. To remove doubts and to avoid reiteration he inserted a clause to cover the masculine-feminine and the singular-plural complex and to include bodies corporate as persons.[1] In the eighteen-thirties Symonds noted that some judges were finding themselves able to take care of singulars and plurals and of masculines and feminines without any statutory direction. In 1850 all doubt was removed by Brougham's Act, now replaced in a much expanded form by the Interpretation Act of 1889 which itself seems ripe for revision. Vice-chancellor Knight-Bruce was not perhaps quite serious when remarking that a company authorized by Local Act to build one market might now claim the right to build two.

It had been a major advance in English nomography when Bills began to specify their precise effect upon previous enactments and to abandon 'blind repeals'. As Coulson observed, a vague phrase like 'so much of any Act as is inconsistent with this Act shall be and is hereby repealed' meant nothing; 'that would be the result anyhow'. The Statute Law Committee, created in 1868 by Lord Chancellor Cairns, did much to improve the sign-posting of the law. Under its direction an Index to the Statutes in Force was officially printed, arranged on principles laid down by Thring; it was accompanied by a Chronological Table of all the Statutes, showing all repeals and amendments. Thenceforward it was possible to 'legislate in daylight'.

Two other improvements of the statute-book were promoted

[1] See, for example, 9 Geo. IV. c.54, s.35.

by that same Committee. The first was the expurgation of obsolete, spent and unnecessary enactments—Bacon's 'statutes which are sleeping and not of use and yet snaring and in force'. Appearing almost yearly (sometimes indeed twice yearly) between 1861 and 1898, and steadily, though less frequently, thereafter, some forty Statute Law Revision Acts have eliminated thousands of unwanted enactments. Cautious doubts were removed by an elaborate saving clause long preserved out of loyalty to tradition but now greatly simplified. This process has diminished the justification for the reproach that the law, like the tyrant Mezentius, tied the living to the dead. Folk who today complain of the survival of obsolete laws seem to be referring to enactments over which it might be found premature to read the burial service—such, for instance, as the Lord's Day Observance Acts; statute law revision has to be careful not to touch topics which have not yet ceased to be controversial. Secondly the Statute Law Committee has linked this process with the official production of successive editions of 'Statutes Revised', containing only the living law. If these inevitably expensive volumes do not satisfy the historian, the academic lawyer or even the legal practitioner, if they can never displace the annotated texts of specialist textbook writers, they may remind the Legislature of its duty to lay its cards on the table.

As long as you have a Parliament, said Stephen, you will always have to be consolidating and revising, just as you repair a house. He thought that ordinary laws ought not to be allowed to last longer than a generation; 'the very language changes'. Almost the sole remedy upon which all the reformers have been agreed has been the need to consolidate statutes, i.e. to re-enact in a single measure all the enactments on one subject, usually a principal statute which has been frequently amended —Bacon's 'reducing of concurrent statutes heaped one upon another, to one clear and uniform law'. Sheer administrative convenience must often have emphasized the need, and yet the administrators (without whose aid a consolidation could not proceed) are sometimes too busy or too reluctant to alter the form of statutory provisions with which they have become familiar. Sir Mackenzie Chalmers enjoyed repeating the playful answer he got when he suggested to an official the consolidation of the Food and Drugs Acts; 'why not leave them alone? We know all about them inside the department and the public finds out in the police-court'. Symonds had been optimistic. It had taken Hume only eighteen months, with the aid of a single clerk, to reduce three hundred customs statutes to ten; if all the departments were required to apply the same process to the statutes affecting them, the whole of the law might be cleared in a similar time. Nobody, however, should be so naive as to suppose that the process is a matter merely of scissors and paste; to draw a good consolidation Bill upon a difficult subject, said Thring, will take two or three months of the time of a good draftsman; 'the labour is immense'. Re-statement is hardly possible without amendment, and one amendment invites others. The special facilities offered at Westminster to a modern consolidating Bill, and in particular the new procedure (under an Act of 1949) for making corrections and minor improvements by a form of subordinate legislation, have been most valuable. The re-writing of income tax enactments in 1952, the cleaning up in 1959 (admittedly with some amendment) of the general and local Acts governing the reorganized railway system and the modernization of the statutes about roads and bridges (largely based on a Highway Act of 1835)—these examples show that the movement which began with the Elizabethan Statute of Labourers has not come to a halt. There was a temporary set-back in 1896 when the re-writing of the Post Office Acts was thwarted—much to the indignation of Lord Thring—by legislators who took the view that the re-wording of some references to postal packets appropriate to the era of the mail coaches was an alteration and not a mere re-enactment of the law. In the field of consolidation as also in that of expurgation progress is hampered if the legislator will not trust the integrity of the draftsman. The pace, moreover, is conditioned by the limits of man-power available in the draftsman's office where the current demands of the Government's controversial Bills must have priority.

Mention, by the way, of the work and influence of the independent and non-political Statute Law Committee could suggest that the improvement in statutory form during the past hundred years has not owed so much to the Houses of

Parliament or to successive Governments or even to legal practitioners as to the draftsmen themselves and to extra-mural interests. Stephen once contributed to the *Nineteenth Century*, an article on 'Law Reform by Private Enterprise'. He pardonably mentioned his own digests of the criminal law and of the law of evidence and spoke without bitterness of a major consolidation to which he had devoted much time as 'one of the large number of omnibuses which never managed to get through Temple Bar'; its prospects had been so remote that it was never even taken out of the stable. His suggestion that law reform might be financed out of the surplus funds of the four Inns of Court found no favour. Nevertheless it was Stephen's digest of the law of evidence that gave Chalmers the idea of similarly gathering together the whole of the law relating to bills of exchange. Chalmers read a paper on the subject to the Institute of Bankers. The Institute and the Associated Chambers of Commerce instructed him to draft a Bill which (thanks largely to the help of his friend and master Lord Herschell) reached the statute-book as the Bills of Exchange Act, 1882. This Act, like his two other successes (sale of goods and marine insurance) and like Sir Frederick Pollock's Partnership Act, was not mere consolidation of enactments but codification; it brought into a single measure also the common law and the relevant judicial decisions. If the parliamentary history of his Bills was not free from occasional disappointments, Chalmers would philosophically reflect that legislation was cheaper than litigation.

The primary purpose of Thring's drafting office was to secure sound results in uniform law-making for the future. The trouble with the English statute-book is the mountainous deposit of laws untidily enacted in past centuries. From this embarrassing inheritance the newer legislatures are happily free; for them there are other opportunities of uniformity. The Parliament of Northern Ireland, making a fresh start, has adopted the law-making procedures and the drafting principles of the Parliament at Westminster. No conspicuous standardization has emerged in the legislation of the former Crown Colonies, now mostly independent. Their laws were often drafted locally by the Attorney General and his staff. Since there existed in the background (however seldom employed) the technical power of disallowance, the local legislation would be communicated to the Secretary of State in London; there would thus be a chance to suggest revision if any flaw were detected. Rarely (perhaps mainly in the field of labour law) Whitehall might circulate a Model Ordinance. Lately there has been organized in London a course for legal officers from the Commonwealth overseas. Assisted by an impressive list of experts, the course covers legislative drafting and the somewhat different technique of treaty drafting. It is said to find that practical exercises afford the best training.

The Westminster Parliament is normally classified as unitary; schemes for creating separate legislatures for Wales or Scotland or for developing some quasi-heptarchical organization of regional legislatures within England have not yet matured. For Federal systems we must look overseas. In India, for example, the Legislative Department of the Central Government's Ministry of Law has prepared Model Bills on common subjects for adoption, if approved, by the several State Legislatures. In North America a conscious movement towards uniformity of laws has been richly rewarded. Canada and the United States have proceeded on parallel lines, the two countries having similar problems inherent in the division of sovereign powers between Central and Provincial (or State) legislatures.

In 1890 the State of New York passed a law to appoint commissioners for promoting uniformity of legislation throughout the USA. The commissioners were to examine subjects of national importance in which the several States seemed to be in conflict; they were to find the best way of making these laws uniform and to advise whether New York should invite other States to send representatives to a convention where uniform laws might be drafted for any State to adopt. The American Bar Association, having previously set up a special committee for this purpose, recommended the States to appoint commissioners. The National Conference, which first met in 1892, can be proud of the results. Its Standing Committee receives proposals for legislating on particular matters; it reports whether the drafting of a uniform law is desirable and feasible; if the report is favourable, tentative drafts are prepared by specialists and circulated throughout the country; if, after criticism and amendment, they are approved, the Conference recommends their adoption. Nearly a hundred such Bills have emerged, a few being also put forward by outside organizations. The statistics of adoption naturally vary from State to State and from Bill to Bill; South Dakota, for instance, has been far more receptive than Oklahoma. The Negotiable Instruments Act seems to have had the warmest welcome, but statutes about warehouse receipts, transfer of stocks, bills of lading and declaratory judgments have found ready acceptance.

Here was a movement in which judges, legal practitioners and academic lawyers took part. Anyone engaged in commerce could easily be persuaded that at any rate commercial law could with advantage be uniform from coast to coast. Canada followed her neighbour's example. When the Canadian Bar Association was formed, one of its five specific objects was 'to promote uniformity of legislation throughout Canada so far as consistent with the preservation of the basic system of law in the respective provinces.'

The Provincial Governments were prevailed upon to appoint representatives and in 1918 the first Conference of Commissioners on Uniformity of Laws (re-named next year 'Uniformity of Legislation') throughout Canada was organized. The happy coincidence that the Conference met at Windsor in 1942 while its counterpart in the United States was meeting not far off at Detroit facilitated the holding of a joint session at which views and experiences could be fruitfully exchanged. A similar joint session at Washington in 1950 was equally profitable. The method of operation in Canada is simple. A subject is referred to the Conference by the Bar Association. If action is approved, one or more jurisdictions will be invited to report. The report, with or without a draft Bill, is discussed at the next annual meeting of the Conference; if a draft Bill is found acceptable to a majority of the jurisdictions, it is recommended for adoption. Primarily the Conference promotes uniformity in the existing statute law, but sometimes it has prepared and recommended measures on topics not yet covered by legislation, e.g. on the law of survivorship, on the abroga-

D

tion of the rule in Russell v. Russell, on the publication of regulations and on proceedings against the Crown. Sometimes, too, the recommended Bills have, as in the case of those dealing with fire and life insurance, had the benefit of help from an outside agency. The annual report of the Conference's proceedings tabulates the substantial list of Model Statutes and shows how far each has been adopted; it mentions any amendments which are being considered and it summarizes the year's judicial decisions affecting the Acts. A collection of nearly forty Model Statutes, consolidated up to date, was published by the Conference in 1962. Attractively and clearly printed, with enviably generous spacing, it makes a handsome volume. Besides all this the Conference has issued some concise Rules of Drafting; the original set, adopted in 1919, was re-issued in 1942 with some re-grouping but no notable change of principle. Similar advice was published in 1951 by Mr Elmer Driedger, Q.C., Parliamentary Counsel and Deputy Minister in the Department of Justcie, for the guidance of officers of that department and of any other persons who might find it useful. One might compare these Canadian developments with the production of Bill-drafting Manuals in many States of the USA where various types of legislative services (whether the help comes from an Attorney General's office or from some other agency) show the increasing appreciation of the value of competence in law-making. In any comparison of the drafting arrangements in Congress with those of the United Kingdom it will not, of course, be forgotten that at Westminster the official draftsman is employed solely on Government Bills (or on Bills to which the Government is disposed to show favour) whereas in Washington, where the legislative and executive functions are constitutionally separated, there are no Government Bills nor is there any front bench of Ministers. The private member who wants to introduce a Bill of his own at Westminster will have to find his own draftsman; he may perhaps get help from the parliamentary agents who draft Private Bills—a form of Bill which must, of course, be dis-distinguished[1] from a Private Member's Bill.

[1] The term 'Private Member's Bill' explains itself. 'Private Bills' are applications for some special power or benefit not available to the general community

Macaulay, when he was framing laws for India, had no high opinion of rules for drafting. An academic course on legislation, likely to be mainly concerned with the discipline of judicial construction and interpretation (and in the United States with the inexhaustible problems of constitutionality), will be an imperfect substitute for practical training, by trial and error, under a master craftsman. A Drafting Manual is not a do-it-yourself booklet. Nevertheless, where all the guides agree, the directions must be worth following. Symonds was a disciple of Bentham; Coode (whose *Legislative Expression* accompanied the Poor Law Commissioners' report in 1843) must have known their ideas; Thring studied Coode; Ilbert followed Thring. In the United States Mr Reed Dickerson, in Canada Mr Elmer Driedger, speak the same legislative language. Mr Dickerson's forbidden circumlocutions and redundancies have affinity with Symonds and his Glossary of Proscribed Words. All the experts inculcate brevity. We think of Jane Austen's letter to her sister Cassandra—'I am going to write nothing but short sentences; there shall be two full stops in every line'. The occasion of her resolve is uncertain, but its merits in the context of law-making are obvious, despite the Horatian tag *brevis esse laboro, obscurus fio*. Contrast the characteristically crisp short sentences of a codification by Chalmers with some of the sections of the Bankruptcy (Scotland) Act, 1913, whole pages with hardly a full stop. All the experts would endorse the opinion of Symonds that the draftsman must begin with some kind of analysis; 'it is almost impossible with a good analysis to draft a bad law'. Sound logical arrangement may have to give way to political convenience; the ideal sequence is best seen today in England in the lay-out of a non-controversial consolidation statute. All the guides warn us to avoid preambles and to eschew the bastard proviso. The would-be law-maker is admonished to prefer the singular number to the plural, the active voice to the passive, the present tense to the future. He is to be careful of the imperative 'shall' and the

—e.g. petitions from a borough or county council for some variation or extension of powers in general Public Health or Local Government Acts. Promoted by different firms of 'parliamentary agents', Private Bills nevertheless exhibit much uniformity through the reluctance of parliamentary committees and officials to multiply precedents or to tolerate divergence from 'Model Clauses'.

permissive 'may'. He is cautioned against using 'said' and 'such' when 'the' and 'that' will do. He is referred to the literature about 'and/or', an expression which Sir Alison Russell said should never be allowed to corrupt the statute-book. Sometimes, when the guides agree, we feel that their recommendations are matters of taste and habit rather than of logical selection; but, if we want uniformity, we must submit to drill.

In the forefront of all the instructions will be Brougham's Golden Rule—never use different words for the same thing or the same word with different meanings. The warning illustrations are familiar. If you say 'ship', don't afterwards say 'vessel'; if you say 'contributions', don't afterwards say 'payments'; if you say 'notice served upon', don't afterwards say 'notice given to'. Not but what Lord Blackburn conceded the possibility that an enactment might vary its expressions 'to improve the graces of the style and to avoid using the same words over and over again'.[1] Lord Goddard, too, reasonably supposed that different words might creep into a Bill by way of successive amendments without any intention to change the meaning.[2] The Golden Rule stands, however, as Lord Blackburn later re-stated it; 'when the Legislature changes the words of an enactment, no doubt it must be taken *prima facie* that there was an intention to change the meaning'.[3]

Another of Brougham's rules was that the reader should never have to look forward to some subsequent page in order to find a meaning. This is the logical convention adopted in the Canadian Model Bills where the short title and the glossary of terms are found at the beginning; in the Public General Statutes passed at Westminster a less perfect sequence prevails.

Avoid repetitions, said Ilbert; provide a generic term for lists of species and stick to it. Bentham had said it first; 'if frequent mention is to be made of a class of persons for which there exists no separate or other authentic denomination, fix upon some short appellative and employ it on every occasion'.

---

[1] Hadley v. Perks (1866) L.R. 1 Q.B. at p. 457.
[2] Lines v. Hersom [1951] 2 K.B. at p. 686.
[3] R. v. Buttle (1870) L.R. 1 C.C.R. at p. 252.

A random example from a war-time Food Control Order will illustrate the value of a label or nickname:

In this Order—
'specified article' means macaroni, spaghetti, vermicelli, noodles and any similar product.'

A pre-Victorian draftsman would have repeated the whole shopping-list over and over again as in the categories of fish and ships cited by Symonds.

Be all that as it may, the rules and conventions of statutory expression are not inviolable. The symmetry of legislation, as Thring said, has to be reconciled with the independence of Parliament. In 1746 an Act declared that in future a statutory reference to 'England' should be deemed to include the Dominion of Wales. The patriotism of Welshmen no longer tolerates the assumption; statutes now speak of 'England and Wales'.

Although an ancient lawyer once declared that a well drawn clause in a Bill gave him as exquisite a pleasure as a stanza of Spenser, we are not to expect the literary touch in law-making. The *Oxford Anthology of English Prose* contains three excerpts from judgments delivered in the courts, none from statutes. Modern Bills, said Rickards, are shaped so as to pass, not to be read as good compositions. Symonds described the Irish Church Temporalities Act of 1834 as 'a splendid specimen of Irish eloquence in the legal way', its rhetoric 'quite Demosthenian'; he dismissed it nevertheless as 'without doubt the worst type of conglomeration and wordiness'. Perhaps this was unkind. Bentham wanted legislation to afford an agreeable sensation to the ear; he said that eloquence could aid utility. Law must have its dignity; what in the late war we called 'the black-out' appeared in legislation as 'the obscuration of light'. Thring, who was third classic and a fellow of his college at Cambridge, fancied that his use of words owed something to the teaching he received from Benjamin Hall Kennedy at Shrewsbury. In the last fifty years three senior Parliamentary Counsel to the Treasury have been fellows of All Souls. Draftsmen drift into drafting; it is hardly a career of original choice, though, once adopted, it develops dedication. In the United States at any rate its financial prospects are not felt to be the most alluring to the foremost graduate of a law school. But universities do now teach the making, as well as the application, of law. The fame of the Student Legislative Bureau at Harvard, the Legislative Research Centre at the University of Michigan and the Legislative Research Fund of New York's Columbia—to name a few institutions only—has crossed the Atlantic. Harvard, amongst others, can claim that it does extensive drafting; a number of Harvard men go from the Law School into drafting offices in Washington and elsewhere; others, finding themselves in the legislature of a State which has no paid drafting staff, turn their acquired skill to good purpose. Mention of Columbia University recalls a bit of ancient history (the kind of private enterprise that Stephen had in mind) which perhaps will bear re-telling.

In 1911 the late Professor Joseph P. Chamberlain wrote to President Nicholas Murray Butler, offering to create at Columbia a bureau for the scientific study of legislative drafting. The offer was accepted. What became the Columbia Legislative Drafting Research Bureau, at first experimental, was administered by a board of three members—John Bassett Moore (afterwards Judge of the Permanent Court of International Justice), Harlan Stone (then Dean of the Columbia Law School, subsequently Chief Justice of the Supreme Court at Washington) and Chamberlain himself. Its major objects were the improvement of legislative methods, the possible undertaking of drafting projects for responsible agencies outside the University, the inclusion of the study of law-making in the Law School's programme and therewith the specialized training of selected students in legislative drafting. Next year a House Committee on the Library of Congress considered schemes for establishing a Legislative Reference Bureau. The witnesses included Lord Bryce, the British Ambassador, who explained the working of the Parliamentary Counsel Office in England. There was no general acceptance of the notion that an experienced draftsman could be useful, though it seemed that the two Houses of Congress would not care to share a drafting service. When in 1913 the notion was again discussed, there

THE DRAFTING OF LAWS 55

were dissentient voices. A Senator from Georgia found the idea astonishing; the time had not yet come, he said, nor was it ever likely to come, when the Senate would need a schoolmaster to teach it how to draft a Bill. There were symptoms of a distrust of 'university professors'. The Columbia Fund decided to try a voluntary demonstration. In 1916 it sent Milton Beaman (earlier the Librarian of the Library of Congress) to Washington to give Congress what help he could. Legislation happened then to be pending for the creation of the United States Shipping Board. Invited to comment on the departmental draft, Beaman made suggestions for eliminating inconsistencies and for improving arrangement, expression and administrative detail. After two years of this pioneer work, with Congressmen inclining to the view that their committees ought not to be dependent on the generosity of an outside body, however willingly furnished, Beaman was formally appointed (under the Revenue Act of 1918) Legislative Counsel to the House of Representatives, while the late Thomas Parkinson (recently professor of legislation at Columbia and first Director of the Fund) was given a similar post with the Senate. Beaman remained at the Capitol for another thirty years, living to see the success of a venture which owed much to his own character and competence. Meanwhile at Columbia the Law School managed, as Chamberlain had hoped, to integrate the teaching of law with the practical service of law-making.

However skilled the teacher, however careful and devoted the draftsman, infallibility is not assured. 'With regard to any work that I have done', confessed Stephen, 'I have always found it full of mistakes; you look at the thing when it is finished and when it has passed out of your control and you are struck with horror to find that there is an oversight for which you cannot account.' Any textbook on Statutes is likely to contain a section on statutory errors, though these will not all be the fault of the draftsman. Perhaps the printers will accidentally have omitted the little word 'not' and another statute is needed to re-insert it. More than twenty words are repeated *per incuriam* in an inconspicuous corner of an Act of 1920; the error had lain hidden in the earliest print of the Bill and remained unnoticed. Many such mishaps are averted when draftsmen work in pairs; as Callis said long ago, *oculi plus vident quam oculus*. At hectic moments of a session 'a few words shoved in at two o'clock in the morning' may cause mischief which there is no time to repair. If legal practitioners criticize drafting, their own can be vulnerable. Thring treasured two gems, the first an amendment contributed by an eminent Q.C.:

'*Dogs trespassing on enclosed land.* Every dog found trespassing on enclosed land unaccompanied by the registered owner of such dog or other person who shall on being asked give his true name and address may be then and there destroyed by such occupier or by his order.

Monday, May 28, 1865.'

The second, a definition enshrined in the Darlington Extension and Improvement Act, 1872, Thring described as 'the result of the combined efforts of a Parliamentary Committee, Parliamentary Counsel and parliamentary agents', a case of too many cooks spoiling the broth: 'The term "new building" means any building pulled or burnt down to or within ten feet from the surface of the adjoining ground . . .'[1]

More than a century ago a writer suggested that, where a mistake in a statute was the fault of the State, the State ought to contribute towards the expense of any resultant litigation. Sometimes, where the complications of revenue law create problems of its application, the taxpayer is treated indulgently over his costs. Lord Justice Scrutton would have liked to go further. 'I regret', he once said, 'that I cannot order the costs to be paid by the draftsman of the Rent Restriction Acts and the members of the Legislature who passed them and are responsible for the obscurity of the Acts.'[2] Other distinguished judges have protested against the tortuosity of income tax enactments and have declared that the citizen is being taxed under laws which he cannot possibly understand. It is not the fault of the draftsman that many subjects of law involve repulsive complications. The following passage from the

---

[1] 35 & 36 Vict. c. cxii, s.4. By 'Parliamentary Counsel' Thring would have meant members of the Parliamentary Bar.
[2] Roe v. Russell [1928] 2 K.B. at p. 130.

National Insurance Act, 1949 (taken, of course, out of its context) is believed to have been set as an intelligence test in a Cambridge examination paper:

'For the purpose of this Part of this Schedule a person over pensionable age, not being an insured person, shall be treated as an employed person if he would be an insured person were he under pensionable age and would be an employed person were he an insured person.'

If in that sentence some loose ends of the insurance scheme are neatly tied up, those who have to administer the Act will be satisfied. Thring quoted the Duke of Wellington as having admitted that he could never understand an Act of Parliament 'in the raw state'. Some people, said Bentham, have to know all the law, some only the part that concerns them. Witnesses before the Select Committee of 1875 were asked if our laws could not be so simply stated that ordinary folk could understand them. F. S. Reilly, an experienced draftsman though not of Thring's staff, instanced the London cabmen; he thought they studied the laws affecting them and probably drew correct conclusions, 'but then they have plenty of time to devote to the purpose which other classes have not'. A more serious answer came from Sir Thomas Archibald, a justice of the Queen's Bench and afterwards of the Common Pleas; 'I do not apprehend that you can ever make any Act of Parliament so plain and clear that unlearned persons will fully understand it without skilled assistance'.

It is too late now to blame the judges for the common law's jealousy of statutes. 'In Blackstone's time', wrote Maitland, 'we see an inveterate dread of legislation; he seems to think it above the skill of earthly lawyers seriously to improve away the faults of the common law without depriving "the subject" of a bulwark or at least a palladium.' Pollock's comment is often quoted; 'some of the rules of interpretation cannot well be accounted for except on the theory that Parliament generally changes the law for the worse and that the business of the judges is to keep the mischief of its interference within the narrowest possible bounds'. The efforts of judges and juries to avoid enforcing the savage penalties of an archaic criminal code have not escaped notice. The *Spectator* referred in 1848 to 'the stupidity or tenderness of judges who, when the law has said that a man who steals a horse shall be hung, acquit the woman who steals a horse or the man who steals a mare'.

'On one point alone', observed Thring, 'Lords, Commons and judges are alike agreed, namely on the incompetency of the officials entrusted with the task of drawing Acts of Parliament.' The judges, however, are not always intolerant. Lord Denning, in particular, has shown his sympathy.

'Whenever a statute comes up for consideration, it must be remembered that it is not within human powers to foresee the manifold sets of facts which may arise, and even if it were, it is not possible to provide for them in terms free from all ambiguity. The English language is not an instrument of mathematical precision; our literature would be much the poorer if it were. This is where the draftsmen of Acts of Parliament have often been unfairly criticised.'[1]

In the same spirit Lord Macnaghten had earlier reminded us that we do not live in Utopia where a perfect language may readily be had.[2] Maybe Thring would not have felt the need of these doughty defenders. A good draftsman, he might well have maintained, will always manage to find 'proper words in proper places' provided that his clients will make up their minds what they want of him. He must, of course be allowed sufficient time. Legislative pressure, as Thring and his successors have known only too well, provides a basic contrast between the earthly and the ideal commonwealths. In Utopia, Sir Thomas More assures us, the laws are few.

[1] Denning L.J. in Seaford Court Estates Ltd. v. Asher [1949] 2 K.B. at p. 498.
[2] Income Tax Commrs. v. Pensel [1891] A.C. at p. 576.

Chapter III

PROCEDURAL LINKS BETWEEN COMMONWEALTH PARLIAMENTS

BY C. A. S. S. GORDON

In the latter half of 1895 the Legislative Assembly of Western Australia passed a bill, the main object of which was to enable any person who had cause of action against the Government to proceed for the recovery of damages without previously obtaining leave from the Crown; one of the Bill's clauses contained the restriction that in cases of accidents on Government Railways no suit could be brought for compensation in excess of £1,000. The Bill was duly forwarded to the Legislative Council, whence it was returned with an amendment striking out the figure '£1,000' and inserting '£2,000' in lieu. The Speaker of the Legislative Assembly ruled that it was a breach of the Assembly's privileges for the Upper House to make an amendment in a Bill whereby, either directly or indirectly, an additional burden might be imposed upon the people, and the Assembly accordingly disagreed to the amendment. When the Bill was returned to the Council, the President of that body gave a contrary ruling and the Council insisted on its amendment, with the eventual result that the Bill was laid aside.

This chain of events, by no means unexampled in the history of intercameral relations, was nevertheless unusual in one of its consequences. Sir James Lee Steere, the first man to hold the office of Speaker of the Legislative Assembly and a jealous champion of the rights of his House, was unwilling to allow the matter to rest undecided. Four years previously the Assembly had adopted, and the State Governor approved, a code of Standing Orders, the first of which stipulated that in all cases not provided for, resort should be had to the rules, forms and practice of the Commons House of the Imperial Parliament, which should be followed as far as they could be applied to the proceedings of the Assembly. It was in the light of this provision that the Speaker had given his ruling, and on 8th October he wrote a letter to Sir Reginald Palgrave, the then Clerk of the House of Commons, asking whether he had been correct in his interpretation of the proper relationship between the two Houses in matters of financial privilege. Palgrave's reply of 15th November can have been no disappointment to him, containing as it did the words: 'You acted precisely as the Speaker of the House of Commons would have acted.'[1]

The Standing Order provision which applied the procedure of the House of Commons in cases of doubt was not peculiar to Western Australia; similar rules found their place in the Standing Orders of all the other existing Australian legislatures, not to mention those of other Colonies, such as Jamaica and Ceylon, whose parliamentary institutions were of longer standing than any Australian House. Yet despite the intended helpfulness and deceptive simplicity of the rule, its observance must at times have caused difficulty to Colonial legislators. Knowledge of the practice of the House of Commons, as anyone who has served there will testify, is not a matter of mere intuition; it is not exhaustively contained even in the 1,145 pages of the current edition of Erskine May, still less in the slimmer volumes of its predecessors. Even so, Mr Speaker Steere's plea for guidance from the very fountain of authority appears to have been the first of its kind, and it is perhaps surprising that no similar request is recorded in the files of the Clerk of the House of Commons between 1895 and the concluding years of the first world war. Few, indeed, were received even then, and the next development in the dissemination of Westminster practice arose not from any action on the part of the overseas legislatures, but from an initiative taken in London.

[1] *Western Australia: Votes and Proceedings of the Legislative Assembly*, July 7, 1896, p. 2.

In 1927 a Conference was convened at the Colonial Office, at which Governors and officials from many parts of the Empire discussed Colonial administration in all its aspects. A paper was read to the Conference by Mr (later Sir) Bryan Fell, a Senior Clerk in the House of Commons, drawing attention to the influence which parliamentary procedure in its broad sense could exert on constitutional developments. In the course of the ensuing discussion, during which the assembled officials touched upon many facets of the usages followed in different legislatures, it was recognized that no absolute uniformity in these matters was feasible; it was nevertheless agreed that there ought to be some measure of practical assimilation in procedure, both as regards Standing Orders and also in relation to ceremonial. It was accordingly recommended by the Conference that model Standing Orders should be drawn up to serve as a basis upon which that assimilation could be achieved.[1] An inter-departmental committee of officers of the Commons on the one hand and the Colonial Office on the other was duly appointed, and set about the task of compiling such a model.

In a few months, the model was completed.[2] It consisted of 58 Standing Orders, embodying a code of procedure on the Westminster pattern, but with the rules and restrictions regarding such matters as questions and the process of legislation set out in much greater detail than in the Standing Orders of the House of Commons itself. The latter, so far from being a comprehensive description of the practice of the House, are in effect a series of modifications which the Commons have found themselves compelled, since the middle of the last century, to make to their former usages in order to conduct their increasingly complicated business; the purpose of the model Colonial Standing Orders, however, was to gather into minimal compass the necessary fundamentals of an all-embracing code. It was recognized that a model of this length could not possibly provide for every contingency, and indeed that there would probably be no single Colony in which every one of its

[1] *Colonial Office Conference, 1927: Summary of Proceedings* (Cmd. 2883), pp. 46–7; *Appendices to Summary of Proceedings* (Cmd. 2884), App. IX, pp. 84–9.
[2] *Draft Code of Model Standing Orders for the use of Colonial Legislative Councils, etc.* (Colonial Office, Miscellaneous No. 393, November 1928).

detailed provisions would be appropriate; for this reason, while the inter-departmental committee was still sitting, Sir Lonsdale Webster, the then Clerk of the House, suggested in a letter to the Secretary of State that the authorities of Colonial legislatures might be told that questions about procedure, in solving which it was felt that the experience of the Imperial Parliament might be useful, should, if the authorities thought fit, be submitted to him. Apart from the possibility of such communication of ideas being useful to the enquirer, Webster expressed the view that in time, if his suggestion were followed, information would accumulate at Westminster which might be used in a more general way. In ensuing years full advantage was taken of Webster's suggestion, and the numerous procedural enquiries which were received from Colonial sources were faithfully dealt with by Fell and subsequently, after Fell's retirement in 1937, by Mr (later Sir) Edward Fellowes, who afterwards became Clerk of the House.

The end of the second world war brought a change both in the volume of enquiries received and also in the type of enquiry made. No longer was it merely the concern of Colonial authorities to seek clarification of existing procedures; constitutional development brought in its train the necessity for altering the procedures themselves, amounting sometimes to a complete revision of existing Standing Orders. The strain that these new demands imposed on the Department of the Clerk of the House of Commons was considerable; not only had the work previously performed by Fell and Fellowes been additional to their normal departmental duties, but in the years after the war the whole scope of the work of the Department tended to increase owing to procedural changes agreed upon by the House itself. Moreover, it was soon found that discussions concerning the revision of Colonial procedures were not best carried out by correspondence, and new ground was broken in 1946 when, at the request of the Ceylon Government, Fellowes visited that country in order to undertake the necessary consultations on the spot. He repeated his journey in 1947, spending some three and a half months at the opening meetings of the bi-cameral Parliament newly instituted at Colombo. Similar visits were also paid in the years immediately following to the Sudan, the Gold Coast and Nigeria; in the latter country Fellowes had the experience, then unprecedented for a Clerk, of taking the Speaker's Chair at some of the sittings of the House of Representatives.

It was clear that it would not be possible for the Clerk's Department to continue indefinitely to dispense with the services of one of its senior Officers for such long periods, and in 1952 suggestions were made, first privately and later during a debate in the House,[1] that a new post should be created within the Department for the specific purpose of performing these and other duties in relation to Commonwealth legislatures. It was agreed that the Clerk who performed these duties should be a Clerk at the Table; in this way, it could be ensured that the advice would not be merely academic, but would derive from a personal experience of the stresses to which the occupant of the Clerk's chair is subject during the day-to-day proceedings of the legislature which he serves. Approval for the creation of the post was accordingly given, and the first appointment to it was made in April 1953.

It was originally envisaged that the Fourth Clerk at the Table (the designation of the holder of the new office) should not spend more than six months in any year overseas; in fact, during the years in which the post has been in existence, he has averaged on his travels only about one-third of that amount. His journeys are always by invitation, the expenses being borne not by the House of Commons but by the country visited; this, although it has its inconveniences, at least serves to acquit him of any suspicion of procedural imperialism. Such a suspicion would indeed be fatal to the effective performance of his duties. In the years when the model Standing Orders were in frequent use, they were constantly criticized on the ground that their makers' intention to achieve flexibility had not been fully carried out, and that they had the effect of imposing sophisticated Westminster procedures upon legislatures which were neither large nor complex enough to require them. Through his own experience of seeing Commonwealth legislatures at work, the Fourth Clerk is perhaps more aware than most of the need

[1] H.C. Deb. (1951–52) 502, cc. 363–72.

for such flexibility, and it has not been unknown for him to advise the rejection of a Westminster procedure formerly enshrined in the model. One example of such advice relates to the method by which the question on an amendment is put from the Chair. The practice of the House of Commons, and the terms of the model Standing Orders,[1] require that when the House is debating an amendment to leave out words from a motion, its decision is eventually taken upon the question 'That the words proposed to be left out stand part' of the motion—an inversion which has puzzled many Members, who understandably fail to see why, having argued hotly for the merits of such an amendment, they then should be called upon to vote 'No'. For some years now, Commonwealth authorities who have sought the guidance of the Fourth Clerk on this matter have been consistently advised that the decision can be more conveniently made upon the question 'That this amendment be agreed to', a form which now appears in the Standing Orders of several legislatures.

The impression might be gained from the foregoing that the Fourth Clerk is in effect a mere travelling draftsman; but the framing of Standing Orders is only the initial part of his work. More often than not, the revision of a Colonial Assembly's Standing Orders goes hand in hand with a stage of major constitutional development; this, in its turn, is frequently followed by an election, as a result of which many new Members are returned, of whom a large proportion are innocent of any previous parliamentary experience. To such a Member, the reading of a series of rules is not a very informative process; flesh must be put onto the bare bones, and for this reason, after such a thoroughgoing amendment of Standing Orders, the Fourth Clerk is often invited to the territory concerned in order to give a series of talks to the new Members, explaining how the Standing Orders may be expected to operate. In this way, the multifarious detail of parliamentary procedure can be related to its general objects—the achievement of some sort of certainty, both in the foreknowledge of what business is to be taken, and also in the recording of the decisions which have in fact been arrived at; the protection of the rights of minori-

[1] Model S.O. No. 47.

ties; and, equally important, the protection of the majority against obstruction. It may happen, in such circumstances, that the Speaker himself is as much of a neophyte in the ways of the legislature as is any other Member; this can be and has been used as a pregnant illustration of the advantage which can accrue to a Member through knowledge of his Assembly's procedure, since by acquiring such knowledge at the same time as does the Speaker he can attain all the greater certainty as to how the Chair itself is likely to act in any given circumstances.

A further use to which a visit by the Fourth Clerk can be put is the discussion of procedural and administrative detail with the Clerk of the legislature visited. There are many problems which are too insignificant to be the subject of a letter, but which come readily to mind during the course of conversation. From this it may emerge that the difficulty is not great enough to be worth bothering about; on the other hand, the Fourth Clerk may be able to point out that it has been encountered, and satisfactorily solved, in some other Commonwealth parliament. No code of Standing Orders, however comprehensive, can, or even ought to, include all the operating detail which goes to the proper working of the offices of the Speaker and Clerk of a legislature. In this sphere as in any other, more ground can be covered in half an hour's talk between colleagues than in months of voluminous correspondence.[1]

An early result of the activities of the Fourth Clerk, both as draftsman and expositor, was the discontinuance of the model Standing Orders. One of the duties laid upon the first occupant of the post had been the continuous review and upkeep of the model, and a revised draft was produced in 1953. Although in many respects an improvement upon its predecessor, the main result achieved by this revised version was to convince all concerned of the uselessness of the exercise in the new situation. It was now possible for the Fourth Clerk to devise new provisions to suit each new set of circumstances, and

[1] For more detailed treatment of the work of the Fourth Clerk, see author's article in *Journal of the Parliaments of the Commonwealth*, Vol. XLVI, No. 1 (January 1965), pp. 53–7.

therefore, with the approval of the Clerk of the House, the revision and use of the model was discontinued in 1954. Nevertheless, in recording the decease of this honourable institution, it must be emphasized that not all the details contained in it have perished; for instance, the list of inadmissible types of questions to Ministers still finds its place, with only slight variations of detail and additions, in every newly-drafted set of Standing Orders (it is not without interest in this context to note that the most frequent variation of form and content is to be found in the provision relating to questions upon matters *sub judice*, a topic which has caused recent difficulty to the House of Commons itself). Moreover, despite these variations of detail, a general uniformity has now been achieved in the substance of the matters for which the Standing Orders provide.

For convenience and ease of reference, a set of Standing Orders is usually divided into chapters or sections; the first of these will include various Orders of primary importance, such as those which deal with the forms to be observed in the taking of the oath of allegiance, the general duties of the Speaker and the Clerk, and such basic matters as the officially accepted languages (and, if there are more than one, the means employed for their interpretation), the quorum and the order of proceedings at the opening sitting of a new Parliament or new session. The next section may be expected to contain provisions as to the days on which the legislature will usually sit, and the times at which, on any of these days, it will normally meet and adjourn. In the smaller Colonies, such matters are often left to be determined *ad hoc* by the Chair, but as a legislature grows both in the number of its Members and the responsibilities it undertakes, it will understandably require the days and hours to be laid down in detail, subject to variation only by resolution of the House itself. It is also usual to prescribe, in respect of each sitting, the order in which the items of business comprising it may be expected to be taken.

In a third section, under the general heading 'Business of the Council', one may expect to find the rules, if any are required, relating to the degree of precedence accorded to Government business; in the smaller Colonies, as indeed, for the greater part of the year, in the House of Lords at Westminster, it is not usually necessary to accord to the Government any precedence at all in this respect over private Members, but the increasing volume of the business of Government will often make it necessary for a legislature, which has before had no provision of this nature, to set aside one or more days in the week exclusively for business sponsored by the Government. It is customary, in this chapter, to include the rules governing the presentation of papers by Ministers wishing to apprise parliament of some matter within their responsibility, the presentation of petitions from members of the public, and questions to Ministers. The latter must comprise not only the many restrictions on the substance of questions to which reference has already been made, but also provision regarding the notice which is required and the power given to the Chair to alter the text of questions so as to bring them into order. Any rules which may be needed regarding statements in the House by Ministers, the raising of matters of privilege, and the making of personal explanations by Members are also here included.

The next section normally deals with the most fundamental part of the work of any deliberative assembly—the rules of debate. These invariably conform to the accepted practice at Westminster, whereby debate is founded upon a motion formally moved and, if necessary, seconded. In most cases such a motion requires notice; provision must also be made whereby, before a decision is finally taken upon it, the motion may, if desired, be amended. This is the appropriate place for the rules which govern the precedence accorded between motions sponsored by one Member and another, and which provide for the introduction, at comparatively short notice, of debates on matters of urgency which have suddenly arisen. And besides these questions of substance, there are also details of regulation. These include such matters as the circumstances in which a Member may speak more than once during the same debate, and the occasions when, and in what manner, he may legitimately be interrupted by another Member when he is speaking. Restrictions are also necessary regarding the contents of speeches; it is, for instance, undesirable that the behaviour of certain categories of persons, such as the Queen or her Representative in the territory, judges, and Members of either Chamber of the legislature, should be subject to casual personal criticism during the course of a debate. It is also normally provided that Members who are not actually speaking should behave in such a way as not to impede the orderly conduct of the business of the House.

Few Chambers have gone as far along the road to perfection in the behaviour of their Members as has the House of Lords, which has declined to delegate to the occupant of the Woolsack any powers over the individual Peers of whom it is composed. Accordingly, a code of Standing Orders can hardly avoid containing a chapter setting out rules for the conduct of the Chair in the case of disorder arising, with provision for the suspension, for a longer or shorter period, of the disorderly Member. Full power is normally conferred on the Chair to order any Member who is guilty of tedious repetition to resume his seat, or even, if he continues to defy the rulings of the Chair, to direct his withdrawal for the remainder of the day's sitting; suspension over any greater period, however, when the House is empowered to exercise it—and not all Colonial constitutions confer such power, a matter which must always be considered when drafting this particular Standing Order—is invariably imposed by a vote of the House alone.

The remaining sections will normally deal, in greater or lesser detail, with the methods by which votes are recorded; the procedure whereby a Bill is taken through all its stages until it eventually receives the Governor's assent; the procedure for voting the financial Estimates, which, in accordance with the Westminster pattern, is normally used as an opportunity for debate upon, and criticism of, the administrative performance of the Government; the appointment, organization and procedure of Committees; the admission of strangers to the Gallery; and finally, the question of procedure to be followed in cases of doubt, to which reference was made at the beginning of this chapter.

As has already been mentioned, the Fourth Clerk at the Table spends on the average two months of each year in visiting Commonwealth legislatures; it must not be imagined, however, that his time during the remaining ten months is equally divided between correspondence with countries which he has been unable to visit, on the one hand, and his work at the Table on the other. It is not only the staff of the House of Commons who have seized upon the advantages of mobility and swiftness conferred by modern air transport; the same cause has led to a great increase in the number of overseas Clerks on visit to Westminster. Provided that discussions can take place at all, their venue is often of secondary importance; moreover, when Standing Orders are being written at a time when the drafting of a territorial Constitution has not reached its final stage, there are certain advantages in working in London, where a few moments' conversation on the telephone with the Legal Department of the Colonial Office may be sufficient to allay a perplexity which could not otherwise be resolved save by a lengthy exchange of letters. But without question the main influence which attracts Clerks of overseas Parliaments to London is the possibility of observing Westminster itself at work. An early visitor of this nature, in the years following the War, was Mr M. N. Kaul, shortly after his designation as the first Clerk of the new Central Parliament of independent India. During the weeks which he spent in London, sifting every detail of Westminster procedure to see whether or not it could usefully be applied in the new circumstances in India, there can have been few Clerks in the House of Commons to whom his penetrating questions were not addressed; and it was during the course of his conversations with Mr Kaul that the writer of this chapter, at that time a very new and inexperienced Clerk, obtained his first insight into the problems of overseas legislatures which, while sharing roots with our own, have undergone diverse evolution in detail. It was in these years also that Sir Gilbert Campion (later to become Lord Campion), the then Clerk of the House of Commons, formulated a scheme for temporary exchanges of Clerks between the House of Commons and other legislatures in the Commonwealth. Since the purpose of such exchanges was to be not merely the acquisition of knowledge by the visiting Clerk but also the imparting of it to his hosts, it was Campion's suggestion that Clerks on exchange should be prepared to perform definite duties so as to replace, partially or wholly, a member of the staff of the legislature visited; he further envisaged that the normal period of an exchange should be one year, and that there should be no strict reciprocity between Westminster and the other legislatures—in other words, that during a year when one British Clerk was visiting Canberra, the House of Commons might be receiving overlapping visits by, say, one Clerk each from Ottawa and Wellington. This scheme, and possible variants of it, were discussed at length between the authorities of the House, the Commonwealth Relations Office, the Treasury, and various Commonwealth Governments; and in November, 1951, a step towards implementing one part of it was made by the Australian House of Representatives, whose then Clerk Assistant was sent to observe and assist the House of Commons for a term of six months. Regrettably, a period of acute financial difficulty prevented the sending to Canberra of any British Clerk in exchange, and the matter was allowed to rest during the years following, despite the improvement of the financial situation.

But the period which witnessed the frustration of Lord Campion's scheme marked the inception of another, non-reciprocal, system, which has in contrast expanded and continues to flourish. In 1949 two Clerks from the Legislative Assembly of Southern Rhodesia came to Westminster for periods of approximately two months apiece, during the course of which they attended in the offices of the Clerk's Department and observed its working from within. In the following year a similar attachment was served by the Clerk of the Singapore Legislative Council; from then on, there have never been less than three such visitors, and indeed usually more, during the course of any single year. Permanent provision is now made for eight regular attachments during a calendar year, and the syllabus has been extended and formalized. During a period of eight weeks, the attached Clerks are given desks in each of the main offices of the Clerk's Department in turn; from this point of vantage, they are able to observe how the work of the office is conducted, and are encouraged to ask questions on any aspect of it which may excite their curiosity. A week is also spent in the offices of the House of Lords, whose procedural arrangements and problems are in many cases more relevant to those of the legislatures in the Commonwealth than are those of the House of Commons; the pace is less hurried, there is less pressure on the time of the House, and the proceedings are in general less formal. This is also true of the Parliament of Northern Ireland; and it has recently become the accepted practice for such attached Clerks as wish to do so to pay a visit of about a week to Stormont during the time of their attachment.

It might be thought that in view of the procedural differences between the House of Commons and other Commonwealth legislatures a course of this kind would not be in the best interests of the visiting Clerks, since its effect would be to familiarize them with a great deal of detail which they would then need to unlearn when they returned to their own legislatures; this, however, would be to misunderstand the basic nature of the system. The main utility of the attachment is to enable the visitors to observe close at hand the operation of a going concern, which the House of Commons can fortunately still claim to be despite, or even because of, its seven hundred years of existence. In the matter of questions to Ministers, for instance, the returning Clerks will not have to apply at home precisely the same rules of order and restrictions as their colleagues need to operate at Westminster; on the other hand, they will undoubtedly be required to expound and justify their own rules to their own Members who, from time to time, bring in questions which are not in order, and the many colloquies of this nature which they will have witnessed in the Table Office at Westminster may well stand them in good stead when searchfor the soft (but firm) answer that turns away wrath. And while the attachment lasts, there is always the Fourth Clerk at the Table in the background. With his own knowledge both of the procedure at Westminster and also of the rules of the legislature of the visiting Clerk, he is usually able to explain why the Commons procedure has not been, or indeed ought not to be, adopted in a particular instance in the overseas House. Discussions of this nature are, of course, more valuable if the attached Clerk has already a reasonable knowledge of his own procedures; it is therefore preferred that any Clerk coming to

Westminster on attachment shall have had at least one year's experience in the service of his House (although it has not always been possible to achieve this desirable goal, particularly in cases where a legislature or second chamber has been newly set up, or where a constitutional change has involved a great increase in parliamentary staff).

Visits of Clerks from the Commonwealth are, of course, by no means confined to these formal attachments. It may be necessary, as has already been observed, for a Commonwealth Clerk to come to London at some period during the negotiation of a new Constitution for his territory; and leave, or other reasons, may bring him to England for a period which permits a short incidental visit to Westminster. No opportunity is ever lost on these occasions of showing the visitor whatever he may wish to see, and discussing with him any points of procedural import which may have arisen either at Westminster or in his own House. Between 1949 and the time of writing, eighty-seven Clerks have been on the formal attachments described; the number of shorter visits would defy computation.

It is perhaps of interest to note that the last few years have seen the revival of the concept of exchange. Although the Clerks who come on attachment are genuinely regarded as colleagues rather than pupils, it cannot be denied that the prime object of the attachment system is to teach, and that this aspect of the scheme has made it not entirely acceptable to the older and more experienced parliaments of the Commonwealth, some of whom have over the years since 1949 sent few or no Clerks on formal attachment to Westminster. It was for this reason that the present Clerk of the House of Commons decided to put forward a modified version of Lord Campion's scheme of exchanges. The main difference between the old and new versions is the amount of time involved. It is now recognized that few legislatures would be able to spare one of their own staff for a period as long as a year, especially if the exchange is not expected to be simultaneous; but it is acknowledged also that in many cases visiting Clerks would be willing and eager not merely to sit acquiring information in the offices of the Clerk's Department, but to partake actively in some degree in the work of those offices. Several such exchanges have now been made, for periods varying between a fortnight and three months, and in each case the Clerk who has come to London has been formally listed as a Temporary Clerk in the Department of the Clerk of the House. He has thus become, during his time at Westminster, in every sense an Officer of the House, and has enjoyed the same amenities and status as are accorded to House of Commons Clerks; similar facilities have been extended to those Clerks from Westminster who have travelled on exchange visits overseas.

At this point it may be objected that although due attention has been paid to Clerks and their requirements, very little has been said about Members. For this the writer makes no apology; it is his intention to describe the procedural links between Commonwealth parliaments, and a Member who cares deeply for matters of procedure is the exception rather than the rule. He is elected by his constituents to further their interests by all the means in his power; so, of course, are all his fellows, and in making provision that the wishes of the greatest number can in some degree be met, the rules of procedure invariably fall foul of the individual Member who wishes, for doubtless admirable reasons, to claim more than his own share. Accordingly, while it is apparent to a Clerk, who spends his professional life in interpreting and ensuring the implementation of the rules of procedure, that those rules have a value in themselves, and make a positive contribution to the quality and usefulness of parliamentary debate, a Member who has been prevented by a particular rule from achieving a purpose dear to his heart may, in his exasperation, take the view that the Standing Orders are a mere obstruction to his own high purpose, to be dispensed with and evaded if this can possibly be done. A more subtle Member, however, will sense the advantage of applying in this context the principles of Judo, whereby a fighter can use to his own advantage the strength which is exerted by his opponent. It has been a heartening experience to successive Fourth Clerks at the Table, when expounding to Members of newly constituted legislatures the procedures which have been drafted for their use, to observe the acuteness and the searching nature of the questions which have been raised at the end of every one of the talks which they have given—a clear indication of the value accorded, by Members of emerging legislatures, to a real working knowledge of the rules.

But it is not easy, even for the most diligent Member, to comprehend all the possible nuances of a complicated Standing Order, no matter how carefully drafted; and when, during the course of a debate in an Assembly which has not evolved its own rules, a procedural difficulty arises, the Chair may, in understandable ignorance, give a ruling as to the interpretation of a particular Standing Order which goes quite counter to the established practice of the House of Commons, upon which that Standing Order was in all probability based. A good example of this can be found in the practice relating to the asking of supplementary Questions. In theory, a supplementary Question asked in the House of Commons is subject to precisely the same rules and restrictions as a Question of which notice has been given; in practice, however, a good deal of elasticity needs to be used by the Chair, whose occupant, not being endowed with the gift of prophecy, is not normally able to determine the content of a supplementary Question until it has actually been asked. The Speaker at Westminster will therefore normally only interrupt a supplementary Question, or refuse to allow one to be answered, when it is clear that some fundamental rule (such as the raising of a matter *sub judice*) is being infringed. In Colonial Standing Orders, however, where codification of the practice is necessary, a provision is usually inserted to the effect that the Chair may refuse any supplementary Question which in his opinion introduces matters not relative to the original Question; and it has happened in some legislatures that the Chair has interpreted this provision with such exactitude as to make the asking of a supplementary Question in any terms other than those of the original Question virtually impossible.

The opinion has been expressed, notably by the Select Committee on Procedure, that in recent years the House of Commons may have become over-tolerant of the supplementary Question which is but tenuously related to its original; but even that Committee conceded that without some degree of flexibility being retained by the Chair, the Question hour would lose its interest and liveliness.[1] The best way of avoiding excessive rigidities in the application of House of Commons rules, while at the same time indicating the bounds beyond which permissiveness in applying them should not be allowed to go, is to make arrangements for as many Speakers and Members as possible to come to Westminster and observe for themselves both the virtues and the faults displayed by the parent assembly in the interpretation of its own procedures. It is thanks to the work of the Commonwealth Parliamentary Association that this can in large measure be done.

The Colonial Office Conference of 1927, to which reference has been made, was convened at the initiative of the then Secretary of State for the Colonies, the late Mr L. S. Amery; and it was to an earlier suggestion by this far-seeing man that the Commonwealth Parliamentary Association also owes its being. In 1911, the year of the Coronation of King George V, Mr Amery proposed that facilities be provided for parliamentary delegations from all parts of the Empire to be present at the ceremony,[2] and the Empire Parliamentary Association (as it was then called) was formed as a result of discussions between the assembled delegates. Originally comprising six branches only, the Association now has over ninety, varying in size and importance from main branches, that is to say, branches formed by Members of the legislatures of the fully self-governing Commonwealth nations, to subsidiary branches, derived from the legislatures of countries which are not yet self-governing. The general aim of the Association is to promote understanding and co-operation among persons engaged in or formally associated with legislatures within the Commonwealth; the means laid down for the promotion of such understanding are, firstly, the exchange of information and visits, and secondly, periodical conferences, whether of the whole Association or of its members within a particular region. The understanding and co-operation which it is sought to promote range far beyond mere matters of parliamentary procedure. Debates at the Association's general conferences, which now take place

[1] Second Report of Session 1964–65, para. 11 (H.C. 188, p. viii).
[2] In an Address to the Royal Colonial Institute; see L. S. Amery, *My Political Life*, Vol. I, pp. 350–1.

annually, are related to every conceivable matter in respect of which Commonwealth co-operation might be relevant, and provide a valuable forum for the exchange of political and practical ideas between the assembled parliamentarians; and the visits by members of one branch to the country of another, while of course providing the visitors with excellent opportunities to see another Parliament at work, are in general used for conveying to the visitors information about the political and economic life of the country visited, rather than the minutiae of the procedure of its legislature.

There is, however, an important procedural side to the Association's activities. It has now become customary for the General Council of the Association in London to arrange, in the early summer of each year, a course for the benefit of about thirty members of overseas branches. The members of each course attend in London a series of lectures on aspects of the life and work of Members of Parliament; some of these, dealing with the work of a Member and the organizations, such as the political parties, by which that work is affected, are delivered by Members of the United Kingdom Parliament, and others, relating to the machinery of Government and its interaction with Parliament, by civil servants; but about half the lectures deal with matters of procedure, and are given by Clerks from either the Lords or the Commons. It is, of course, each lecturer's basic aim to give to the assembled Members a full and accurate account of how the procedure which he is describing operates at Westminster; but this is prevented from becoming a mere academic exercise by two factors. In the first place, it is now usual to allocate almost as much time for the asking of questions at the end of each lecture as is given to the lecture itself; in this way, the lectures develop into genuine discussions rather than mere expositions. Secondly, during the period when the members of the course are at Westminster, facilities are given for them to sit in the Gallery of one or other House on most days on which Parliament is sitting; in this way, they can relate what has been described to them in the Association's lecture room in the morning to what they see passing before them in the afternoon on the floor of the House. While the course is in London, there are manifold opportunities for any procedurally-minded member to seek out whichever Clerk is responsible in the House of Commons for particular matters which he wishes to explore; and the lectures conclude with a period known as the 'Brains Trust', half of which is devoted to the answering of political questions which have emerged from the lectures, and the other half to procedural questions—the 'Brains' contributing to the latter being usually the Clerk of the House of Commons and the Fourth Clerk at the Table. The members of the course also spend some days in observing in session the Parliament of Northern Ireland and one other of the smaller peripheral legislatures (usually either Tynwald of the Isle of Man or the States of Jersey).

Mention should finally be made of one other organization which plays its part in forging and strengthening procedural links between Commonwealth legislatures—the Society of Clerks-at-the-Table in Commonwealth Parliaments. This Society was founded in 1932 by Mr Owen Clough, on his retirement from the post of Clerk of the Senate of South Africa. Its membership is confined to Clerks and other Officers of Commonwealth legislatures, and its main object is to provide a means by which knowledge of the practice of the various legislative chambers of the Commonwealth may be made more accessible to Officers of other such legislatures. Although the Houses of the United Kingdom Parliament, and a number of other legislatures besides, make financial contributions to the Society, sufficient funds have not up till now been available to allow for interchanges of visits and conferences among the Society's members in the same way as among those of the Commonwealth Parliamentary Association; the main organ by which the objects of the Society are achieved is a journal called 'The Table', published annually, in which descriptions of matters of procedural import which have occurred in individual legislatures during the previous year are intermingled with articles of general parliamentary interest. Opportunities for meeting have, however, been found when a fair number of members of the Society have been fortuitously gathered together (as, for example, in London on the occasion of Queen Elizabeth's Coronation in 1953); and although it is unlikely that annual conferences of the whole of this body, on the lines of those of the Commonwealth Parliamentary Association, can ever be envisaged, consideration is actively being given to the possibility of more frequent meetings of a reasonable proportion of its membership.

From all the foregoing, two things will be readily apparent —in the first place, that the procedures of most legislatures in the Commonwealth are based, to a greater or lesser degree, upon the practice of the Parliament of the United Kingdom, and secondly, that machinery exists whereby this relationship may be continued and improved. The question may, however, be asked whether it is necessary or even desirable that this should be so. In many of the emerging territories of the Commonwealth, developments such as the institution of a presidential form of government, or of a one-party state, have marked a substantial deviation from the system of Parliamentary democracy as practised at Westminster, and it is not unreasonable to question whether the evolution of the new system is best served by preserving the forms of the old. Indeed, it can be argued that if an apparently freely-elected Parliament has not the power to do what can be done by its Westminster counterpart, its very existence is mischievous in that it provides opportunity for the authorities to manipulate its apparently democratic machinery for the practical suppression of democracy itself, as, for example, by using it to create an appearance of permitted opposition where none is in fact allowed. To this one can only answer that such a hypocritical attitude seems far removed from any of the existing one-party states in the Commonwealth. The role of parliament in these polities is, for the time being at any rate, subordinate to that of government; no one pretends that it is otherwise, but equally no responsible authority has claimed that this is a state of affairs desirable in itself and worthy to stand for all time.[1] Moreover, for every Commonwealth legislature whose debates may have lost some fire and effectiveness through the absence of formal party criticism, another could be adduced where the multiplicity and vigour of the parties makes the Chair's task

[1] Cf. the thoughtful analysis of the difficulties of a one-party legislature in *Report of the Presidential Commission on the Establishment of a Democratic one-party State* (Government Printer, Dar es Salaam, 1965, paras 39–60).

of ensuring the carrying-on of Government business far more burdensome than that of protecting the rights of minorities. A framework which can stand up to both these contrasting stresses is all the more likely to be sound, and it is this writer's opinion that in the great majority of parliaments, where neither of these extremes obtain and where both the disciplines and the freedoms of democracy are cherished as having value in themselves, the checks and balances which have contributed to the making of the United Kingdom Parliament can hardly be bettered. Be that opinion right or wrong, the fact remains that procedural information and advice continue to be sought from Westminster; and as long as this demand exists, the means are likely to be there to satisfy it.

Chapter IV

THE POSITION OF MEMBERS OF PARLIAMENT

BY JOHN CRAIK HENDERSON

All the countries of the Commonwealth shew to a greater or lesser extent how much, in form at least, they owe to the Westminster model.

In Commonwealth countries the privileges of Parliament and of Members and the procedure of Parliament itself is generally founded on those of Britain. The British parliamentary inheritance in the Commonwealth countries is the most significant expansion of a political way of life in the contemporary world. No homeland provides to colonies and former colonies throughout so great an area such a complete and enduring structure from the groundwork of common law to parliamentary conventions.[1] In many of these countries too there exists a feeling for and appreciation of the qualities that are required to make parliament efficient and the pillar of liberty and tolerance and this too is derived from the long history of British parliamentary government but one cannot expect in some of the emerging African countries that instinctive regard for real democracy, for the rule of law and for rights privileges and duties which is the result of centuries of a parliamentary form of government. Democracy is a word much used but with less understanding of its true meaning than almost any other word in the language.

The older countries of the Commonwealth, possessing a common heritage, naturally are closer to ourselves and our

[1] See Alexander Brady (*Democracy in the Dominions*, p. 498).

parliamentary traditions than countries whose inhabitants are accustomed to the rule of the Chief.

It is the individual members of parliament who during successive generations create the traditions and outlook of their respective parliaments and unfortunately too little is known of the beliefs, training and background of the present members of Commonwealth parliaments, their standing in their respective communities and their relationship to their constituents.

Differences too arise in the parliaments of the Commonwealth from dictatorship, single party government, federation and a presidential form of government as distinguished from our constitutional monarchy.

Where there is dictatorship or a one party government—and often these go together—then obviously there is a complete break with British traditions of Government even though the forms of government may still closely follow Westminster. In these countries the position of the member must be quite different—there can be no attempt directly or indirectly to control the executive and questions if asked must obviously be such as would not offend the dictator or government. The relationship of the member to his constituents must also be quite different.

The distinction between a Presidential form of government and a constitutional monarchy can be one more of form than of essential effect. The Indian constitution for example is a Presidential one but in most respects it more closely resembles the British constitutional monarchy than the Presidential system of the United States.

Federation also involves considerable differences both in form and in the position of the members of the Central and State parliaments. In a federation much of the constitution is concerned with the division of rights and the relationship between the Central and State governments. Australia, Canada, India and Nigeria are examples of federal government and some of the historians of these countries feel that the existence of State governments detracts from the importance of the Central government and of the individual members.

One wonders if we had parliaments for Scotland and Wales as well as for Northern Ireland and possibly also regional parliaments whether this would not detract from the importance of Westminster in particular and from parliamentary government in this country in general. It could be argued that the decline in the importance of the central parliaments in Canada or Australia—if true—is due more to distance than to federation but it can also be argued that Britain is too small for a number of Parliaments and this would involve a loss of respect for parliamentary government and the members of parliament.

In some of the Commonwealth countries, owing to the great distances from the seat of government perhaps, the State government is to the people of that State more important and certainly more personal than the Central government. Leslie F. Crisp discusses this in *Parliamentary Government of Australia* and seems to feel too that the long distances members have to travel to Canberra necessarily involves the neglect of their businesses with the probable result that some of those who might be regarded as the most suitable members are prevented from standing.

Crisp also says, at p. 64, 'It is at least noteworthy that there has been a coincidence in time of decline in the legislative importance of the private member with an increased call of electors on private members' time'. I think these remarks would also apply to this country though perhaps more to the long hours which should be spent in the House through the increase in the business of the House than to the demands by constituents on the time of private members—heavy though that is. The result, whatever the cause, is that many men who might have proved valuable and excellent members have been and will be prevented from standing for parliament and becoming members by the time occupied by parliament and the difficulty of carrying on their own business. Brady says of Canada:

'But it is doubtful whether their discussions exert an influence on national thought and political behaviour comparable to that of their overseas prototypes, or whether the House of Commons performs adequately the function which Walter Bagehot so much emphasized, that of teaching the nation what it does not know. The Federal Parliament would seem to be less effective than the British in providing to the nation real leadership and political education. It adds to the stirrings of thought, but among the populace its influence is restricted by the endemic penalty of federalism, namely the dissipation of public attention between the national and the provincial legislatures, between federal and local issues. Provincial politicians are always zealous to attract attention to themselves; the most skilful succeed. The provincial is often more impressive than the national stage because it is in nearer view.'

He also seems to feel that the parliament in Ottawa does not get the attention or perhaps have the authority of Westminster due to

'the diffuse and sprawling quality of the democracy. It too like Westminster receives in the Metropolitan press the fierce light of publicity but in the more local and regional press it commonly obtains scant attention except when its debates pertain to regional affairs or when some nation-shaking issue is involved.'[1]

Distance, the French-Canadian position affecting both Ottawa and the regions, and federalism all seem to detract somewhat from the importance and influence of the Central parliament in Canada. Perhaps it is true that parliament from its long history and the comparatively small size of Britain and Northern Ireland has greater influence and is more regarded in this country than probably in any other country in the world, but even here the respect and attention which parliament and the individual Member of Parliament used to receive, seems less. One has only to read the papers for years before the First War to realize this—debates were more widely reported and considered. This no doubt is due to many causes—the rise of a popular press which, when it reports parliament, is more interested in personalities and incidents than in the views expressed. It is no doubt too due to the motor car and television (blamed for most of the faults of today).

I think too the standing of members has fallen, but this may be due to (a) parliament making it difficult to carry on

[1] *Democracy in the Dominions*, p. 77.

work of one's own and thus closing the door to many able men who might have contributed to the standing of parliament, (b) that Members of Parliament tend more and more to be 'career politicians'. In *Parliament: A Survey*, I said at p. 93:

'The proportion of career politicians has greatly increased. A career politician is likely to become a ministerial "yes man". If he is a good party man in the House, always supports the Government, listens to the Whips and speaks only to order and never says anything to annoy his own front bench, in due course he may rise to the front bench with £5,000 a year and many perquisites. But if he takes the wrong turn, questions the decisions of his leaders, or, horror of horrors, speaks or votes against his Party, he will almost certainly find himself dropped at the next election and without salary or even possibly a trade or business to which to turn. This must lead to the strengthening of the powers of the front bench over the back benches, to the increase in the power of the Executive and to the loss of independence by Members of Parliament.

'Also the offices of profit under the Crown and otherwise have greatly increased. All Members receive £1,000 which in fact with free travelling and other perquisites is worth considerably more. There may be eighty or ninety Members in receipt of salaries as Ministers and in addition there are rich prizes: profitable offices of various kinds with the nationalized industries, as governors and judges, and these prizes go to the well-behaved Members of the Party. This all builds up the power of the leader of the Party over his followers in Parliament. For good behaviour—titles and jobs; for independence—loss of his seat and often his income and his future. Gold may be the root of all evil but sometimes it makes a man able to be independent and to vote with his conscience and against his interests. Lack of money but possession of a wife and children are very powerful advocates for loyalty to the potential spreader of the morning slice of bread.'

And in the present Wilson Government the number of Ministers in the House of Commons has been increased still further and also the remuneration of members. I think the evil effect of this increase in remunerated offices open to Members of Parliament has not been fully realized.

In the Commonwealth countries too payment of members seems to be general though it is sometimes called Expenses but the proportion of offices of profit in the lower house does not appear on the surface to be as great.

The remuneration of members in the Commonwealth countries varies greatly but always tends to increase, but an exception to the general rule was that in Nigeria in March 1962 as a result of consultations between representatives of both Houses the salaries of members were reduced by 10 per cent. The salary is now £900 per annum but there is also a travelling allowance of £266 per annum tax free. It is understood that there is a scheme in hand to increase the salary to £1,500.

The payments of members are sometimes difficult to determine. In New Zealand for example on October 16, 1964, the salary of members was increased to £2,150, but in addition the basic expense allowance was increased to £425. Members were entitled also to further payments depending on the type of electorate—a member for a wholly urban electorate receives an additional £25 whilst a member for predominantly rural electorates receives £300. There is a further sessional allowance of 15s. for each sitting day whilst Parliament is in session and a night allowance of £2 10s. for each night that a member must be absent from his home outside Wellington by reason of his proceeding to and from Wellington by the ordinary means of transport available to him (one wonders what 'ordinary' means) for the purpose of attending Parliament and for each additional night for which he must be absent from his home whilst he is in Wellington for that purpose.

In Ghana there appears to be no specific salary for members but they receive a tax free allowance of £50 per month in order to cover their basic expenses.

In Canada members of the House of Commons receive a sessional allowance. In 1954 payment was raised to $10,000, of which $2,000 represented a Tax Exempt allowance.[1] The

[1] MacGregor Dawson, *The Government of Canada*, 4th Edition, p. 360.

allowance is now $12,000 with in addition an expense allowance of $6,000 and retiring allowances on a contributory basis are now given to members of the House of Commons.

As one knows in some cases the member or senator has also a private office and secretary and if we are to have professional politicians there is something to be said for this. Members of Parliament here have either at their own expense to have an office and secretary or make use of the rather inadequate facilities connected with the House. It is an advantage to have somewhere where one can see constituents and others in privacy and where letters can be dictated and filed but in this country it would be quite impossible to supply accommodation for members in the present Palace of Westminster, but the new extensions will provide more accommodation.

To return to Canada, MacGregor Dawson at p. 366 refers to an unusual provision that a member is allowed 21 days unexcused absence but for every day over that $60 is deducted (that was in 1954, the figure may be different as may the other figures quoted when this book is published), but he adds 'both the interpretation and the enforcement of these rules are so lax that they have little effect'.

In Australia members of both Houses receive £A2,750 p.a. with allowances and free air and rail travel on parliamentary business.

It is perhaps safe to say that however called and however the remuneration may vary the countries of the Commonwealth generally pay their members, though the Bahamas and Jersey are at least exceptions.

It is to be expected that members of *our* Parliament will tend more and more to become professional politicians. I think this is unfortunate. The less monastic the atmosphere and the more the member is a member first of the community and only second of parliament the better for the country but in spite of long holidays, though shorter than in the past, the member more and more finds it difficult to give the time to his profession or business which is normally necessary. Unless the volume of work and hours of sitting can be modified one has to admit that the prospect is that politicians are likely to become 'full time' members, though some of the smaller countries, once they have found their feet, might find it possible to regulate the number of meetings or more important the times of meeting, to allow more opportunity of combining professional or business work with the work of the House, but Brady writing in 1952 said of Australian members that few men enter the legislature for whom politics is a life-long vocation—'Approximately 25 per cent of the members in every fresh Parliament are new-comers'.

In 1948 the membership of the House of Representatives in Australia was increased to 122. Brady seems to think that the smallness of the Chamber was due in part to the fear that it would have been difficult to get a sufficient number of first-class candidates with a larger House. One can appreciate in countries with a small population and perhaps a population which contained a smaller proportion of established men or men with an inherited background and a sufficiency of income the problem would be greater. In the United Kingdom at least until recently there were enough men with independent means or with businesses which enabled them to combine satisfactorily their own and parliamentary work who were willing or anxious to join the House of Commons through a desire for public service and in earlier years perhaps because it was a good club whose membership then carried a certain degree of prestige.

So far as the franchise is concerned, and that to some extent affects the choice and type of candidate, the new African Commonwealth countries shew some differences from this country, though generally men and women get the vote at 21. Even in the older Commonwealth countries the Westminster model may have had some influence on the franchise but possibly these countries had as much influence if not more on us and there are many distinctions.

In Australia for example the Secret Ballot was adopted by South Australia in 1856 and subsequently followed by many countries, In Great Britain the Ballot Act of 1872 was passed which provided for secrecy in voting. In Australia too compulsory enrolment was introduced prior to the first world war and compulsory voting in 1924. Again Australia was ahead of this country in giving women the vote in 1902 but there was a discrimination against aborigines subsequently modified.[1]

In Canada the franchise was on a property basis but seemed to cause no feeling of hardship.

In New Zealand in 1879 manhood suffrage on a residential and freehold qualification was attained. By the end of the century the property franchise was not merely swept away but in 1893 New Zealand took the lead among English speaking States in giving to women the parliamentary suffrage.[2]

So far as the older Commonwealth countries are concerned we cannot claim, at least so far as regards the breadth of the franchise that Westminster was the model. Rather it seems that they generally were in advance of us.

It is difficult at this stage to say much about the new African states for whilst their constitutions often are wide and liberal unfortunately it appears at least in some cases that the actual result falls far short and that though one may vote this may be limited (a) by choice to candidates of one party or (b) to some degree of pressure, if all is to be believed, of a rather formidable nature.

Generally in form at least most Commonwealth countries have one man one vote but in an article recently it was said:

'The fight against colonial rule in Commonwealth Africa was characterized almost uniformly by the slogan "One man one vote". Is the addendum "One party" to the slogan a post independence afterthought?'[3]

But in the Commonwealth even where the franchise is constitutionally wide and the opportunity of standing is unhindered what are the chances of a man who wants to become a Member of Parliament being successful?

In *Parliament: A Survey* Mr Bulmer-Thomas dealt with how the parliamentary aspirant here gets chosen. Generally speaking in this country any person who is a British subject and over 21 years of age is entitled to stand for Parliament if he can get people to sign his nomination paper and if he can

[1] See Brady, p. 191.   [2] Brady, p. 266.
[3] *The Round Table 1962–63*, p. 240.

put up his deposit, but even then his chance of being elected is remote unless he has the support of one of the great parties but any candidate has the same rights of speaking, of getting police protection where necessary and of protection from victimization of his supporters.

There is of course nothing wrong in the fact that an independent member has little hope of being elected unless perhaps he has become well known as a member of the House and subsequently stands as an independent. The two cases I best remember of a real independent being returned were Mr Pemberton Billing in the first world war and a prohibitionist in Dundee. One or two Communists too have been elected but they had the support of the Communist party.

In the Commonwealth the position varies greatly—generally in the older countries the same methods would apply and a man would be unlikely to be elected unless he belonged to one of the great parties but the success of the Social Credit Party in Canada is in some ways an exception. In a country with single party rule it would be essential that the prospective member belonged to the Party and was generally acceptable to the leaders of the Party.

In this country we have been brought up in the belief that the parliamentary system we know is the best method yet devised and is evidence of advanced political development and of an educated electorate and perhaps more of an electorate with an unconscious but real understanding of politics. This may appear complacent and over generous to the electors here but looking back over the past sixty years there does seem some justification for this judgment on the British electors.

To a lawyer it might seem dangerous and unsound to leave great questions including decisions involving life or death to a jury with no special qualifications for sifting evidence and little or no knowledge of law, yet the jury system has on the whole been a great success and certainly in criminal cases probably better than might have been obtained from a single judge and something of the same kind is the surprising wisdom of the electorate here even though they might seem to have little knowledge of politics or the issues at any general election.

But can such a parliamentary system succeed except after

very many years? It may be wrong to assume that the emerging African countries have yet attained that degree of political experience and that a form of government more in keeping with the rule of the Chief to which they are accustomed may not be more suitable as a starting point on the slow march towards full free and independent parliamentary government and that we cannot expect that such new countries will at once produce—even if allowed—the type of elector produced here.

In some cases it may be unrealistic to condemn an African nation for forming a one-party State. No doubt it is more democratic in the true sense to have anyone able to stand for parliament and for there to be an Opposition, but this calls for a more advanced form of democracy than may be possible in some newly emergent African States with a tradition of the rule of a chief which, I believe, allowed full and free discussion until a decision was made; after that opponents as well as supporters were expected to support whatever had been agreed.

Since writing this Sir Alan Burns has drawn my attention to *The Missionary Movement from Britain in Modern History*, by Canon Max Warren, where the author says at page 80:

'The African is fully entitled to insist that his method of 'palaver', by which unanimous opinion is arrived at after a long and patient discussion, is just as democratic as, if not more democratic than, the counting of heads and making the decision depend on a majority opinion.'

One is afraid, however, that a one-party system is likely to lead to absolute dictatorship unless the Head of State (President or whatever he may be called) is subject to election after a fixed time and that such elections are fairly and honestly conducted and held. France is an example of how somewhat dictatorial powers can be controlled to some extent by fixed elections of a President.

If one-party States are not to become arbitrary dictatorships with a completely subservient parliament—if one at all—and no freedom of speech, something requires to be done and it is interesting to read of what Tanzania has done, though we shall require to wait to see whether it works.

On January 28, 1963, President Nyerere of Tanganyika issued the following statement:

'On the 14th January I made public the decision of the National Executive of TANU that Tanganyika should become a democratic one-party State. At the same time I made it known that I had been empowered by the National Executive to appoint a Presidential Commission which would be charged with the task of considering the changes in the constitution of the Tanganyika African National Union and in the practice of government that might be necessary to bring into effect a democratic one-party State in Tanganyika.'

The Commission was set up and the chairman was Mr Kawawa, Vice-President. Among others were Mr Kambona, the Foreign Minister, and some other African citizens of the Republic. On the union of Tanganyika and Zanzibar, four Zanzibaris were appointed to the Commission. The report, which is dated March 22, 1965, is well worth reading.

From the point of view of this Chapter, paragraphs 50 to 60 inclusive are perhaps most important, dealing as they do with their recommendations as to how the candidates for parliament should be selected.

Time alone will show whether candidates will be chosen because of their qualifications or merely for unquestioning loyalty to the government, but it is an interesting experiment and appears to show a desire even in a one-party State for a certain freedom of choice.

What today are the outstanding rights and privileges of a member of parliament in this country? In a chapter such as this it is only possible to sketch a few of these. Perhaps the most important is generally the right to be free in the House to ask questions which may be most distasteful to the Government, to bring pressure on his Party through committees of his Party and generally speaking to be free from arrest or actions in respect of anything said by him in the House.

A member here will also have the right, if lucky in the ballot, to introduce a Private Member's Bill and it will be his duty and right to help or criticize a Bill on its way through the

House and we shall consider presently how far even in one party legislatures the procedure of the House is followed in its three readings and Committees and Report stages of a Bill.

The old view used to be that the legislature controlled the Cabinet but though this still happens occasionally it is usually indirectly by individual members through the Whips or expression of opinions in party meetings or even sometimes in the smoke room. More and more, however it is the Executive which controls the legislature and one is perhaps surprised that more attention has not been given to the increase in paid posts by the Wilson Government. It was bad enough before but now members can hold more paid offices, and when one adds the number who by loyal and faithful and unquestioning service may hope for other posts the power of the Executive to control the members of its own party becomes apparent.

Whilst I feel the tendency to professionalism is inevitable I am sure the result will be bad for parliament but worse for the country. The professional politician lives so much in an artificial world of divisions, tactics and personalities that he is often incapable of seeing the wood for the trees and where the needs of the country are lost in the tactics of politics. It would seem that even in some of the older Commonwealth countries the same tendency may be seen.

With regard to freedom from arrest, Erskine May (17th ed.) at p. 43 says

'Certain rights and immunities such as freedom from arrest or freedom of speech belong primarily to the individual members of each House and only secondarily and indirectly to the House itself'

and he quotes from the Journals of the House of Commons (May 20, 1675) 'that the reason of that privilege' (freedom from Arrest) 'is that Members of the House of Commons may freely attend the public affairs of that house without disturbance or interruption'.

At the commencement of each session it has been the custom of the Speaker 'In the name and on behalf of the Commons to lay claim by humble petition to their ancient and undoubted rights and privileges; particularly that their persons may be free from arrests and all molestations'.[1] One would have thought this clear but apparently for example in 1429 treason, felony and surety of the peace were excepted and May appears to consider that all criminal cases are excluded and that may be understandable where the offence would generally be regarded as criminal such as murder or rape and not political.

A surprising decision of the Committee of Privileges during the War was that the privilege of freedom from arrest did not apply to a member detained under 18B of Defence Regulations.

I spoke in the House against this decision at the time and I still consider the decision wrong. It is understandable that the House should not claim protection for a member where he is charged, without any political motive, with a criminal offence but surely the House would and should claim privilege for the arrest and detention of a member without trial and whether at the instance of King or Executive, and it is difficult to follow the argument that because the privilege is not claimed in criminal cases it follows that it also does not apply where a member is imprisoned at the instigation of the Home Secretary and held in prison without a trial and without any criminal charge being brought against him. In time of war there is always a danger of law or privilege or rights being adversely affected. In this country the danger may or may not be serious but it should prevent us being too censorious of the actions of some of the newer countries, for I can imagine no greater danger to parliament than that members could be arrested and detained without trial at the instigation of the Executive.

Reports vary as to freedom from arrest of members in Commonwealth countries. In most Commonwealth countries the rights and privileges are based on the rights of the British House of Commons. In Nigeria 'the privileges and immunities of the Nigeria Legislatures derive not from any inherent authority reposed in them but from Statute and as such they form part of the general and public law of the Federation of the Region of which the Courts are bound to take judicial notice'.[2]

[1] May, pp. 44 and 45.
[2] Nwabueze, *Constitutional Law of the Nigerian Republic*, 1964, p. 217.

Incidentally the Nigeria (Constitution) Order in Council 1960 set forth in the Second Schedule The Constitution of the Federation of Nigeria and in Chapter III dealt with Fundamental Rights including freedom of conscience and expression and personal liberty, and this provision of Fundamental Rights is something not inherited from this country. As Professor de Smith said in *The New Commonwealth and its Constitutions* at p. 162 ... 'Neither in the British Constitution itself nor in any of those Commonwealth Constitutions in which British influence had been predominant was there to be found any comprehensive statement of human right.'

In New Zealand too and other Commonwealth countries the rights and privileges are defined by statute. The New Zealand Legislature Act of 1908 Sec. 242 provides that the House shall possess the privileges possessed by the House of Commons in 1865 except where a privilege would be repugnant to the Constitution Act.[1] 1865 was the year when the provision was first enacted. In Canada the rights and privileges too are statutory and based on those of the British House of Commons.[2]

Ghana is interesting and has already since independence passed through various phases and the position of the Member of Parliament has been altered both in form, and, if reports are to be believed, also and more unfortunately in practice. Under the Ghana independence Act and the subsequent Ghana Constitution Order in Council signed by the Queen on Feb. 22, 1957 expressly or by implication the rule of law was to apply.

It was provided in Section 45 of the Constitution order that:

'It shall be lawful by laws enacted under this order to determine and regulate the privileges immunities and powers of the Assembly and its members but no such privileges immunities or powers shall exceed those of the Commons House of Parliament of the United Kingdom or the Members thereof'

but the good intentions of the Order seem to have been quite abortive.

It is remarkable what care has been taken by this country to

---

[1] See Kenneth Scott, *The New Zealand Constitution*, p. 62.
[2] See MacGregor Dawson, *The Government of Canada*, 4th ed., p. 371.

provide a liberal Constitution for the new independent countries and how at least in some cases within a few years the result is very far from what was intended.

It may seem for example a good and safe provision, as was provided in Sect. 32(1) of the Ghana Constitution Order in Council, that no amendment of the constitution was to be valid unless passed by a two-thirds majority of the Assembly but it has not proved so. Such a provision can be useless where the ruling party is able to displace judges, detain in custody important opponents and where undue influence and threats if not worse can be used with impunity as is alleged with regard to certain countries.

One interesting provision in the Constitution Order of Ghana was Sect. 27 which gave the Ghana Supreme Court exclusive jurisdiction to decide 'All questions which may arise as to the right of any person to be or remain a member of Parliament'. In this respect Ghana did not follow the Westminster pattern.[1] It may have been that it was thought that an independent judiciary would be able to approach such questions in an independent fair and judicial way but such hopes must have been extinguished when the President dismissed the Chief Justice because presumably his Court had acquitted three men charged in connection with the Kulungugu attack.

The Ghana Preventive Detention Act which was passed on July 6, 1958 permitted detention without any trial for a period up to five years and after an attack was alleged to murder or capture Dr Nkrumah the Government assumed emergency powers under the Preventive Detention Act and many members of the Opposition were arrested, including two members of the House of Assembly. The Ghana National Assembly Act, 1961, gave authority to unseat any member who was absent without the Speaker's permission from twenty consecutive sittings. This provision was used to unseat Professor Busia, leader of the Opposition.

Another provision of the Act also authorised the unseating of any member who was detained under the Preventive Detention Act.

The position therefore of any member who opposed the

[1] See Elias on *Ghana and Sierra Leone*, p. 47.

Government was a dangerous one. He could without trial be detained and because he was detained he could be unseated.

Incidentally in November 1963 President Nkrumah announced his intention of asking approval by a referendum . . . (1) To give the President power at his discretion to dismiss a Judge of the Supreme Court or a Judge of the High Court at any time for reasons which appeared to him sufficient, and (2) that there should be one National Party in Ghana and that party should be The Convention People's Party.

The referendum took place in January 1964. The result was: Yes 2,773,920; No 2,452.[1] To misquote the Duke of Wellington . . . 'If you believe these figures you will believe anything'.

Ghana of course had been proclaimed a Republic on July 1, 1960, and Dr Nkrumah became the first President. Both had been approved by a referendum. The republican Constitution contained many interesting points and has been amended to give effect to the referendum of January 1964.

In a short article it is impossible to deal at all fully with such a wide subject particularly where the position of the member in some of these countries is liable to suffer dramatic changes within a short time and in some cases has. Another difficulty is that the form and reality seem in some cases to differ considerably.

I have dealt perhaps more with the older Commonwealth countries and I have gone to the other extreme and dealt with Ghana as the first of the new African Commonwealth countries and perhaps the one that started with an apparently democratic constitution in which it was provided or inferred that members of parliament would be free to express their views without danger, that the rule of law would prevail and parliamentary elections and parliament itself would be conducted more or less on the model of Westminster. Ghana has moved rapidly away to a position where the President appears to be a virtual dictator, where there is one party government and opposition of opponents or members may involve arrest and certainly exclusion from Parliament, though fortunately there is no evidence of the execution of opponents merely for being opponents but where

---

[1] See Dennis Austin, *Politics in Ghana 1946–60*, p. 414.

much of the procedure and form of Westminster is still retained with a Speaker, a mace and the three readings of a Bill.

I wish I could have dealt more fully with some of the other countries and particularly with India—one of the most interesting and important as it must be in a country of such size and with such differences of religion and tongues.

When elections were held for the first time after independence in Central and State Parliaments in India at the end of 1951 and beginning of 1952 there was adult franchise and an electorate of over 174 millions. It was a great achievement in these circumstances that the elections proceeded in an orderly fashion.

India may have in many respects a parliament of one party, though as the result of free elections, but democratic principles, freedom of speech, and to a great extent the rule of law have been upheld. It will be a great triumph if India which follows the British parliamentary system, though with many and important variations, can survive the strains and difficulties with which it is surrounded, and the deaths within such a short time of Mr Nehru and Mr Shastri.

Perhaps one of the most valuable and important rights of a member of the House of Commons is his right to ask questions. It is not perhaps fully realized by the public in general that this is one of the greatest safeguards of liberty and methods of controlling the arbitrary acts of ministers and curbing our very efficient bureaucracy when it becomes too bureaucratic.

Members' questions range over a wide field and though the clerks at the table have full power to sub-edit questions, the Speaker's responsibility in regard to questions is limited to ensuring compliance with the rules of the House. In practice, however, few members find that they are prevented by the rules or in any other way from asking any question they desire unless they seek information about matters which are in their nature secret.[1]

It is of course the oral answer and supplementary question that are most important and the supplementary question can be very effective and in Westminster, though the Speaker might like less supplementaries, in fact considerable latitude is allowed.

It is doubtful whether in any other legislature questions have

[1] See Erskine May, p. 352.

been so fully and so usefully employed. This may be due to less expertise in the art or that constituents do not bring to the attention of their member the sort of question which is a good basis for questions.

It is difficult to get exact information as to how far the relationship between the constituent and his Member which exists in this country, applies in other Commonwealth parliaments, but my impression is that it is different, even in the older Commonwealths, and in some of the newer Commonwealths quite different, as of course it must be where there is dictatorship, or virtual dictatorship, or where there is a one party parliament. I have even heard of a member who made quite a good income by charging his constituents or others £1 for each question asked.

Supplementary questions seem not to be used as effectively in other legislatures and this is probably due at least in some part to the action of Speakers who are inclined to be more strict and to refuse to allow Supplementaries which are thought not to be strictly relative to the original question and answer and what is relative has been interpreted so strictly in some countries as to discourage supplementaries. It is difficult to imagine any one thing in parliament which shows that members are free to criticize and speak than the use of questions to check and control the acts or failures of ministers including the Prime Minister. No Minister likes questions and these are also certainly disliked by the civil service but it is to be hoped that we at least shall never see this right of members stopped or curtailed.

The former Justice Robert Jackson wrote in 1955 as quoted in *The Times* in 1965 with regard to certain differences between the United States and ourselves as follows:

'I have been repeatedly impressed with the speed and certainty with which the slightest invasion of British individual freedom or minority rights by officials of the Government is picked up in Parliament, not merely by the Opposition but by the party in power, and made the subject of persistent questioning, criticism and sometimes rebuke. There is no waiting on the theory that the judges will take care of it.

'In this country, on the contrary, we rarely have a political issue made of any kind of invasion of civil liberty. . . . In Great Britain, to observe civil liberties is good politics and to transgress the rights of the individual or the minority is bad politics. In the United States, I cannot say that this is so.'

These remarks are I think just and perhaps they apply to many other countries—naturally 'persistent questioning criticism and sometimes rebuke' are not possible in a dictatorship or easy in a one party legislature but even where there is freedom to do so without fear of arrest the rights do not seem to be used to the same extent but one fears that even here the right may in the future be less and less used especially by members of the Government Party, though no doubt opposition members will still persistently question and criticize but the most effective questioning and criticism is often that by a member of the Government Party.

At Westminster another right of a member is of introducing on certain Fridays a Private Member's Bill but this is a right of only such members as are lucky in the ballot. Some important changes in the law have been effected by such Bills. For example Sir Alan Herbert in 1937 introduced a Marriage Bill which was passed as the Matrimonial Causes Act 1937. This Act provided additional grounds for divorce and was most important. There are undoubtedly great differences of opinion as to whether it was wise to make divorce easier by giving such additional grounds but it shows at least what an important right this can be for the member lucky in the ballot.

The Ghana Constitution Order in Council 1957 Sect. 41, provided that any member could introduce any Bill and that this would be debated and disposed of according to the Standing Orders of the Assembly except that the Assembly was not to proceed upon any Bill which in the opinion of the Speaker or member presiding would dispose of or charge the Consolidated Fund or other public funds in Ghana or revoke or alter any disposition thereof or charge thereon or impose alter or repeal any rate tax or duty except with the recommendation or consent of the governor-general, but today it is impossible to believe that any Bill could be introduced and proceeded with which had not the support and approval of the government. In other legislatures members have the right of introducing Bills but it is difficult to find any evidence of this right having been responsible for the passing of any important legislation.

Another method of law making is by delegated legislation. In *Parliament: A survey* this was discussed in an interesting and able chapter by Sir Cecil Carr and in a chapter of this length it is sufficient to refer any interested readers to Sir Cecil Carr's chapter. Such delegated legislation can be far reaching and as pointed out in Erskine May at p. 608 during the war of 1939–45 the phenomenon of a three tier system appeared—first the enabling statute, secondly Orders in Council or regulations made under the statute, and thirdly orders or other instruments made under the Orders in Council or regulations.

It must be apparent that such form of law making can be dangerous. With an ordinary Bill, before it becomes law its terms are known and approved or criticized but with delegated legislation that is generally not so and parliament itself when passing such enabling statute often has little realization of the extent to which the powers may be used. The justification or pretended justification is that it lightens the burden on the legislative machine and unfortunately such delegation has been followed by other countries. In this country, at least during the War, there was such a spate of delegated legislation that even the most conscientious member could not possibly digest these and in some other Dominion parliaments the same thing happened.[1]

The principal method of legislation is by the passing of a Public Bill. The first reading is now purely formal and the real debate on the merits of the Bill occurs on the Second Reading. This is the big occasion in connection with an important Bill. 'The Second reading is the most important stage through which the bill is required to pass; for its whole principle is then at issue.'[2]

The Bill then goes into Committee of the whole House or of a standing Committee of between 20 and 50 members, where any member may propose an amendment.[3] The Committee consists

---
[1] See Dawson, *The Government of Canada*, pp. 251–2.
[2] Erskine May, p. 524.
[3] See Erskine May, pp. 478–9.

of members specially named but they are in the number of their members and the mode of choosing them more representative of the House as a whole than in a select Committee.[1] The Bill as amended is reported to the House when amendments can again be moved. The Bill is then read a third time and if passed then goes on to the House of Lords.

This procedure for passing Bills has generally been followed by the other countries of the Commonwealth except that overseas Parliaments have nothing equivalent to our Report stage. If further amendment is required a Bill is usually re-committed.

Odomosu in *The Nigerian Constitution: History and Development 1963* under the heading 'The Passage of a Bill', at p. 159, says the 'Procedure for passing a Bill follows generally the Westminster model' and 'after the Bill has been read a third time it is sent to the Senate where it undergoes similar stages. Finally the Bill receives the Governor-General's royal assent, when it becomes law'.

The passage of a Bill through parliament which is of a controversial nature, will involve opportunities for an energetic member but also if it affects his constituency, some anxiety and work. If he supports the Government in power he will want amendments passed to safeguard or help his constituents and will endeavour in private with the Minister responsible and with other members of his party also affected to get some amendment made and he will also find himself involved in a large correspondence with constituents who are affected by the Bill. He may even have deputations and callers at the House.

If on the other hand he is an Opposition member he may try to persuade the Minister to amend but if any political issue is involved he is unlikely to succeed. In that event he will want to oppose in Committee and possibly also desire to catch the Speaker's eye and speak on the Second Reading, but on an important Bill unless his constituency is particularly affected he is quite likely to be unsuccessful. In which case his opposition would be mainly shown in Committee where if it is a Committee of the whole House he should have little difficulty in speaking in opposition to certain parts of the Bill.

In this country there does not seem generally to be a 'lobby'

[1] Erskine May, p. 673.

in the American sense and different views are expressed as to the pressures brought to bear on members of other Commonwealth legislatures.

The more one studies the legislatures of the Commonwealth, the more surprising is the similarity in form of the procedures and 'trappings' of the various legislatures to Westminster, though the practice may and does in many instances differ greatly.

In recent years the term Politician has become in many countries almost a term of abuse but this is wrong. Many men are politicians because they are anxious to do public work and have as high principles as in any profession or trade. No doubt there will be many who regard parliament as giving possibly an easy way for the ambitious and able man to notoriety, if not fame, only equalled by, if not so well paid as, the popular pop star.

Much of the criticism of members arises from their getting too involved in the tactics of politics and of the few who give the appearance of constant jockeying for position. The lack of independence which often follows from a good salary as a member and no trade or profession to fall back on also helps to create this image but the great majority of members are still as decent and hard-working and conscientious as any other similar class of the community, and this I should imagine is also true of the member in many of the legislatures of the world but it will be bad for the world if with whole time professional politicians the standard falls and with the increased power of the Executive and Whips, the independence of members declines.

Whether one of the Westminster exports is the traditions, outlook and behaviour of members, I do not know but I would like to think that at least in some respects the British Member of Parliament has contributed something important to the legislatures of the Commonwealth. A friend of mine said to me recently that the Westminster model seems to succeed best in the cricket-playing countries. If this is so, the Lords and Commons cricket matches may be more important than one realized.

Chapter V

THE PARTY SYSTEM

BY IVOR BULMER-THOMAS

The statutes and other documents which comprise the written part of the British constitution, and the official reports of parliamentary debates, studiously ignore the existence of parties. When a candidate stands for Parliament he does so as John Bull, trade union official, of Wilson Road, Bexley Heath, or whatever his name, address and description may be; when he arrives in Parliament he speaks there as Mr Bull (Beaconsfield), or whatever constituency he represents. All attempts to simplify the voter's or the reader's task by including his party in the description have always been resisted. This studied indifference to party affiliations conceals the fact that in modern times the struggle for place and power between contending parties is the greatest reality of British political life. No candidate, with the single exception of the Speaker (a special case) has secured election to the Parliament of the United Kingdom since 1945 other than as the chosen representative of a party; and those members who have achieved a brief independence by incurring expulsion or renouncing the whip have been given short shrift at the ensuing general election. In Parliament almost every vote is taken on party lines; and, though a member may on most occasions abstain from voting without attracting more than raised eyebrows, to vote against his party would be treated as a sign of lunacy or criminality. It is from the majority party that the Prime Minister is drawn, and from his own party (save in times of national emergency) that he almost invariably selects his colleagues, while the policy eventually pursued is the resultant of the clash between the parties.

If we are to consider whether the British parliamentary model is suitable for other countries it is impossible to omit this vital feature of it. Let us consider what has actually happened in countries having a historical link with the United Kingdom.

In the countries peopled mainly by persons of British stock the party system has been transplanted with success and has worked as well as it does in the mother country itself. The origin of the Canadian parties ante-dates the creation of a united federal Canada in 1867, and ever since that event Canadian politics have polarized around the Conservative (since 1942 Progressive Conservative) and Liberal parties. The government at the time of the union was a coalition, but the Liberals withdrew within a year; and, except for another period of coalition at the end of the first world war and the years immediately following, Canada has ever since had a succession of Conservative and Liberal governments. Strong and stable parties based on clear-cut principles have enjoyed gifted leaders who have played some part not only in their own countries but on the world stage. The Conservatives were in power from 1868 to 1874 (exactly reversing the British experience in the United Kingdom) and from 1878 to 1896, led throughout until his death in 1891 by that most fervent admirer of the British connection, Sir John MacDonald; from 1911 to 1917 led by another great imperialist, Sir Robert Borden; from 1930 to 1935 by the redoubtable R. B. Bennett (later to take his seat in the House of Lords as Viscount Bennett); and most recently from 1957 to 1963 under J. G. Diefenbaker. The Liberals have been no less fortunate in their leadership. They provided the government of Canada from 1874 to 1878 with Alexander Mackenzie at their head and from 1896 to 1911 under the formidable Sir Wilfrid Laurier. From 1921 to 1930 and again from 1935 to 1957 they were again in power, and throughout the whole of this long period to his retirement in 1948 they were led by one man, William Lyon Mackenzie King. His mantle fell at length on Louis St Laurent, who was obliged to yield place to a Conservative government under Mr Diefenbaker in 1957 and in the following year handed over the Liberal leadership to the Oxford-trained Rhodes scholar, Mr Lester Pearson. The Conservatives then outnumbered the Liberals by 113 to 105, but were in a minority in the whole House of 265. Mr Diefenbaker remedied this state of affairs in 1958 when he led the Conservatives to their greatest victory in Canadian history, gaining 208 seats (including fifty in the Liberal stronghold of Quebec) to the Liberals' forty-nine. The Liberals edged their way back to office in 1963, and maintained their precarious position in 1966, but out of five general elections in eight years only that of 1958 was decisive. The results in the general election of 1966 were: Liberals 131, Progressive Conservatives 97, other parties 35, independents 2.

The clarity of the two-party system in Canada was blurred after the first world war by the rise of the National Progressive party drawing its support from the western farmers, but Mackenzie King modified his policies to accommodate them, and after his striking electoral victory in 1926 they practically became merged in the general Liberal body. A new party, Social Credit, based on the economic theories of Major Douglas, swept Alberta in 1935 and has since played some part in the national scene; while the rise of the Cooperative Commonwealth Federation, a social democratic party, which has achieved power in Saskatchewan, added a further complication, and its formation of the New Democratic party in 1961 in concert with the Canadian Labour Congress could be as significant for the future as the formation of the Labour Representation Committee in 1900 has proved for Great Britain. It won the not inconsiderable number of twenty-one seats in 1966. If these complications are ignored and a broad view of Canadian political history since 1867 is taken, it stands out as a copy-book example of the working of the party system. The fact that the party system has functioned so smoothly in producing a succession of stable governments under good leadership has incontestably been a major factor in the growth of the Canadian economy and the emergence of Canada as a world power. There was no inevitability in the process. The existence in Quebec of a large body of citizens differing from their fellow-Canadians in origin, language, religion and feeling contained elements of potential conflict such as have made the party systems of other countries creak and break down; but French-speaking Canadians have been content to support either of the two great parties rather than to create their own, and they have twice provided leaders of the Liberal party who have also been Prime Ministers of the dominion.

Owing to a succession of changes of name, re-grouping, alliances and splits the course of Australian party politics is not so easy to chart, but in the outcome it has proved hardly less satisfactory than the Canadian system as a means of settling political differences and determining policy. In the Australian states before federation in 1901 the main element in the political scene was the struggle between protectionists and free-traders, competing with each other for the support of 'centre' voters, but they were political groups rather than organized parties. The formation of the Australian Labour party in 1891—it is the oldest Labour party in the Commonwealth—and its success in gaining control of the federal government for short periods in 1904 and 1908-9 by taking advantage of divisions among the older political groups, led most of the protectionists and free-traders to join together and form a new party known at first as 'the fusion' but from 1913 as the Liberal party. In this manner Australia came to possess by 1909 a clearly-defined two-party system. The Labour party was the more highly disciplined and in 1908 adopted the caucus system whereby binding decisions on how members should vote were taken at private meetings of the party, and ministers or their 'shadows' elected; but this rigid discipline did not prevent a serious split during the first world war. After the Liberal defeat at a general election in 1913 Labour had its first taste of real power. The Prime Minister, Andrew Fisher, promised Australia's last man and last shilling to the war effort, and when he went to London as High Commissioner his successor, William Morris Hughes, came to the conclusion that it was necessary to introduce conscription; but he failed to carry a majority of the party with him and withdrew from it with those who supported him over conscription. They described themselves as National Labour, and Hughes formed a coalition government composed of Liberal and National Labour ministers. In a short time Liberals and National Labour coalesced to form the Nationalist party.

The two-party system based on the confrontation of Nationalists and Labour did not last long, for in 1919, following earlier moves in the states, a Country party was formed to represent the interest of farmers. This party has never attempted to represent more than a sectional interest, but it is, of course, in Australia a very powerful interest. The rise of the Country party at first weakened the Nationalist cause, and led to a revival of Labour's fortunes, but in 1923 an alliance was struck between the Nationalist and Country parties, and through coalition governments this dominated the political scene until 1929. Labour then won a sweeping victory, but (as in Great Britain) the sweets of victory were turned bitter by the great depression. The Labour party shed sections at each extreme, and in 1931 was defeated at the polls. The United Australia party was formed at this time by a combination of seceders from Labour with the Nationalists; the Country party agreed with it in general principles but declined to fuse with it.

The United Australia and Country parties dominated Australian politics until 1937, and the former Labour minister, J. A. Lyons, who had been chosen leader of the UAP, managed, despite increasing difficulties, to remain Prime Minister until 1939. At this point Robert Gordon Menzies, who had abandoned a brilliant legal career, took over from him the leadership of the United Australia party and was Prime Minister at the outbreak of the second world war. The reviving fortunes of Labour brought it back to favour at the next election, and the Labour party was in power from 1941 to 1949. The members of the United Australia party felt it necessary to refurbish the party's image, and in 1944 it was wound up and a new Liberal party constituted. This was not, of course, the same body as the old Liberal party which existed from 1913 to the end of the first world war, though a line of descent can be traced, and the name (like that of the Italian Liberal party) denoted a political stand more Conservative than Liberal by English measurement. The Liberal and Country parties entered into an alliance, won the elections of 1949, and through coalitions have governed the Australian Commonwealth in the whole long period since that date. The Liberal-Country dominance was facilitated by a third split in the Australian Labour party, which after several years of dissension, became open in 1955. The split took place over the attitude to be adopted to Communism. Roman

Catholics of Irish origin had always played a big part in the Australian Labour party, and their hierarchy led the demand for more effective measures to prevent infiltration by Communists. One result was the formation of the Australian Democratic Labour party. The Liberal-Country coalition has by now won six consecutive general elections, and Sir Robert Menzies, who passed the previous cumulative record for the tenure of the highest office as far back as 1954, had been Prime Minister in all for eighteen years. When he laid down his responsibilities early in 1966 and went into honourable retirement he was succeeded as leader of the Liberal party and as Prime Minister by Mr Harold Holt.

Despite the fluid character of Australian party politics, the general picture left by Australian history since the Commonwealth came into being is that of a strong Labour party based on the trade unions opposed by an alliance of two conservative parties, which have taken different names at different epochs. Outwardly the system is tripartite, but in practice it is a duality. The system has evolved notable leaders who have not allowed the rest of the world to forget Australia's existence—notably W. M. Hughes; Stanley Melbourne Bruce (now Viscount Bruce of Melbourne), the Nationalist Prime Minister from 1923 to 1929; J. B. Chiffley, Labour Prime Minister after the second world war; and above all R. G. Menzies. It has provided Australia with strong and stable governments who can be trusted to keep their international engagements. Though it has also thrown up some leaders with less secure reputations, it has laid the basis for the development of Australia as a great producer and leading member of the comity of nations.

New Zealand was given self-government in 1852, and the emergence of a party system was at first impeded by the struggle between the central government and the provincial councils and by the Maori wars. When these constitutional and racial issues had been settled, politics took on the pattern of a struggle between the Conservatives and the groups calling themselves radical or progressive. In the prolonged depression which began in 1879 the Conservatives were voted into power and held office for twelve years, but at the turn of the year 1890–91 Sir Harry Atkinson's government was overthrown by the progressives under John Ballance, who began to call themselves Liberals. About this time the trade unions started to take an active part in politics. At first they supported the Liberal party, which remained in office for twenty-one years, led after Ballance's death by Richard Seddon and Sir Joseph Ward, but in 1910 they decided to set up a Labour party. This was a contributory factor to the defeat of the Liberals in 1912, when the Conservatives, who had by then taken the title of the Reform party, returned to power under William Ferguson Massey. A coalition ministry of the Reform and Liberal parties was formed in the first world war, but the Liberals withdrew in 1919. Massey was able to stay in office, thanks to the division of the opposing forces between Liberals and Labour, until his death in 1925, when he was succeeded by Joseph Gordon Coates. In the general election of that year the Reformers won a sweeping victory, largely at the expense of the Liberals, and although Labour won only twelve seats it soon gained some by-elections and became the official opposition. The Liberals returned to office in 1928—under the veteran Sir Joseph Ward who retired shortly before his death in 1930—and in 1931 his successor, George William Forbes, formed a coalition government of Liberal and Reform ministers to deal with the economic crisis. Faced with the rise of Labour, the Liberal and Reformers then fused their organizations in the National party, and New Zealand thus came to possess once more a two-party system. Labour, under the leadership of Michael Joseph Savage, won a sweeping victory in 1935, and its triumph was confirmed in 1938. On Savage's death in 1940 during the second world war Peter Frazer became leader and Prime Minister, but in 1949 Labour was defeated by the National party under Sidney George Holland. The National party remained in power for eight years. In 1958 Labour resumed office with Walter Nash as Prime Minister, but the National party, now with Keith Jacka Holyoake as its leader, recovered the favours of the electorate in 1960, and has since been in power. In a broad view of New Zealand's party history we see the early opposition of conservatives and radicals disturbed by the rise of a new party based on the trade unions, and we see the parties re-grouping so that a two-party system of Nationalists and Labour is established. It is a story similar to that of the mother country, and the New Zealand parties have, no less than the British, proved themselves responsive to the needs of the hour and capable of throwing up leaders and policies equal to the occasion.

In the oversea countries of mainly British stock the British party system has therefore been transplanted with few differences and has functioned well. Two strong parties contend for the right to form the government; they may change their names and their policies over the years; they may be disturbed by the rise of a new party, and new groupings may take place, but at the end there are still two strong parties seeking the favour of the electors, hardly troubled by such smaller parties as may arise; and these two strong parties have provided strong and stable government, often for long periods without a break. It is a more chequered story when we turn to the formerly dependent territories of non-British stock.

In the first place we naturally turn to the Indian sub-continent, not merely because of its vast population but because the Indian experience has been a guide in many other countries formerly under British rule. The India sub-continent illustrates pre-eminently two principles which continually recur. (1) Because the main political interest for many years has been the achievement of self-government, all other considerations such as divide parties in Great Britain are subordinated to nationalism. All the loyalties of the politically conscious section of the population are given to that body which looks most likely to secure the termination of foreign rule. It would weaken the nationalist cause, and would be considered disloyal, to work for any rival body. The basis for a party system on the United Kingdom model thus cannot exist before the achievement of independence. All the energies and loyalties of the local political figures are given to a single organization dedicated to the task of ending foreign rule. When independence is achieved, political power has naturally to be conceded to that body which has done most to achieve it. Independence is therefore achieved as a one-party state. Parties which have power are reluctant to share it, and do not consider it their duty to create an opposition; while the force of inertia also operates, for the formation of a new political party is a major task, and the party which has achieved independence tends to retain support even when economic, educational and social questions take the place of nationalism as the main interest in political life. There is thus a tendency for countries which have gained their independence of foreign rule to begin their independent life as one-party states. (2) The second principle runs counter to the first. The peoples of the formerly dependent territories of the British Commonwealth rarely constitute a nation, and frequently they are not an economic or even a geographical entity. It is only gradually that the administrators become conscious of the differences among the peoples they rule, and it has been the policy of successive British administrators to weld the peoples for whom they are trustees into a national unity. This has proved an immensely difficult task, and the ancient divisions of race, tribe and religion have always been hindrances and sometimes insuperable impediments to the creation of national unity. It may thus happen that when parties arise it is not on the basis of social and economic differences as in the party systems of the United Kingdom, Canada, Australia and New Zealand, but on the basis of race or religion or a combination of both. The strife between these parties may be so sharp that there is no way of resolving their differences except by keeping them apart, that is, by dividing the area which it was hoped to create into a national unity.

This is what has happened in the Indian sub-continent. When the Crown took over the administration in 1857, it became the ruler of many vast populations differing in language and religion and divided by caste. It became the aim of British policy, at first unconscious and then conscious, to fuse this great amalgam of peoples into a nation. In the outcome amazing success was achieved in creating nationhood, but there was one problem that defied solution, the difference between Hindu and Muslim, and eventually two states were created.

The first body in the sub-continent having the character of a political party was the Indian Association founded by Surendranath Banerjea in 1876, but of far greater ultimate importance was the establishment in 1885 of the Indian National Congress. Its founder was an Englishman, Allan Hume, but it soon became the main vehicle of Indian nationalist aspirations. It was intended in the first place to be a sort of Indian Parliament where grievances could be discussed even if no action could be taken; but the permanent organization for the convening of such congresses had the character of a party. The first congress was attended by seventy-two delegates, and in retrospect it can be seen as significant that only two of them were Muslims. The second was attended by 440, but only thirty-three Muslims were among them. In 1906 the Muslim League was formed as a counterpoise to Congress, and relations between politically-minded Hindus and Muslims deteriorated. After the return of Gandhi from South Africa, and his application in India of the policy of non-resistance, the Indian National Congress grew in importance. In 1923 the Swaraj party was founded by supporters of the Congress to contest elections to the legislatures provided under the Government of India Act, 1919. It was led by the Pandit Motilal Nehru and Chitta Ranjan Das, and its aim was to wreck the constitution by obstruction. (The parallel with the Irish party in the House of Commons after 1886 is not out of place.) It was merged in the Congress organization in 1926.

The Simon Commission, appointed in advance of its time in 1927 to review the working of the 1919 Act, pointed out:

'Political thought in British India today is derived from Europe. The keen intelligence of the educated Indian has been stimulated by study of Western institutions. It is remarkable how the theories and phrases of political science as expounded in England and America have been adopted and absorbed'.[1]

When they came to their recommendations, however, Simon and his colleagues had to admit that communal feeling had stultified the development of a true party system.

'The minds of all were fixed on the future. Every community and every interest was thinking of what its position would be under the next constitution. The result was to intensify communal rivalries. Every community tried to consolidate its

[1] Cmd. 3568, p. 406.

position. Groups tended to coalesce on communal lines. Communal advantages were sought in the regulation and recruiting of the services.... In such circumstances, the growth of political parties on a basis related to the actual problems of India and to different attitudes of mind towards the solution of practical difficulties could not take place. Parties were aligned in accordance with their views as to the best tactics for securing the next advance.'[1]

These considerations led the Simon Commission to pose the basic question which is the theme of this book.

'It was in any case a difficult and delicate operation to trans plant to India forms of government which are native to British soil, and what was needed was that the new institutions should have time to take root and to grow naturally. The British parliamentary system has developed in acordance with the day-to-day needs of the people, and has been fitted like a well-worn garment to the figure of the wearer, but it does not follow that it will suit everybody. Custom and convenience have retained in it various provisions which, formed for one purpose, are in practice used for another. Many of its detailed contrivances work only because there is the will to make them do so, or because there is a general understanding that they will be used in moderation.

'British parliamentarism in India is a translation, and in even the best translations the essential meaning is apt to be lost. We have ourselves in attending debates in the Assembly and provincial councils been more impressed with their difference from than their resemblance to the Parliament we know.

'While the principles and practice of the British parliamentary system are accepted by educated Indians as the best example of democracy in action, they are being applied in a country where the conditions and the mental habit of the people are very different.'[2]

The Simon Commission refrained from saying outright that British parliamentary institutions were unsuitable for India, but

[1] Cmd. 3569, p. 6.   [2] Cmd. 3569, pp. 6–7.

H

it emphasized the long time that those institutions had taken to mature.

'Ultra-democratic constitutions are propounded, although the long process which was a necessary antecedent to democracy in Europe, viz., the breaking down of class and communal and occupational barriers, has only just begun. Indian political thought finds it tempting to foreshorten history, and is, unwilling to wait for the final stage of a prolonged evolution. It is impatient of the doctrine of gradualness.'[1]

In the outcome the modest proposals of the Simon Commission were outstripped by events, and the Round Table Conference was followed by the Government of India Act, 1935, which made provision for eleven autonomous governors' provinces in British India and for an all-India federation. Elections for the provincial legislatures were held in 1937, and brought the differences between Congress and the Muslim League to a head. Claiming to be a non-communal body representing Muslims as well as Hindus, and working for a unitary, independent sub-continent, Congress under the leadership of Gandhi with Jawaharlal Nehru as his chief lieutenant secured large majorities in six of the eleven provinces and proceeded to form exclusively Congress ministries which were in practice strictly under the control of the party machine. Until that time the Muslim League had also aimed at an all-India solution, and its leader, Mohammed Ali Jinnah, had supported cooperation with Congress, but the claim of Congress to represent all Indians and to set up exclusively Congress ministries exasperated him; and the League's electoral successes justified its claim to speak for the Muslims.

In 1940 the League came out in favour of the partition of India between the predominantly Hindu and predominantly Muslim areas, and after all attempts to find a unitary solution had failed the inevitability of partition was recognized in the India Independence Act, 1947. The advancement of the date for British withdrawal made it impossible for the administrators to effect an orderly transfer of power, and a panic mass migra-

[1] Cmd. 3568, p. 406.

tion accompanied by hideous slaughter took place. In the outcome power was effectively handed to the Congress party, now led by Jawaharlal Nehru, in India and to the Muslim League, led by Jinnah, in Pakistan.

In India the Congress party received a massive vote of confidence at the general election of 1951–52. It won no fewer than 362 out of the 489 seats in the Lok Sabha (Lower House). The Communists, though far behind with only twenty-three seats, emerged as the next biggest party, but only in Madras and Travancore did they achieve any real measure of success. The Praja Socialists were next in strength with twenty-one seats, and the Jan Sangh, a militant Hindu party, won three. Dissatisfaction with the dominating role of Congress was more adequately expressed by the eighty Independents who were successful than by the other parties. At the next general election in 1957 the results were much the same. Congress won 371 seats in the Lok Sabha, the Communists twenty-nine, the Praja Socialists nineteen, the unqualified Socialists seven, the Jan Sangh four, and there were sixty-four Independents. A conservative party known as the Swatantra (Freedom) party was formed by C. Rajagopalachari, a former governor-general, in 1958, and it contested the general election of 1961. The results were: Congress, 361; Communist, twenty-nine; Swatantra, eighteen; Jan Sangh, fourteen; Praja Socialists, twelve; Socialists, six; Independents, fifty-four.

The Congress party at the same time secured majorities in all the state assemblies and formed all the state governments. Only on two occasions has an Indian state had a non-Congress administration, and in the elections for the Lok Sabha only in four districts out of nearly 300 has any other single party ever secured more votes than Congress.

The above figures show that India since independence has been effectively a one-party state, but it is only fair to add that this has come about without any improper pressure on voters. The opportunities for forming other parties and voting for other candidates exist, but the hold of Congress on the Indian masses is profound and so far scarcely shaken.

There have been two occasions in recent years when the stability of the Indian political system might have been severely tested—on the passing of Nehru in 1964 and on the sudden death of his successor, Lal Bahadur Shastri in 1966, immediately after signing at Tashkent an agreement with Pakistan designed to end the friction between the two countries. On both occasions the transfer of the leadership of party and State was swiftly and smoothly effected; and the fact that on the second occasion the choice fell on a woman, even though that woman was Nehru's daughter, Mrs Indira Gandhi, emphasizes the confidence of Congress in itself.

The history of party in Pakistan has been more stormy. It might have been less so if Jinnah, who became the first governor-general, had not died in 1948 and if the first Prime Minister, Liaquat Ali Khan, had not been assassinated three years later. It would also have helped if Pakistan were a continuous landmass instead of consisting of two parts 900 miles apart. While the constituent assembly was labouring to produce a federal constitution, elections were held for provincial assemblies between 1951 and 1954. In Punjab, the North-west Frontier province and Sind the Muslim League won big majorities, but in East Bengal it was overwhelmingly defeated by a united front of non-League Muslims and others. The League began to split into factions in the west, and after a crisis in 1954 the governor-general dissolved the assembly, and appointed a non-party government with Muhammad Ali as Prime Minister, assisted by two non-League figures, Khan Sahib from the North-west Frontier Province, and H. S. Suhrawardy from East Bengal; the government was given the task of preparing a new constitution, including the making of West Pakistan into a single political unit on the same footing as East Pakistan. There was much argument, in the courts and elsewhere, about the validity of these actions, but the elections were duly held in 1955 on the basis of parity of representation between East and West Pakistan. The Muslim League was returned as the largest party, but did not have a working majority. Muhammad Ali resigned, and his Finance Minister, Chaudri Muhammad Ali, succeeded as Prime Minister and brought members of the East Pakistan United Front into his government. At the end of 1957 Firoz Khan Noon formed a coalition government out of the Republican party, founded by Khan Sahib, two sections of the Awami

League, founded by H. S. Suhrawardy, and some smaller groups. The Republican League suffered when its founder, Khan Sahib, was assassinated in 1958, and the Muslim League recovered some of its lost ground. Chaudri Muhammad Ali formed a new group, the Nizam-i-Islam. The political situation in East Pakistan deteriorated so greatly that the Speaker and Deputy Speaker of the Provincial Assembly were bodily attacked; a resolution declaring the former to be of unsound mind was passed, and the latter died of his injuries. On October 7, 1958 President Mirza—Pakistan had become a republic two years before—dismissed the central and provincial cabinets and assemblies, declared political parties illegal, and imposed martial law under the administration of General Muhommad Ayub Khan, who later succeeded him as President. Martial law was terminated in 1961, and at the same time a new constitution vesting all executive authority in the President was announced. Under it 'basic democracies' elected by adult suffrage formed an electoral college which chose the President and members of the national and provincial assemblies.

With the new constitution parties were again tolerated. The Muslim League remained the strongest single force, but split into two sections—the 'Conventionists', supporting and supported by the government, and the 'Councillors', led by Khwaja Nazimuddin, who joined the opposition. The opposition forces were weakened in 1963 by the death of H. S. Suhrawardy, and it is pleasing to record that, although he had been the outstanding opponent of the new constitution, and had spent nine months of the previous year as a political prisoner, on the occasion of his funeral President Ayub Khan ordered flags to be flown at half-mast on government buildings. The first elections under the new constitution—to elect 40,000 Basic Democrats in each of the two provinces—were arranged for the autumn of 1964, and as they approached Khwaja Nazimuddin brought the opposition parties together into a loose combination known as the Combined Opposition Parties. They had an agreed programme including direct election by adult suffrage and a substantial transfer of power from the President to the Assemblies. The main task of the Basic Democrats was to elect a President (and thereafter members of the Assemblies). President Ayub

Khan was supported for re-election by the major section of the Muslim League, and the day before the COP met to select a candidate the National Awami party declared their support for Miss Fatima Jinnah, sister of the architect of Pakistan. The other parties thereupon had little option but to declare for her also, though the Jamaat-i-Islam was reluctant to admit that a woman could ever be head of a Muslim state. The opposition was weakened by the death during the campaign of Khwaja Nazimuddin. The elections for the presidency were held on January 2, 1965, when President Ayub Khan received 49,647 votes and Miss Jinnah 28,343, a sufficient indication of the relative strength of the government and opposition parties.

Ceylon occupies an intermediate position between the virtually one-party state of India and the temporary collapse of the party system in Pakistan. As an island it is a natural geographical entity, but the diversity of its peoples and religion have encouraged the proliferation of parties. The dominant political body when Ceylon received independence in 1948 was the United National party founded and led by Don Stephen Senanayake until his death in 1952, but a large number of competitors soon sprang up. In 1951 S. W. R. D. Bandaranaike resigned from the government, and in the following year he founded the Sri Lanka ('Blessed Ceylon') Freedom party with a socialist outlook. This has ever since been the chief opponent of the United National Party, led after his father's death by Dudley Senanayake, and these two far exceed in importance any of the other parties. In 1956 the Sri Lanka Freedom party joined with three other parties of the left to form the People's United Front, and the Front won the general election of that year. A split took place in the P.U.F. in 1959, and Bandaranaike lost his majority. He was assassinated soon afterwards by a Buddhist monk. W. Dahananake who succeeded him as Prime Minister resigned from the Sri Lanka party in 1960 and formed the Ceylon Democratic party. Two elections were held in that year. The first, in March, was contested by more than twenty parties, and the United National party secured a narrow victory over the Sri Lanka party with fifty members against forty-six; the Ceylon Democratic party was totally unsuccessful, and Dudley Senanayake became Prime Minister again. His efforts to win the support of the (Tamil) Federal party, with fifteen seats, was unsuccessful, and within a month he was defeated. New elections were called for July, and in these the Sri Lanka Freedom party won seventy-five seats out of 151, against thirty won by the United National Party. Mrs Bandaranaike widow of the assassinated statesman, became Prime Minister—the first woman Prime Minister in the world. The government soon lost popularity through its attempts to take over assisted schools, to form public corporations for the purpose of running the newspapers, to nationalize life insurance and to expropriate installations of the oil companies. Though nominally possessing half the seats in the House, and being able to call on the votes of six nominated members, Mrs Bandaranaike's government ran into trouble. In 1964 she prorogued Parliament for four months and entered into discussions with the United Left Front for a coalition. In the event only representatives of the Trotskyite Sama Samaja ('Equal Society') party were taken into the government. Far from consolidating Mrs Bandaranaike's majority the formation of the coalition had the effect, along with the socialistic measures, of drawing seventeen of her former supporters across the floor of the House. Her government was defeated by seventy-four votes to seventy-three on a vote of no confidence, and in the ensuing general election held in 1965 the (Tamil) Federal party, the Tamil Congress, the Sri Lanka Freedom Socialist party and the People's United Front agreed to support Mr Senanayake's United National party against Mrs Bandaranaike's coalition. The result in terms of seats were:

Mr Senanayake's coalition		*Mrs Bandaranaike's coalition*	
United National party	66	Sri Lanka Freedom party	41
Federal party	14	Lanka Sama Samaj party	10
Sri Lanka Freedom socialist party	5	Communist party	4
Tamil Congress	3		
People's United Front	2		
	90		55
Independents	6	National Liberation Front	1

Mr Senanayake thus obtained ninety supporters against Mrs Bandaranaike's fifty-five, with seven members uncommitted.

Though Mrs Bandaranaike was reluctant to yield up the reins of power, she eventually recognized the verdict of the electors, and Mr Senanayake became Prime Minister again.

Even if the Ceylon scene may perplex British and American observers by the multiplicity of party names, in practice it has been virtually a two-party system, and the way in which Mrs Bandaranaike, as a result of pursuing unpopular policies, was overthrown by proper parliamentary and electoral process, is a good example of the working of that system.

Among the former colonial territories of the British Empire Nigeria is pre-eminent in having a population which probably equals that of the United Kingdom itself; but this population is made up of peoples of diverse tribes, languages and religions, and apart from the coast the frontier does not coincide with any ethnic, geographic or economic boundary. It was almost inevitable, therefore, that parties in Nigeria, when they arose, should be based on tribal divisions, which are to a large extent geographical divisions, and the great question when full independence was finally achieved in 1960 was whether the country would remain an entity once the unifying force of British power was withdrawn.

The federation was divided at the outset into Eastern, Western and Northern regions with the federal capital of Lagos as a separate entity. These corresponded to the great ethnic divisions, the Hausa and Hausa-speaking Fulani, Muslim in religion, being mainly in the North, the Ibo mainly in the East, and the Yoruba mainly in the West, sometimes Christian but mainly pagan and animistic in their religious outlooks, with a high proportion of the educated, Westernized Nigerians in Lagos. Eastern and Western Nigeria became self-governing in 1957, the Northern region, which had always been more conservative and less politically articulate, in 1959. After a plebiscite, a new Mid-west region was created in 1963 for the non-Yoruba people of the Western region around the old kingdom of Benin.

The parties have followed these divisions. The first in the field was the National Council of Nigeria and the Cameroons, which was founded in 1944 by Dr Nnamdi Azikiwe. Until 1946 he was its general secretary, from 1946 to 1960 its president.

He was the chief spokesman of the demand for independence, and when independence was granted in 1960 he became the first Governor-General and later the first President of the federation. Though intended to be an all-Nigerian party, the NCNC has always been strongest in the Eastern Region, and after leading the opposition in the Western House of Assembly in 1952 to 1953, Dr Azikiwe was Premier of the Eastern Region from 1954 to 1959. The Action party was founded to represent the interests of the Yoruba in the Western region, and in due course the Northern People's Congress was formed to speak for the more traditional peoples of the northern part of the country. These three parties have dominated the respective regional legislatures, and by reason of the weight of population the Northern People's Congress, though slowest off the mark, has been the predominant element in the federal Parliament.

After the first federal elections held in 1959 a coalition government drawn from the NPC and the NCNC was formed with Sir Abubukar Tafawa Balewa, a leading figure in the Northern People's Congress, as the Prime Minister. (He had been holding that post for the two years before independence.) The opposition in the federal Parliament was provided by the Action party, and Chief Awolowo gave up the post of Premier of the Western region, in which he was succeeded by Chief Akintola, in order to lead it. A serious split in the Action party led to a crisis in the Western region in 1962, when Chief Akintola was deposed from the leadership by the party's national executive. He asked for a dissolution, but the Governor refused and deposed him from the office of Prime Minister. (The Federal Supreme Court later declared the deposition invalid.) The resulting disorders led to the proclamation of a state of emergency, and when it was lifted Chief Akintola again became the premier in a coalition government. In 1963 Chief Awolowo, the Action party's national leader, after a long trial, was sentenced to ten years' imprisonment for an alleged attempt to overthrow the federal government; a few days earlier, his deputy, Chief Enahoro, who had been refused asylum in Great Britain, had been sentenced to fifteen years' imprisonment on similar charges. After the split Chief Akintola formed the Nigerian National Democratic Party and established links with the Northern People's Congress, while the Action Party was led in the West by Chief Adenbegro in association with the National Council of Nigerian Citizens (the dominant party in the East) under the name of the United Progressive Grand Alliance.

Except for these troubles in West, up to this point the party system in Nigeria may be considered to have worked successfully when all the differences resulting from race, language and religion are considered. With Sir Abubakar Tafawa Balewa at the head of the executive, there had been an impressive continuity in the federal government which had been a source of great stability in the troubled African continent. Unhappily this appearance of strength and stability was shattered at the beginning of 1966. In retrospect ominous pointers of what was to come can be seen in the general election of October 1965, in the Western Region. This was marked by loss of life, by charges of 'rigging', and by an announcement on the part of Chief Adenbegro's supporters, unwilling to accept or even to believe the verdict returned by the ballot boxes, that he had formed an interim government. He was taken into custody to give him an opportunity of denying it, and it was significant that the Chief Justice strongly criticized the support given to him by the Premier of the Eastern Region. Further acts of violence culuminated on January 15th in the audacious coup by a group of officers of intermediate rank in which the Federal Prime Minister (Sir Abubakar Tafawa Balewa) and the Northern and Western Premiers (Sir Ahmadu Bello and Chief Akintola) were murdered. The facts that the officers concerned were mainly Ibo, and that the Western Premier had allied himself with the Northern, whose fate he shared, were immediately recognized as the key to the ghastly situation. Once more the strength of tribal loyalties and jealousies had been demonstrated. Civil administration was suspended in favour of military government. It is impossible, as these words are written, to see the outcome, and futile to conjecture when the normal processes of civilian government will be resumed; but even on the morrow of this bloodbath, and with charges of 'tyranny' and 'corruption' ringing in the ears, it would be churlish not to recognize the impressive record of Nigeria in its first five years of independence.

The same cannot unfortunately be said of Ghana, known in the days of its dependent status as the Gold Coast and regarded in those years as the show-piece of the British Colonial Empire. The United Gold Coast Convention was founded in 1947 by Dr J. B. Danquah, a barrister and member of the Legislative Council, to work for self-government. Unhappily orderly progress towards that goal was marred by serious riots in 1948 and the report of the subsequent commission of inquiry, and the constitution of 1950 based on this report practically gave the territory a cabinet responsible to the legislature. This constitution was nevertheless not accepted by the organizing secretary of the United Gold Coast Convention, Dr Kwame Nkrumah, who broke away from it and in 1949 founded the Convention People's Party with the slogan 'Self-government now' and a programme of 'positive', that is, violent, action. At the first general election under the new constitution the CPP won a sweeping victory, gaining thirty-three out of the thirty-eight elective seats. Dr Nkrumah became Leader of Government Business and from 1952 was recognized as Prime Minister.

The United Gold Coast Convention, a smaller opposition party called the National Democratic party, a few non-party men and some former members of the CPP joined together in 1952 to form the Ghana Congress party, but nothing further came of this movement. A still more advanced constitution was brought into effect in 1954, and about this time signs of party divisions along tribal and geographical lines, as in Nigeria, but not to the same marked extent, began to appear. The area which British colonial administrators sought to mould into a unity consisted, in fact, of three distinct parts—the southern coastal belt (the original Gold Coast colony, itself divided into eastern and western regions), Ashanti and the Northern Territories—with marked differences in language, religion and customs. At the first elections under the 1954 constitution the CPP won seventy-two of the 104 seats. The Northern People's party, which won twelve seats, was recognized as the official opposition. Later that year the National Liberation Movement was formed. Strongest in Ashanti, it was based on the economic interests of the cocoa producers and advocated a federal structure in contrast with the centralized government demanded by the CPP. This question became a matter of acute contention for some years. Party politics took a violent turn, and the propaganda secretary of the National Liberation Movement was murdered. In 1956 the NLM, the Northern People's party and other opposition groups formed an alliance, and Professor K. A. Busia was elected leader of the 'National Liberation Movement and its Allies'. Dr Nkrumah's government put forward proposals for independence, and at an election held to test opinion on the issue the CPP again won seventy-two seats out of 104 in the legislature. The Gold Coast duly became independent under the name Ghana in 1957.

After the achievement of independence the various opposition groups coalesced in the United party. As a step towards getting rid of the entrenched clauses in the constitution, legislation setting up five regional assemblies—because their consent by a two-thirds majority was necessary—was introduced by Dr Nkrumah's government; the opposition boycotted the elections, and the CPP obtained overwhelming majorities in these assemblies. An allegation that members of the opposition had conspired together to secure the assassination of Dr Nkrumah set the pattern for the next few years; the leader of the opposition, Dr Busia, was exonerated, but the majority of the commission of inquiry decided that such a conspiracy had taken place, the chairman dissenting. Dr Busia left the country for an academic post in the Netherlands. Over the opposition of the United party Ghana became a republic in 1960, Dr Nkrumah adding the post of President to his responsibilities as Prime Minister. Effective power was placed in the hands of the President. Dissensions within the CPP in 1961 led Dr Nkrumah to take over direct control as general secretary and chairman of its central committee. The situation took a turn for the worse in 1962 when the throwing of a hand-grenade during the President's visit to a northern village led to the arrest, along with two others, of the Minister of Foreign Affairs, the Minister of Information and the executive secretary of the CPP. This had legal repercussions—including the dismissal of the Chief Justice, Sir Arku Korsah, because a special court over which he presided found these three not guilty—and on the political side it led the CPP to demand the outlawry of other parties. On December 31,

1963 President Nkrumah announced that he had approved amendments to the constitution by which Ghana would become a one-party state and that party the CPP. Two days later there was a further attempt on the President's life. On this occasion Dr J. B. Danquah was arrested, and he subsequently died in prison without any charge being preferred against him. A referendum on the proposed amendments to the constitution was held in January 1964, and in the manner of such things 2,523,385 votes were reported as cast in favour compared with 2,452 against. A 'general election' was fixed for June 1965, but as no candidate appeared in opposition to the 198 nominated by the central committee of the CPP it was not necessary to hold it. The opposition within Ghana has since been effectively silenced.

In East Africa Kenya provides another example of the way in which tribal loyalties have impeded the growth of a true party system on the British model. African nationalist aspirations were at first canalized in the Kenya African Union founded in 1944. Its first leader was Mr James Gichuru, but in 1947 he handed over the leadership to Mr Jomo Kenyatta. After the Mau Mau outbreak all party political activity was proscribed, and the Kenya Africa Union was banned in 1953. When the ban on parties was lifted in 1960, the Kenya National party founded by Mr Ronald Ngala and the Kenya Independence Movement led by Mr Tom Mboya competed for the votes of Africans, while the European settlers' leader, Mr Michael Blundell, started a New Kenya Group on a multi-racial basis and the Unity party stood for the retention of European privileges; but of more ultimate significance was the foundation of the Kenya African National Union. The new party elected Mr Kenyatta as its president, but as his movements were still restricted Mr Gichuru became the acting leader. It was clearly the old Kenya African Union with a scarcely changed name. The formation, or revival, of this party soon drove the Kenya National party and the Kenya Independence movement off the political map, but KANU, as it became generally known, was mainly based upon the Kikuyu and Luo tribes, and this roused fears and suspicions in other tribes, especially the Masai and the Kalensin. The result was the formation of the Kenya African Democratic Union, soon known as KADU, by Mr Ngala. About the same time Sir

Ferdinand Cavendish-Bentinck resigned the post of Speaker of the Legislative Council in order to found the Kenya Coalition on a multi-racial basis; the aim was formally the same as that of the New Kenya party, but Sir Ferdinand Cavendish-Bentinck made more appeal to Europeans, Mr Blundell to Africans.

The strength of these parties was tested at elections held in 1961 under a new constitution. Of the 'free' seats, that is, the elective seats not reserved for any one race, eighteen were won by KANU and twelve by KADU, with three Independents. Of the 'reserved' seats, the New Kenya party took eight, the Kenya Coalition three, the Kenya Indian Congress three, the Kenya Freedom party one and Independents five. These reserved seats did not conceal the fact that on a basis of universal suffrage the contest would lie between KANU and KADU, with the former in distinctly the stronger position. KANU refused to take part in the government of the country until Mr Kenyatta was freed from all restrictions, but KADU did not feel obliged to carry its support for Mr Kenyatta's freedom to the same lengths; Mr Ngala accepted the post of Leader of Government Business and some of his associates were also given office. KANU soon saw the disadvantages of having no hand on the governmental machine, and one of its members agreed to become Minister of Health and Social Affairs. There was for a time a truce between the two African parties, but this broke down when Mr Ngala announced that he hoped to get internal self-government without an election or a conference—which would have deprived KANU of any of the credit.

Mr Kenyatta was released towards the end of 1961. Until that point he had not identified himself with either of the African parties. He made it his aim to bring about their unification, but he found the differences too great, and accepted the leadership of KANU. He was soon elected to the Legislative Council and became leader of the opposition.

The Secretary of State for the Colonies invited delegates from all the main Kenya parties to attend a constitutional conference in London in February 1962, and it was dominated by the clash between KANU, desiring to see a centralized state, and KADU, aiming at the devolution of power to regions as the best means of preventing Kikuyu domination. KADU's point of view was substantially accepted by the United Kingdom government, ever zealous for the protection of minorities, and seven regions with their own assemblies were created. The constitution came into force in April 1963 and elections were held under it in May. They were contested not only by KANU and KADU but by the African People's party, newly founded by Mr Paul Ngei, who had failed to find a satisfactory home in either of the other two African parties. In the elections for the House of Representatives KANU won sixty-four seats, KADU thirty-two, and the APP eight and there were eight Independents. The dream of a multiracial Kenya had by this time faded. It was accepted that Kenya's future was to be an African state, and the European and Asiatic parties disappeared from the scene.

Fortified by this result, Mr Kenyatta agreed to form a government from the ranks of KANU, and KADU went into opposition. At this point the principle of the bandwagon came into play. With power in the hands of KANU ministers, the attractions of other political affiliations began rapidly to fade. Mr Ngala stood out as long as he could, but he had the mortification of seeing his supporters melt away, and on November 10, 1964 KADU was merged in KANU. From that point Kenya has been effectively a one-party state, though without any legal compulsion or formal suppression of the opposition. In a paper written on August 13, 1964 Mr. Kenyatta had argued that a single-party state was inevitable in Kenya, but he added that if the situation became favourable for a multi-party system his government would not put any legislative obstacle in the way.

In Uganda the main obstacle to the growth of a genuine party system after the Westminster pattern has been the existence within its framework of the kingdom of Buganda with its own traditional forms of rule and desire to preserve its identity. The main channels of nationalist aspirations in the nineteen-fifties were the Uganda People's Union, the Uganda National Congress and the Democratic party; the last-mentioned differed from the others in being a moderate party strongly influenced by Roman Catholicism. In 1960 the People's Union and a section of the National Congress merged to form the Uganda People's Congress, and this has since been the dominant party in the territory. Another section of the National Congress merged with the Uganda Freedom Union and the United National party to form the United National Congress, which has had strong Protestant support; the Uganda National Congress was itself revived in 1961, while dissident sections of the parties comprising the United National Congress formed the Federal party in 1961. Of more practical importance than these last-named groups is the Kabaka Yekka, which was formed in 1961 to protect the position of the Kabaka of Buganda.

The Kabaka's government attempted unsuccessfully to preserve the special position of Uganda by a federal solution, and when the British Government declined to meet its wishes it boycotted the elections held in March 1961. In these elections the Democratic party led by Mr Benedicto Kiwanuka won forty-three seats against thirty-five gained by the Uganda People's Congress under Mr Milton Obote, but the result was illusory as half the successes of the Democrats were in Buganda and were due to the boycott. At a constitutional conference the following September agreement was reached on all the main issues, and at elections in April 1962 the Uganda People's Congress won thirty-seven seats, the Kabaka Yekka, fighting as its ally, won all the twenty-one Buganda seats, and the Democratic party won twenty-two. A new coalition government with Mr Obote as Prime Minister and four Buganda ministers was then formed, and Uganda became fully independent on October 9, 1962. Effectively Uganda has since that date had a two-party system, which has worked without undue incident.

In Tanganyika nationalist aspirations were almost wholly centred in the Tanganyika African National Union, which under the able leadership of Mr Julius Nyerere promised to bring the country to fully independent status smoothly and with general goodwill. There was no rival to TANU—though the All Muslim National Union founded in 1959 to some extent fulfilled the role of a party for the Muslim immigrants—and the goal was achieved on December 9, 1962 when Tanganyika became an independent republic within the Commonwealth. From that date the path has not been so smooth, but TANU without any legal compulsion behind it still enjoys a monopoly on the mainland. Since 1964 Zanzibar has been united with

THE PARTY SYSTEM   129

Tanganyika in the republic of Tanzania. Its path to that goal was stormy. As in some other territories, parties had developed on a racial basis. The interests of the ruling Arab class in the sultanate were represented by the Zanzibar Nationalist party, those of the Africans and of that section of the population which is of mixed African and Persian descent by the Afro-Shirazi party. The Zanzibar and Pemba People's party was founded as a breakaway from the Afro-Shirazi party. In the elections of 1961 the Nationalists and the Afro-Shirazis won an equal number of seats, ten each; the Zanzibar and Pemba People's party, with three, held the balance, and by joining forces with the Nationalists formed a coalition with its own leader as chief minister. At the next election, in July 1963, the Zanzibar Nationalist party won twelve seats and the Zanzibar and Pemba People's party six, and the coalition continued; though the Afro-Shirazi party polled a majority of the votes, it had only thirteen seats and remained in sullen opposition. The Umma ('People's') party with a radical, even revolutionary, programme, was formed as a breakaway from the Afro-Shirazi party. The protectorate was granted independence in December 1963 and early in January the Umma party was banned. Within a few weeks the government was overthrown in a violent revolution, the banning of the Umma party being made the pretext. The Sultan fled, a republic was proclaimed with the head of the Afro-Shirazi party as President, and the head of the Umma party became Foreign Minister. These events caused some alarm on the mainland, which was resolved when a union between Tanganyika and Zanzibar was proclaimed.

A general election for the united republic of Tanzania was held in September 1965. No candidate was put up in opposition to President Nyerere as President, but electors were given an opportunity of indicating by a cross if they would prefer someone else. The result was never in doubt. For the elections to the legislature, a commission appointed to report on the establishment of a one-party democratic state had hit on a novel idea. It recommended that the single party, TANU, should put up two candidates for each constituency. This was in fact done in all save six constituencies, and led to many exciting personal contests within the fold of the same party. Not a few members of Parliament, some ministers included among them, failed to hold their positions.

In Rhodesia the evolution of a true party system has been overshadowed by the struggle between Europeans and Africans, and there have in fact been two unrelated party systems. At the general election held in May 1965 the Rhodesia Front led by Mr Ian Smith won all fifty A roll seats (with a mainly white electorate), while the Rhodesia party won ten of the fifteen B roll seats, the remaining five being won by Independents. The claim of the Rhodesia Front to speak for the European electors is thus incontestable. There have likewise been several organizations competing for African support. The Zimbabwe African People's Union, founded in 1961 and led by Mr Joshua Nkomo, was suppressed in 1962. The Zimbabwe African National Union was founded in 1963 by the Revd. Nathaniel Sithole after a split in ZAPU, but it has likewise been suppressed. The Zimbabwe African Democratic Union also has been banned.

In the former colony of Northern Rhodesia nationalist hopes were at first fostered by the African National Congress, founded in 1944, but from 1959 a serious competitor arose in the United National Independence party, and in the test of the general election of January 1964 UNIP, led by Mr Kenneth Kaunda, gained fifty-five seats in the National Assembly while the African National Congress, led by Mr Harry Nkumbula, won only ten. Mr Kaunda became Prime Minister and in the following October the territory became an independent republic within the Commonwealth under the name Zambia. There is also a People's Democratic Congress, a breakaway from the African National Congress. European interests are maintained by the National Progress party, formerly the Northern Rhodesian section of the United Federal party.

The former protectorate of Nyasaland, known since the achievement of independence in 1964 as Malawi, is in practice a one-party state. Under the constitution there is a Parliament of fifty-three members, of whom three occupy special seats reserved for non-Africans. At the elections held in May 1964 all fifty seats open to Africans were won by the Malawi Congress party. Founded in 1959 and led by Dr Hastings Banda, this is the successor to the Nyasaland African National Congress.

The three non-African seats went to the Constitutional party. There are also a small branch of the United National Independence party and a Convention African National party. It has recently been announced that when Malawi becomes a republic in July 1966, it will formally become a one-party State.

It cannot be deduced from the clean sweep made by the Malawi Congress party that there is complete satisfaction among Africans with its performance. This was shown in 1964 when the Prime Minister, Dr Banda, dismissed four ministers and three others resigned; all were expelled from the party. Mr Henry Chipembere and other ministers have since gone into hiding or exile, and a constant polemic has been maintained between them and Dr Banda.

The seeds of party have been sown in the High Commission territories in Southern Africa, but it is too early yet to say how they will develop. There are no fewer than five active parties in Basutoland; at the 1960 election the Basutoland Congress party won thirty of the forty seats in the National Council. Three parties are active in Bechuanaland, and no fewer than seven in Swaziland.

The West Indian territories in the British Commonwealth have a much longer political history, and the party system is on the whole well understood and operated responsibly. In Jamaica two democratic socialist parties—the Jamaica Labour party founded in 1944 and led by Sir Alexander Bustamante and the People's National party founded in 1938 and led by Mr Norman Manley—have long maintained a keen and honourable struggle with each other. The Jamaica Labour party derives its strength from the Bustamante Industrial Trade Union founded by Sir Alexander in 1938, the People's National party from the middle classes and the National Workers' Union. The two parties have alternated in office; when the territory went to the polls in 1962, the Labour party won twenty-six seats and the National party nineteen. At the last elections in Trinidad, in 1961, the People's National Movement led by Dr Eric Williams won twenty seats and the Democratic Labour party ten; there is also a less important Trinidad Muslim League.

Not so far away on the mainland of South America British Guiana presents a sad contrast, but here party has become bedevilled with race and personal ambitions. Three main parties have contested with each other for political power. The People's Progressive party, which is the strongest single party, is based mainly on the Indian immigrants and is led by Dr Cheddi Jagan. The People's National Congress, which is the second strongest party, represents in the main the African element in the population and is led by Mr L. F. S. Burnham. The United Force, which speaks for the American Indians and is led by Mr P. S. D'Aguiar, is the smallest of the three parties but is influential out of proportion to its numbers because its weight, added to that of the PNC, is sufficient to out-balance the PPP. There are also a Guiana United Muslim party, a National Labour Front, a Justice party, and a Peace, Equality and Prosperity party, but these are small and have little influence. The extreme policies of Dr Jagan and the PPP created anxiety, both in the other parties and among the British administrators, about what might happen if independence was given with the PPP in power. The other parties took the view that this would mean the subjection of the Africans and American Indians to the immigrant Indians, and were resolved to prevent it by all means in their power. When a constitutional conference in London in 1962 ended in deadlock the Secretary of State was invited to find a solution himself, and he decided to introduce a system of proportional election as a means of protecting minorities. This was not at all to the liking of Dr Jagan when he realized that it would curb the powers of the PPP, and disorders broke out. Elections by proportional representation were duly held in December 1964. The People's Progressive party gained 45·9 per cent of the votes (an increase in its share compared with the previous election in 1961) and twenty-four of the fifty-three seats; the People's National Congress secured 40·5 per cent of the votes and twenty-two seats; the United Force obtained 12·4 per cent of the votes and seven seats; no other candidates were successful. The voting took place almost strictly on racial lines. Though proportional representation worked, as expected, to the disadvantage of the PPP, it did not by itself resolve the crisis, but the People's National Congress and the United Force were willing to form a coalition. Dr Jagan was unwilling, however, to resign in the face of this combination, and the constitution had to be amended, and his office declared vacant, before Mr Burnham could be invited to form a coalition government in which he made Mr D'Aguiar the Minister of Finance. This coalition has since governed the country, but the territory remains in an uneasy state and although independence has been promised in 1966 it is difficult to contemplate the future without anxiety.

When the desire for independence arose in Malaya, the United Malay National Organization was created to give effect to it; and on the setting up of the federation of Malaysia it formed a coalition, under the name of the Alliance party, with the Malaysian Chinese Association, the Singapore Alliance, the Sabah Alliance, the Sarawak Alliance and the Malaysian India Congress. Led by Tunku Abdul Rahman, the Alliance won 123 of the 159 seats in Parliament at the first Malaysian elections. Opposition is provided by the Pan Malayan Islamic party, with nine seats, the Socialist party, the People's Progressive party, the National party, the People's Convention party, and the United Democratic party. The Sabah Alliance incorporates five parties and is opposed by the Social Democratic party. Sarawak has no fewer than six parties in the lists.

Singapore has since, in 1965, broken away from Malaysia. The government party since independence has been the People's Action party, which won thirty-seven of the fifty-one seats at the general election of 1963. The Socialist Front, which provides the main opposition, is a breakaway from the People's Action party; it gained thirteen seats in the 1963 election. There are also a United People's party and a Singapore People's Alliance.

Even in the small territories party has taken firm root. Seven parties are active in Aden, and Mauritius has been brought to the brink of independence in the course of a struggle between the *Parti travailliste* (mainly Indian) and the *Parti Mauricien*, which has worked for association with Great Britain rather than independence as a means of protecting minorities. It is unnecessary to pursue the ramifications of party into the smallest territories. The time has come to see what lessons can be drawn from this survey.

No time need be taken in arguing that the party system has worked in 'the old Dominions' Canada, Australia and New Zealand in much the same way as in Great Britain. This is universally agreed, and the question at issue is not so much whether the Westminster form of parliamentary democracy can be exported, but whether it can be exported to peoples not of British stock. Is it something that requires for its efficient working qualities that are found in the British people but are not found—not, at any rate, to the same degree—in other peoples? If this were so, it need not imply any superiority—or for that matter any inferiority—in the British character; it would imply only that the British peoples are different from others.

It is undoubtedly the case that the efficient working of the party system cannot be guaranteed. It is not automatic. It does depend on an underlying unity and in an agreement about the fundamental characteristics of society, so that the differences between the parties are differences within a larger unity. In the case of Great Britain the tacit understanding between the parties that sovereignty lies in Monarch, Lords and Commons; that the Monarch is bound to act on the advice of ministers; that ultimate power must reside in the representative chamber; that the ministry must be responsible to that representative chamber; the agreement, moreover, on the broad lines of external policy—these and many other features of the system on which the parties are agreed are far more important than the things on which they differ.

The efficient working of the party system depends, also, on a readiness not to push those differences to extremes. It depends on a recognition that no party has a monopoly of truth or wisdom, that 'the other fellow' has his rights, that some sacrifice of dearly cherished aims (provided that it does not involve sacrifice of the moral law) may be better than civil war or even political stalemate. It depends, in a word, on a readiness to compromise when a party cannot secure its own aims, or cannot secure them without harming the state; and this readiness to compromise is partly based on self-interest, in that the party which is in power today knows that there are limits to what men will stand, and that the party which is in power today may find itself in a minority tomorrow.

The successful working of the system depends, furthermore, on a recognition that there are methods which must not be used to achieve party success. Reliance on intimidation and on corruption are the most obvious. This recognition that there are limits to political action depends in turn on acceptance of the principle that worse calamities can befall a nation than the triumph of the other side.

Is there any reason to think that these qualities are prerogatives of the British race? I see no reason for such a belief; nor do I take a pessimistic view of the working of the party system in the former dependent territories of the British Crown. In general, when all the difficulties are considered, the new parties in most of the territories in question have stood up well to the strains to which they have been subjected.

Two charges that are frequently made cancel themselves out. It is argued that the efficient working of the party system depends on its being a two-party system, with an alternation between government and opposition; and it is pointed out that in some countries of the British Commonwealth there is only one party and in others there is a proliferation of parties. These statements need many qualifications. So far as Great Britain itself is concerned, except for relatively short periods it is a myth of the text-books that there have been only two great parties struggling for power and alternating in office. From 1679 to 1874 there were, indeed, only two *names* of parties—Whigs and Tories, then Liberals and Conservatives—but there were in fact many parties under the broad umbrellas of these names. They were often the personal following of some leader, but from Wilkes's election for Middlesex in 1768 to Chamberlain's break with Gladstone in 1886 the Radicals at least were almost a 'party within a party' among the Whig-Liberals. The break of the Peelites with the Tories in 1846, the formal creation of the Irish Nationalist party in 1874 and the rise of the Labour party in 1900 greatly blurred the simplicity of the two-party system beloved of the text-books; and today it is the turn of the Liberals, refusing to die, to confuse the clarity of the struggle between the Conservative and Labour parties. Furthermore, the myth of alternating periods of office needs considerable qualification. Great Britain was effectively a one-party state from 1714 to 1760, when no one except a Whig had any hope of achieving office. The Tories were in power all the time from 1807 to 1830 with the Whigs almost totally discredited—and virtually in power from 1783 to 1830—while the Whig-Liberal supremacy from 1830 to 1886 was broken by only fifteen years of Conservative rule and a brief period of coalition.

It is true that in many countries of the British Commonwealth there is virtually only one party, but Ghana is the only territory of which it can be fairly said that a one-party state has been set up by law and a genuine opposition suppressed by force. Malawi is a border-line case, for the resignation, dismissal and exile or hiding of ministers indicates that the supremacy of the Congress party is not entirely due to satisfaction with its performance. The Indian National Congress, in contrast, holds its exceptional position in that vast land not by the compulsion of law or of terror but because it has captured the loyalties of the Indian masses to a quite exceptional degree. Its continued supremacy long after the withdrawal of the British *raj* which gave it a *raison d'être* is a political marvel; and so long as it maintains its unique position by the example of its past and the promise of its future, by rational argument and emotional appeal, it does not contradict the essentials of the two-party system any more than the Whig supremacy in Great Britain from 1714 to 1760. The time will no doubt come when a party or parties will arise seriously to challenge the monopoly of Congress—possibly one of the existing parties, of which the Swatantra is the most obvious candidate, possibly by a schism within its own body, possibly some entirely new body. In the meantime it would be churlish not to admire the stability of the Indian political arrangements. Kenya is another one-party state which does not contradict the premises of the party system, for there was a genuine opposition between KANU and KADU, and public support was transferred from the latter to the former. It may well be that in Kenya also a real opposition party will arise—and Mr Kenyatta has promised to put no legal obstacles in its way—but for the time being KANU satisfies the freely expressed wishes of the Kenya voters. The same can be said of the unique position of TANU in Tanganyika, and the experiment of having two candidates in each constituency drawn from the same party and therefore appealing to the electors solely on personal qualities is as interesting as it is novel. The least democratic and least defensible element in the British party system is the selection of candidates. Meeting behind closed doors a small selection committee or delegate conference chooses the man (or occasionally the woman) who will in practice receive the Conservative, Labour or Liberal votes whatever the voters may think about him (or her.) In 'safe' constituencies this means that the member is effectively selected, not by the thirty-thousand or so people who vote for him, but by a small group who happen to be in the right positions when the vacancy occurs. The system of primary elections in the United States is meant to get over this problem in that great country's very different system, under which parties have an official status; and Tanganyika's experiment will be watched with interest for the results it produces. It may not succeed, for if candidates cannot count on the party vote they may come to ask what is the good of party; but it would appear to be a useful corrective where there is effectively only one party.

If the appearance of a one-party state is sometimes illusory, so also is the apparent multiplicity of parties in some other territories. In Ceylon, as we have seen, no fewer than nine parties nominally contested the elections of 1964, but in practice eight of them belonged to one or other of two groups, and the struggle was really one between the United National party and its allies on one side and the Sri Lanka Freedom party and its allies on the other. In Great Britain the general election of 1964 was rightly regarded as a struggle for power between two parties, but no fewer than fourteen parties entered candidates—Conservative, National Liberal, Labour, Cooperative, Liberal, Communist, Welsh Nationalist (*Plaid Cymru*), Scottish Nationalist, (Irish) Republican, Socialist party of Great Britain, British National, Patriotic, British and Commonwealth, Social Credit—and this without counting the Ulster Unionists and the Northern Ireland Labour party separately, or including the candidates standing in the name of such organized bodies as the League of Empire Loyalists, the Anti-Common Market League and the Independent Nuclear Disarmament Committee. The list could be even further extended if we included all labelled candidates (New Liberal, Radical Liberal, Christian Progressive, Christian Socialist, and so on), but they are best regarded as Independents.

In comparison the Ceylon party structure seems relatively simple. The way in which the party system worked in Ceylon to secure the overthrow of Mrs Bandaranaike's government when it had ceased to represent the wishes of the electors is, in fact, almost a classic example of the working of the party system at its best. In many countries the situation that prevailed in Ceylon in 1963 and the early months of 1964 might have led to a *coup d'état*; it is highly to the credit of this young Asian democracy that power was transferred and policy changed by the method of casting votes into an urn.

If we omit Nigeria, on which judgement must now be suspended, it is really only in Pakistan, Ghana and British Guiana that the party system fails to satisfy the tests of a reasonable expectation. The case of Pakistan, born in communal strife and nurtured in a state of war, which had flared up into active fighting just before these words were written, and consisting of two widely separated provinces, is exceptional, and the temporary breakdown of parties there cannot fairly be regarded as proof of the unsuitability of the party system to Asian peoples; in any case a party system seems once more to be taking root. Ghana is a bitter disappointment to those who have known and worked for that territory in the days when its future seemed unclouded, but the reasons for the present oppressive *régime* must be sought in the personalities of individuals rather than in any failure of the party system to meet the needs of Africans. In British Guiana the party system broke down when three main parties representing three different races were competing for power on the basis that the candidate 'first past the post' won the election, partly because the dominant party was determined to exploit its position to the utmost and was not prepared to exercise that restraint in office which is an essential condition of the party system. But the party system is not necessarily bound up with this method of election. On theoretical grounds the case for the alternative vote or some form of proportional representation has often been argued in Great Britain itself; it is no place here to go into these arguments, but the substitution of proportional representation for the old system in British Guiana does seem to have brought some alleviation to its troubles.

It may well prove to be the case that in some territories there may have to be a preliminary period of adjustment before a party system can take firm root. In Great Britain a party system could arise in the second half of the seventeenth century only when the preliminary question whether the King or Parliament was to be supreme had been settled. In some of the territories with which this chapter has been concerned the great preliminary question was whether their constituent elements would fall apart for lack of any real unity once the unifying influence of British power was withdrawn. The question mark was most conspicuous in the Indian sub-continent and in Nigeria. As we now know, the centrifugal forces in the India sub-continent were too strong, but it is possible to hope that Nigeria will emerge as a single strong nation within the geographical bounds laid down by British administrators. As these words are written there is a large question mark over the continuance of Aden in the South Arabian Federation which has its bearing on parties in that region.

The fact that parties in the territories with which we are concerned are so largely based on race or religion seems no bar to the successful working of a party system. If these are the political realities, they are likely to be as good a basis for party divisions as social class or economic conditions. In Great Britain the basis of party has changed considerably over the course of centuries. The line dividing the Conservative and Labour parties is mainly social and economic, but it is salutary to reflect, with G. M. Trevelyan in his Romanes Lecture (1926), that the continuity of the Tory and Whig parties from Danby and Shaftesbury to Canning and Grey 'was to be found mainly in the unbroken connexion of the Tories with the Church interest, and of the Whig aristocrats with the Protestant Nonconformist voters.' Before we condemn the oversea territories for basing parties on race, we would also do well, even if we dismiss Irish nationalism as water over the dam, to reflect on the increased activities of the Welsh and Scottish Nationalist parties in recent years. In 1946 *Plaid Cymru* contested six of the ten Welsh boroughs, seventeen of the twenty-six Welsh county seats, and polled respectably.

Human failures in the working of the party system in the oversea countries often get widely reported, but we shall not conclude that the party system is unsuited for Asia or Africa if we reflect on our own history. Throughout the eighteenth and a considerable part of the nineteenth century bribery and corruption were rife. Members had to pay heavily for the privilege of representing their constituencies and when in Parliament they expected to recoup themselves in favours, honours and sometimes hard cash. It was not, indeed, until 1884 that corruption was effectively exorcized from British political life.

It has sometimes been claimed, even seriously, that the British ability to work the party system is bound up with our national love of games; but we have seen both Indians and West Indians take to cricket as enthusiastically and as successfully as ourselves, and there is no reason to think that we have some secret of character that enables parties to work in Great Britain but not abroad.

A more serious argument is that we cannot expect the Asian and African peoples to acquire in a few decades those political skills which it has taken Great Britain several centuries to develop. There is some truth in this contention. It would certainly have been to the benefit of the formerly dependent territories if the successive steps to independence could have been taken a little more slowly than has in fact been the case. The precipitate rush to independence has made it impossible to keep social, educational and economic advance in step with political advancement. It cannot, however, be argued that the emergent countries will need as long as Great Britain took to develop comparable political institutions. They have all the benefit of our experience, and in retrospect we can only be amazed at the length of time taken in Great Britain to bring about inevitable reforms. Seventy years elapsed before the campaign to modify the 'rotten part of our constitution' (Chatham's words) terminated in the sweeping away of the rotten boroughs by the Reform Act, 1832; though girls were educated along with boys from 1870 onwards, not till 1918 did any woman receive the vote in Great Britain. We can see now how unnecessarily long and how greatly injurious these periods of waiting and controversy were. The emergent countries need not be expected to wait so long. They will, of course, make their mistakes; but, as Aristotle said, the only way of learning to play the flute is to play the flute. No one in his senses will wish to force the British party system upon countries that do not want it. But no better system has yet been devised for settling peacefully great political issues, and when the emergent countries themselves reproduce it, or their own variant of it, we can only wish them well and help them to avoid our own mistakes.

Chapter VI

PARLIAMENT, THE EXECUTIVE AND THE CIVIL SERVICE

BY JOHN FLETCHER-COOKE

I

During the two decades which have elapsed since the end of World War II, the less sophisticated sections of public opinion in Britain, urged on by constitutional theorists both at home and abroad, have accelerated their efforts to secure the export of the 'Westminster Model' to a progressively increasing number of formerly dependent territories.[1] Indeed, the figures for this particular export stand out in sharp contrast with the less satisfactory performances recorded as regards the exports of other goods and services with which Britain was accustomed to supply the world in earlier decades.

It may be appropriate to make two points at the outset. The first is that, on the face of it, this was a perfectly natural, and perhaps inevitable, process. Britain was rightly proud of this delicate piece of mechanism and she revelled in the admiring glances which were directed upon it from almost every part of the world. It seemed to meet all her needs; and what could be more natural than that she should wish to share this boon with her wards.

But, secondly, attention should be drawn to a confusion of thought which has accompanied the general movement towards the independence of formerly dependent territories. The idea seems to have been accepted, almost without question, that

---

[1] 'One thing the British were very eager to export was their particular version of parliamentary government.' Immanuel Wallenstein, *Africa—The Politics of Independence*, First Vintage Edition, New York, 1961, p. 73.

independence could be achieved *only* on the basis of the 'Westminster Model'. This was the approach not only of the grantors, the British, but also, as will be seen later, of the grantees, the peoples of the dependent territories.

There was never any seriously sustained attempt, and certainly not at the policy-making level of successive British Governments, to consider the possibility of granting independence on any other basis than that of the 'Westminster Model'. Representative parliamentary democracy as practised at Westminster became almost synonymous with independence.

But there are numerous independent states in Asia, the Middle East and Latin America, accepted as respectable members of the United Nations, whose constitutional development has never been directly subjected to British influence and whose governmental dispositions bear little resemblance to those embodied in the 'Westminster Model'. Even in Africa, the admission to the United Nations, as a founder member, of Ethiopia should have made the point that independence was not synonymous with acceptance of the 'Westminster Model'.

If those who were pressing for the indiscriminate export from Britain of the 'Westminster Model' believed, or even hoped, that this mechanism would ensure *better* government in the emerging states, than that which is to be found in the other states referred to above, then one is bound to consider whether their beliefs, or hopes, have in fact been fulfilled.

II

It is perhaps inevitable that in evaluating the success or failure of this process, particular attention should be focused on the fate of representative parliamentary democracy in these new states. But to do this would be a mistake. Such a limited assessment would ignore the fact that representative parliamentary democracy is but one, though no doubt the most important, of a whole series of institutions, patterns and attitudes which should be included in the term, the 'Westminster Model'. This whole complex of ideas and institutions represents the Western, and more particularly the British, way of doing things. In addition to representative parliamentary democracy, as practised, broadly speaking, on a two-party basis, this complex includes a belief in the rule of law and the consequential independence of the judiciary; support for academic freedom in universities and colleges; an acknowledgment of the merits of private enterprise and a consequential acceptance of a free trade union movement; respect for the rights of minorities; insistence on an efficient, incorruptible and impartial civil service—indeed the catalogue of accompaniments is endless.

This complicated web of ideas and institutions hangs together. To expect parliamentary democracy to take root and flourish in an environment in which these other supporting factors are not present in adequate measure is tantamount to expecting a house to stand up without proper foundations.

III

Two basic points may be made at this stage. First, it has taken a thousand years or more to distil this complex of supporting ideas in Britain. The fact that 1965 marks the seven hundredth anniversary of Simon de Montfort's Parliament should serve as a reminder that the development of parliamentary institutions in this country has been neither rapid nor without setbacks.

Three examples of fundamental ideas which have encouraged and sustained the growth of the 'Westminster Model' in Britain may be given. First, we in Britain, like others in the West, are heirs to Graeco-Roman civilization. One of the ideas that we have inherited from the Greeks is the principle of the Greek dialectic; a belief that the best way to grope for the truth is by means of the thesis and anti-thesis. This is the basis of our two-party system and of our counting the heads of those who are for or against a particular proposition. But this is not the only way of groping towards the truth. There is another way which finds much favour in the traditions of many of the newer members of the Commonwealth which may conveniently be labelled 'the consensus of opinion approach'. In such an approach, there is no room for the cut and thrust of formalized debates between Her Majesty's Government and Her Majesty's loyal Opposition; rather is the method of proceeding a leisurely and somewhat inchoate series of deliberations in circumstances where time is at a discount.

Secondly, we in Britain are heirs to Western Christendom, from which comes, *inter alia*, an inheritance of respect for minorities. It is true that this fundamental idea has frequently been overlaid during the long history of Western Europe; and never more so than during the past quarter of a century. But always the underlying feeling re-asserts itself that maltreatment of minorities is evil, as is evidenced by the current Nazi trials in Germany.

Thirdly, Western Christendom also bequeathed the idea of individual responsibility from which has sprung a belief in the merits of individual enterprise. Such enterprise flourished exceedingly in Britain during the days of the Industrial Revolution and the underlying force of this idea is still an essential part of the texture of life and thought in Britain.

But it has required centuries for these, and many other fundamental ideas which underpin the 'Westminster Model' to emerge in this country. To what extent, then, has it been possible to export these accompanying ideas with the parliamentary institutions which they sustain? The answer to this question is the second main point to be considered.

IV

It is a commonplace to observe that the member states of the Commonwealth (other than the United Kingdom) embrace developed and developing countries, 'haves' and 'have-nots', whites and coloured, and so on. But for the purpose of evaluating the extent to which the export of the 'Westminster Model' has been successfully achieved, these categories are inadequate.

A more useful distinction can be made between those parts of the Commonwealth to which the 'Westminster Model' went as 'accompanied baggage' and those parts to which it was sent as an 'export'.

In the former category fall not only Australia, Canada and New Zealand but also the Carribbean states including Trinidad and Jamaica. In these areas there was little or no indigenous culture to offer competing ideas. The settlers from Britain took with them all the seeds of the 'Westminster Model' as it is known today. Even in the Carribbean, circumstances were such that British ideas, reinforced from time to time by ideas drawn from other Western cultures, had the field to themselves.

The fact that many of the peoples of the West Indian islands were of different races and colours was far less relevant than the fact that they had been cut off from their own indigenous backgrounds. And so they absorbed over the centuries the ideas and ways of life of those who were originally their masters. Naturally the blossoms of the seeds of the 'Westminster Model' which went oversea as 'accompanied baggage' have a somewhat different appearance there. The size of Canada and Australia demanded federal arrangements to which British experience could make no direct contribution; and the West Indian temperament has added something of colour to the sombre hues of Westminster. But the plant has taken firm root in all these areas and it is beyond dispute that the mechanism can work, even when those who work it are not wholly of British stock.

v

But the 'Westminster Model' has also gone to Asia and Africa. How has it fared in these two continents? Here an important distinction must be made.

The continent of Asia, including those parts which are within the Commonwealth, has a rich inheritance of civilizations and cultures. India, Pakistan and Ceylon, and to a lesser extent Malaysia, can point to achievements not only in cultural fields but also in technical fields which preceded by centuries the advent of the British. Indeed, when the early inhabitants of the British Isles were still living in comparatively primitive conditions, a measure of progress had already been made in many parts of Asia, which in the contemporary idiom, would have entitled them to be described as 'developed'.

Furthermore, during the two thousand years or so which have elapsed since then, the East has itself exported many ideas which have been absorbed into Western culture.

For these reasons Asia has felt less inhibited about receiving and adopting Western ideas than has, as will be seen, the continent of Africa. The supreme example of this is, of course, Japan. But the states of the Indian sub-continent, reassured as it were by the richness of their own backgrounds, have not hesitated to accept British ideas, attitudes and institutions where they felt that these had merit. Mahatma Ghandi, himself, welcomed the independence of the judiciary and the incorruptibility and impartiality of the civil service which the British took to India, while rejecting the 'industrialization' and 'modernization' which were in the same package.

And so, while the complex of ideas which makes up the 'Westminster Model' has had to compete with a rich inheritance of other ideas, attitudes and institutions indigenous to Asia, many of these British concepts appear to have taken root there. The general scene, though inevitably different from that to be found in the old Dominions or in the Caribbean states, is nevertheless, at present, sufficiently close to the 'Westminster Model' as it persists in the place from which it was exported, to justify the claim that it is well founded. The close association with British ideas for some three centuries has left its mark.

VI

But the African member states of the Commonwealth present a very different picture. Here the 'Westminster Model' appears to be wilting visibly. The reasons have already been suggested and may now be elaborated.

All the nineteenth century explorers of Black Africa commented on the absence of any significant technical advance among the inhabitants; no knowledge of the wheel, no alphabets, no written languages, no evidence of great buildings, of irrigation works or indeed of the technical progress of which there was ample evidence in the Far East, the Middle East and indeed, along the North African coast. This latter, which is really a projection westwards of the Middle East, has exchanged ideas with Europe across the Mediterranean for hundreds, if not thousands of years.

But Black Africa, sub-Saharan Africa, differs from virtually all the other so-called under-developed parts of the world in the sense that at no time in the long history of the world was this part of Africa, in the light of all known evidence, in the van of technical progress. This, it is suggested, has had a profound effect on the reception by Africans of the 'Westminster Model' as will now be indicated.

It has already been suggested that the firm establishment of the 'Westminster Model' requires the acceptance of certain fundamental ideas which are essential to its sustenance. These ideas were the sole inheritance of those who peopled the old Dominions and they had virtually no competition in the Caribbean where such indigenous cultures as there were were weak and uncompetitive. While there were competing cultures in Asia—and this may well change the picture in years to come— the three hundred years' association with Britain was strong enough to implant enough of these fundamental ideas to make parliamentary democracy a workable proposition at the present time.

But in Africa these supporting ideas have never really taken root. For example, the principle of the Greek dialectic on which the two-party system is based has never overcome the African principle of proceeding by means of a consensus of opinion. This accounts for the emergence in so many African states of the single-party system. But while this has reduced the parliament to little more than a façade, the traditional African way of proceeding has found a new embodiment in the Party organization. The African Party machine, it will be suggested later, is the village meeting writ large.

Again, the legacies of Western Christendom—respect for minorities and encouragement of personal responsibility and initiative—have never taken root in sub-Saharan Africa. Indeed, where the concept of a single party has not yet succeeded in asserting itself (i.e. in the Federal Government of Nigeria) it is because minorities, based on tribal or geographical affiliations, have realized the precariousness of their position and have formed political associations in an attempt to safeguard their rights.

Similarly Africa's reluctance to accept ideas of personal responsibility and initiative is understandable enough against a centuries-old background of collective decisions. Personal initiative and private enterprise are discouraged by a climate of opinion that has its roots deep in the African past.

But while these supporting ideas which are vital to the successful working of parliamentary democracy have not, as yet, taken root in Black Africa, and while this fact alone would have been quite enough to ensure that the 'Westminster Model' did not flourish there, there has been a more positive factor at work eroding the whole complex of Western ideas, to which it may now be appropriate to turn.

VII

In less than ten years a host of new independent, sovereign nation-states has appeared in sub-Saharan Africa. The Africans take a pride in their new-found nationhood. But they are reminded at every turn that they are still dependent on the outside world for education, expertise, capital, 'know-how' and indeed for the most rudimentary technical advance. They realize, too, perhaps subconsciously that this has more to do with their history than with their colour; for it cannot have escaped their notice that other coloured races have, at different times in their histories, made considerable advances in these matters. The presence of half-a-million Asian 'belongers' in East and Central Africa cannot but remind them that these came to Africa not so very long ago because they had skills which could not then be found in that continent.

Africans, then, are faced with the need to assert their new-found independence. Since, as has been seen, this cannot be done, as yet, in the fields mentioned above wherein they are so patently dependent on the outside world, in what field can it be done? Africans have concluded that it can be done in the field of political, social and economic relationships and institutions.

All the evidence suggests that what is occurring in Africa today is a largely subconscious rejection of the alien 'Westminster Model' and its replacement by a complex of institutions and patterns derived from Africa's rich inheritance in these fields.[1] In short, the basic features of the tribal system are being

[1] '... the history of the peoples of Africa has been one ... of skills in art and government'—Wallenstein, *op. cit.*, p. 11.

projected on to the national canvas of these new African states.

Against the background of this survey of the extent to which the 'Westminster Model' has fared in various parts of the Commonwealth, the lens may now be focused more closely on the Executive and the Civil Service and their relationships with Parliament, with particular reference to the position in Africa.

VIII

It may be appropriate first to make a general point. In the constitutional arrangements which prevail in Britain, as indeed in the constitutional arrangements of other member states of the Commonwealth which have derived their inspiration from the 'Westminster Model', the relationships between the Executive and the Civil Service and Parliament are governed more by 'conventions' and less by 'legislation' than any other part of these arrangements. The composition and powers of legislatures, relationships between two chambers where there is a bi-cameral system, relationships between state governments and federal governments where these are applicable, even the constitutions of party organizations—all these are duly recorded in written documents containing specific provisions for the procedures whereby these matters can be varied.

But the particular relationships now being considered are governed largely by 'conventions'. This can be a source of both strength and weakness; of strength because a 'convention', once firmly established, is far less easy to 'repeal' than a standing order, a law, or even a constitutional provision. A mere counting of heads according to prescribed procedures is not enough. There must be an over-whelming change in the climate of opinion, not easily measurable, before a well-established convention can be varied. But there is also a weakness in this reliance on 'conventions'. Their strength is largely derived from the length of time they have been accepted. If they are not firmly rooted, if they do not have general acceptance as 'conventions' then they may be varied or even abandoned before they have acquired any binding force.

Projected against the canvas unrolled in the earlier part of this chapter, it will be readily appreciated that these 'conventions' are firmly based in the old Dominions and in the Caribbean states where the principles which sustain them have not been subjected to competition from other ideas. In Asia, too, although there are other ideas lurking in the ambush, these principles have not yet been seriously challenged and would seem to dominate the spheres of activity in which they operate. But in Africa, partly because of the comparatively short period of time since they were introduced, partly because of the circumstances in which they were introduced but, most important of all, because of the upsurge of specifically African and competing ideas, these 'conventions' have already suffered serious casualties. Some examples may make this point clearer.

IX

The first 'Ministers' in the African member states of the Commonwealth were expatriate civil servants. While the justification for this arrangement was the attempt to organize the machinery of Government on a Ministerial rather than a Secretariat basis the wisdom of this move, at the stage it was made, is at least arguable. The true significance of the Ministerial system lies in its political rather than its administrative implications. But there was no political significance in creating a Cabinet of civil servants.

It was natural that the new civil service Ministers should accept the principle of collective responsibility. Before they became Ministers they had been trained and accustomed to working as a team, albeit with a greater measure of control and direction by the Chief Secretary than was the case after they attained Ministerial status. Moreover, since they were *ex-officio* members of the legislature, by virtue of their Ministerial office, they went about their tasks as objectively and dispassionately as they had done as senior civil servants; and they were not subject to any political temptations, or indeed opportunities, to hint publicly at differences of opinion in the 'Cabinet', even on those very rare occasions when differences existed. Similarly, they were not really answerable to the legislature for their actions; rather were they accountable to the Governor for the proper administration and effective management of the portfolios which he had entrusted to them. There was no more likelihood of their resigning, or of their being dismissed, than when they were only civil servants.

Again, as experienced civil servants themselves, their relationships with their Permanent Secretaries were far more akin to those prevailing between the Head of a Department and his second-in-command than to those which should exist between a political Minister and his Permanent Secretary.

And, finally, whatever administrative advantages may have flowed from the establishment of a Ministerial form of Government by civil servants (and even these can be questioned) it remains a fact that the Government continued as a benevolent dictatorship reflecting the views of those at the top rather than the aspirations of the man in the street or the peasant in the field.

It was to this highly artificial Ministerial system that the first Africans were introduced as Assistant Ministers and ultimately in most cases, as a minority of Ministers. The true conventions of the 'Westminster Model' with all their political implications had never been established. It is unreasonable, therefore, to criticize Africans for failing to accept and perpetuate them when Independence came.

But there is another point to be made here. Cabinets which existed in the period immediately preceding Independence were composed of two elements representing two different worlds. A majority, and subsequently a minority, of civil service Ministers working closely with a minority, and subsequently a majority, of African nationalists. This cannot be compared with a wartime coalition of duly elected Ministers representing two bitterly opposed political parties who had agreed to sink their differences in the face of an external threat to the State. In pre-Independence African Cabinets one group, the Africans, were dedicated to securing independence from colonial rule at the earliest possible opportunity. Their declared objective was to change the whole structure of the State and to remove their Cabinet colleagues, not only from their offices, but also from the country. The other group, the civil service Ministers, however much they sympathized with African aspirations, could not, by virtue of their training and experience as civil servants, fail to have reservations about the pace of political change. Although the niceties of collective responsibility were, by and large, observed in public, it was a highly contrived atmosphere.

Again African nationalist leaders did not hesitate to attack expatriate civil servants by name or office. While those senior civil servants who held Ministerial posts could have no complaints about this and had, in any event, opportunities of defending themselves in the legislature, the fact that virulent attacks were also launched on middle rank and junior civil servants made an early break in the convention that Ministers alone should be called to account in the legislature for the work of their departments; and that individual civil servants who could not defend themselves publicly should not be subjected to such attacks. To sum up, the circumstances in which African public opinion was introduced to the Ministerial system were not such as to facilitate the institution of those conventions governing the relationships between the Executive and Parliament or establishing the role of the civil service, which are essential to the smooth working of the 'Westminster Model'. The highly charged atmosphere of the period immediately preceding Independence in which this artificial Ministerial system was introduced was hardly conducive to getting the appropriate conventions off the launching pad.

x

It may be convenient now to analyse in greater detail the ways in which the Executive and the Civil Service developed in the period immediately following Independence.

During the late eighteenth and nineteenth centuries a number of new nation-states came into being in Western Europe and in North and South America. Almost all of these attained statehood as a result of the application of organized force. The American War of Independence and the Wars of Liberation in Germany, Greece and Italy as well as the liberation movements in Latin America—all serve as reminders that force was the mid-wife at the birth of these states.

But there are no George Washingtons, Garibaldis or Bismarcks among the African nationalist leaders. The African 'father figure' is more likely to be a scholar or a Trade Union leader.

This absence of force at the birth of these new nation-states has had a profound effect on the behaviour of the new African 'Executives'. The prime task facing the Government of any new nation is to maintain itself. For if stability is not established, no progress can be made in garnering the promised fruits of Independence; and there are many pressures working against the new Government at this stage. The withdrawal of the Colonial Power inevitably removes the major factor which made for the unity of the nationalist movement in the pre-Independence period. Again, it was the writ of the Colonial Power, acting through the network of the Provincial and District Administration, which had treated as a single unit that which had previously been a collection of separate tribal entities. Moreover, the expectations of millions of poor and simple-minded people, even where these expectations had not been inflated by the promises of nationalist leaders, were bound to be disappointed as the cruel realities of independence succeeded the joyous exuberance of the 'freedom' celebrations. But, most important of all, pre-independence politics involved changing the whole structure of the state. The lesson had still to be learned, and it was a lesson which would take a long time to learn, that opposition to the particular policies of any Government must always be tempered by such restraint as will ensure that, in destroying the Government of the day, which is a legitimate objective, nothing should be done which might destroy the state itself.

Faced with such a situation, the new African 'Executives' were far less favourably placed than were the Governments of those eighteenth and nineteenth century states which came into being as a result of the application of organized force. The peaceful passage to independent statehood of the new African states (and where force has entered into the picture, as in the Congo, it has been the result, not the cause, of independence) has deprived them of an important element of cohesion in their new-found statehood. There is something missing, forged in the heat of battle, which provided a spiritual mortar binding together the citizens of the eighteenth and nineteenth century states, particularly during the early years of their nationhood.[1]

Starting with this considerable disadvantage, common to all, in terms of national cohesion, the new African 'Executives' have inevitably faced differing situations in the different states. Where the nationalist movement was 'monolithic' as in Tanganyika, prior to the union with Zanzibar, the dangers of secession were diminished. But where the movement developed as an uneasy coalition concealing deep tribal, ethnic or geographical differences, as in Kenya, the post-Independence Executive was faced with all the risks of secession and possibly chaos.

Again the personalities and inclinations of those who formed the first post-Independence Cabinets were bound to affect the measure of leadership which they could give. Some Ministers were (and still are) bitterly and irrevocably anti-white; others, while taking a legitimate pride in their new-found 'Africanism' were willing to treat non-Africans on their merits and as equals. Some Cabinets were (and still are) deeply divided as regards their reactions to the ideologies of the East and the West; all, however, profess a belief in 'non-alignment'.

In some states, the personality of the leader was such that he would only tolerate 'yes-men' around him; and the Executive became no more than the projection of a single and dominant personality. In others, the leader has encouraged a frank expression of differing opinions in the Cabinet. In others still, the leader has had to tolerate, for a time at least, some among his Cabinet colleagues who could only be regarded as disloyal by any standards. The strength, and persistence in office, of such as these often rests on a particular geographical or tribal influence, carefully nurtured by funds remitted from abroad.

But all these new 'Executives', as the heirs of the out-going Colonial Administrations had to face a variety of pressures.

During the Colonial period, the central Government was the unchallenged focal point of power. It had no competitors. In other parts of the Commonwealth, universities, professional

---

[1] It should also be noted that because this 'military' content is missing in the make-up of the new African states, there is, perhaps, far less likelihood of inter-state hostilities such as has characterized the history of Western Europe and Latin America.

bodies, City Governments, the Churches and many other organizations and institutions representing special interests, brought influences to bear which the Government of the day ignored at its peril and of which it had to take some account, at least. In the British colonial territories in Africa these institutions either did not exist at all or were, in the last resort, under the control of the Colonial Government.

But the new African Governments found at least three possible competing sources of power. In some states, the traditional Rulers were strong enough to make life very difficult for the new 'Executives'; but it would seem to be only a matter of time before their influence is diminished to the point of no return, as it has already been in many states.

But there remain two far more virile and less easily subdued possible rivals for power. The first is the Co-operative Movement. This is strong and growing in most African member-states of the Commonwealth; but as it is wholly in tune with the philosophy of these new African states, far from incurring any displeasure from the 'Executives' it is encouraged and, indeed, largely represents their chosen instrument for economic development.

The third possible competing source of power has met with a very different fate. The idea of a free Trade Union movement, which was deliberately introduced into the British dependent territories in Africa by Colonial Governments, on the instructions of the British Government soon after the end of World War II, has virtually evaporated into thin air. 'Free' Trade Unions have ceased to exist in most of the new African states. The policies of the new African 'Executives' have no place for such a movement which is so obviously a possible focus of competing power. In many states only one Trade Union is permitted and that is directed and strictly controlled by the Government. Of the original Trade Union leaders, a few are themselves members of the new 'Executives' but many hundreds, who had their big moments during the declining years of the Colonial régime, are now languishing in gaol or subjected to indefinite periods of detention.

More generally, the new African 'Executives' have reacted somewhat unpredictably to the pressures crowding in upon

PARLIAMENT, EXECUTIVE AND CIVIL SERVICE

them. Neither the general public nor the Governments have been very sure of the rules of the new political game. No one has been quite sure how much deviation will, or should, be permitted. As those in power, whether they be Cabinet Ministers or civil servants, are inexperienced, they may either be too tolerant or too harsh in their reactions; frequently they will adopt both attitudes at one and the same time. It will be argued later in this chapter that such checks as are exercised on the 'Executives' come, not from the Legislatures, but from the Party organizations.

XI

It may be appropriate to turn now to a consideration of some of the factors affecting the development of the Civil Service in the period immediately following Independence.

It must not be overlooked that by the time Independence was achieved developments in the political field had far out-run the growth and re-orientation of the indigenous public services. For periods of time which varied in the different territories Africans had been holding Ministerial posts of increasing responsibility and familiarizing themselves with the problems of Government and administration. A number of consequences flowed from this.

First, the aspirations of the new African states were symbolized by the new African Ministers. It was they who had given such thought as had been given to tackling the problems which Independence would bring in its train; it was they who, as a result of their journeyings abroad and their contacts with the outside world, had some idea of the magnitude of the tasks with which they were faced.

Secondly, while the majority of the expatriate civil servants who stayed on after Independence loyally supported their new Ministers, it was hardly to be expected that they would be able to make much of a contribution to the attempts which, by then, were being made to finding essentially African solutions to the new states' problems.

Thirdly, as the Africanization of the Civil Service proceeded apace, the new Permanent Secretaries and other senior civil servants found themselves less, rather than more, experienced in their particular fields than the political masters whom they were now to serve. The African Ministers frequently found that their new African civil servants could not cope with the administrative problems involved and as a result, Ministers became, themselves, deeply involved in matters of detail from which they should have been spared. If a Minister's frustration became too great, he would be sorely tempted to by-pass the elaborate arrangements bequeathed him by the out-going British, who had provided in all their Independence constitutions for Public Service Commissions, and recruit directly into the civil service someone whom he thought could meet his requirements, by virtue of prior performance in the political field.

Nor can it be denied that the objective of the former Colonial Service was to provide good government rather than exciting government. It was regulatory rather than creative. It brought integrity and impartiality, efficiency and loyalty to the tasks of preserving law and order and obviating disorder. But to meet the exciting (if some times impractical) aspirations of the new African Ministers a completely different and more dynamic outlook was called for.

Thus at a time when the Civil Service itself was undergoing two major upheavals—an ever accelerating replacement of expatriate officers by Africans and a deliberate attempt to identify these new African civil servants, not with a colonial regime where the ultimate decisions were taken thousands of miles away, but with the aspirations of the people of whom they were a part—the delicate relationships between Ministers and the Civil Service were being forged.[1] It is hardly surprising that the pattern of such relationships has not always followed the essence of the 'Westminster Model'.

XII

But even more important than the unpropitious circumstances in which the out-going Colonial Administrations vainly attempted to establish the conventions which should govern the delicate

[1] For an elaboration of these points reference may be made to A. L. Adu, *The Civil Service in the New African States*, London, Allen & Unwin, 1965.

tri-partite relationships between the Executive, and Civil Service and Parliament, was the growling ground-swell of African ideas seeking to imprint their own particular mark on the new and tender Independence constitutions.

The question has often been asked as to whether the British were well advised to attempt to force their emerging African territories into the matrix of the 'Westminster Model'. In these terms this is the wrong question to ask. For in the pre-Independence days it was the African nationalist leaders themselves who were insisting on this. They then demanded a replica of the 'Westminster Model', complete down to the last detail. Benches in the Legislatures had to be covered in the same green leather as was to be found in the House of Commons. The mediaeval war-club which is meaningful at Westminster, as indicating that the Crown forms an essential part of Parliament, was treated with more respect than it has sometimes received in the Mother of Parliaments herself. Speakers were attired in full-bottomed wigs, gowns and knee-breeches more in tune with the grey skies of northern latitudes than with the steamy tropical heat of equatorial Africa. Any suggestion of variations in these, and many other matters, were brushed aside against a background of clamour for 'the Westminster Model, the whole Model and nothing but the Model'.

If proposals were put forward for restrictions in the franchise, if suggestions were made that a form of government similar to that practised by the then London County Council—itself responsible for the good government and welfare of many more millions than some of the new African states can claim—all such ideas were summarily dismissed as smacking of an attempt to fob the people of Africa off with something 'second-rate'.[1]

There is no reason to suppose that African nationalist leaders were not sincere in their demands for an exact replica of the 'Westminster Model'; there is no reason to suppose that they were not motivated by a genuine desire to make it work in

---

[1] Lord Attlee appears to have met with a similar response in India. Earl Attlee, *Empire into Commonwealth*, 1961, p. 41. 'I recall suggesting to Indians, when I was over there on the Simon Commission that perhaps they would find the American presidential system more suited to their conditions, but they rejected it with great emphasis. I had the feeling that they thought I was offering them margarine instead of butter.'

these new African states. But they, like the rest of the world, under-estimated the strength of African traditions, of African attitudes, and above all, of the perhaps subconscious determination of the mass of inarticulate Africans to give a specifically African flavour to their new-found independence.

However vociferously the African nationalist leaders were demanding the 'Westminster Model' during the period leading up to Independence this was an alien import in the eyes of African public opinion—an import which, as has been indicated, had in any event been received without many of the props, struts and buttresses required to make it effective. Although retained as a sign of respectability, as a symbol of having 'arrived' and above all as a *sine qua non* of admission to membership of the United Nations, it remains as little more than a facade. The true focal point of political power in Africa lies elsewhere.

If Africanism has rejected the 'Westminster Model', what has it put in its place? The clue to this may be found in a consideration of the following.

XIII

There are many hundreds of tribes in sub-Saharan Africa; and their customs, traditions and values vary greatly. But there are certain basic features which are common to the vast majority of these tribes. It is perhaps of greater significance that all Africans are born into *a* tribal system than that they are born into different tribal systems. The concept of the tribe, the implications of being a member of a tribe, the ways of looking at the world embodied in the tribal system—all these patterns of thought are absorbed by every African with his mother's milk. They are part of his natural environment and of his cultural heritage. Even the apparently 'de-tribalized' or 'Westernized' African is still subject to considerable pressures and influences from his tribal background—just as those born in the Western world are subjected to the influences of Graeco-Roman civilization and of Western Christendom. It is, therefore, natural and perhaps at this stage inevitable, that Africans should seek to replace the alien 'Westminster Model' by institutions and processes more evocative of their tribal inheritance, while continuing to retain the outward trappings of the 'Westminster Model'.

In short, the forms and patterns now evolving in the new African states may be regarded as a projection on to the national canvas of the basic principles of the African tribal system. Let us consider certain features of the new African 'Executives' against this background.

XIV

One of the most striking features is the apparent acceptance of the idea of virtually permanent leadership. Some of the new African leaders come from the traditional ruling classes, but the majority do not. But once elected they appear to acquire a charismatic quality which sets them apart from other men. Titles such as President Kwami Nkrumah's 'Osagyefo', President Julius Nyerere's 'Mwalimu' and President Jomo Kenyatta's 'Mzee' may pale into insignificance beside the long string of biblical titles to which Emperor Haile Selassie of Ethipoia lays claim. But they are symptomatic of the conviction that these leaders are men apart. It is interesting to observe that Milton Obote, the Prime Minister of Uganda, seems to have acquired less of this mystical aurore; but then he has a competitor in this field in the person of the Kabaka of Uganda who is the (constitutional) President of Uganda. There is no room for two charismatic leaders in an African state.

The explanation for this general acceptance of the idea of a permanent and quasi-mystical leader derives from the basic African concept of the 'Chief'.

It is frequently forgotten that most African chiefs are chosen by a system of election. Although the choice is limited to those of the right lineage, sex, and sometimes age group, there is usually a choice in which personal attributes are carefully considered. Once chosen, the successful candidate becomes the Chief not only of those who have chosen him, but also, in a sense, of those who are dead and of those who are as yet unborn.

It is most unlikely that a national leader chosen against a

L

background of such ideas will ever be voted out of office, for so to do would be an admission on the part of the people as a whole that they had made a mistake in originally choosing him; and that would involve a loss of face, a commodity which is in even shorter supply in the continent of Africa than elsewhere. If, in fact, the chosen leader fails to measure up to the challenge of the responsibilities with which he has been entrusted, he is still likely to remain in the supreme position of leadership but to be 'manipulated' by other stronger men operating from behind the scenes. If, however, he does take a strong line which runs contrary to the 'consensus of opinion' building up from the grassroots, he will probably be disposed of, as many a bad 'Chief' has been before him, by methods which will not involve the ballot box. History has shown that it is not beyond the resources of Africa to contrive such disappearances from positions of leadership in circumstances which do not involve the loss of face which an adverse vote at the polls would do.

Again, the existence of so many single-party governments in the African states of the Commonwealth, and the belief in the minds of many observers of the African scene that it is only a matter of time before this pattern is reproduced in all such states, means that it is hardly possible to conceive of circumstances in which an African Prime Minister would fail to obtain in the legislature an overwhelming vote of confidence any time he chose to ask for it. In this sense the relationship between the Executive and Parliament in Africa is so different from that prevailing at Westminster that any comparisons would be almost meaningless.

XV

But it should not be concluded from this that the operations of an African 'Executive' *necessarily* represent the dictatorship of a small group of determined 'party' men dominating an inarticulate electorate. In the first place, political parties in Africa are mass parties rather than elite parties. During the period prior to independence the party spearheading the nationalist movement permeated every aspect of life. Farmers' groups, youth groups, womens' groups, the trade union and co-operative movements—every aspect of African life was brought under the party umbrella; and this pattern has persisted after independence. Indeed in recent years the Party organization in a number of states has stretched out even further to embrace civil servants. The reasons for this particular development are to be found in the difficulties which arose in the administration of various local community development schemes, from differences of opinion about the line dividing the Government's responsibility and the Party's responsibility. Arguments about policies and personalities were only resolved when it was clearly demonstrated to all concerned that the individual or individuals primarily responsible for a particular scheme were all good Party men, whether they happened to be civil servants or not.

The same tendency to blur the hitherto clearly marked dividing line between Party officials and civil servants can be found in the appointment, in a number of new African states, of politicians as Regional and Area Commissioners working with and through civil servants.[1]

It was suggested earlier that the traditional African method of groping for the truth was by means of the village meeting seeking to establish a consensus of opinion. Here again can be seen a fundamental feature of the tribal system which has now been recognized at the national level. The institution which provides for the reproduction of the village meeting on a national scale is the Party organization. The Party organization is in fact becoming the real focal point of political power rather than the legislature.[2] The national leader must earn and retain the confidence of the Party organization. He can always command the confidence of the legislature. Indeed, the Party organiza-

[1] This blurring of the distinction between Civil Servants and Party officials is reflected in another way. After the attainment of Independence most nationalist parties in Africa were faced with a serious falling-off in subscriptions. This tendency became even more marked as the new Governments imposed higher taxes. Now there are signs that the new Governments propose to overcome this difficulty by making party subscriptions mandatory. In Zanzibar, for example, it has been decided that up to a maximum of fifty shillings will be taken from the earnings of all citizens as their subscription to the Afro–Shirazi party.—'East African Newsletter', *African Assessor*, September, 1965, p. 10.

[2] For example, it is reported that the Council of Government in Mali acts on recommendations initiated by the Bureau Politique National and that the National Assembly then passes these decisions into law with practically no debate—'Political Revival in Mali', *Africa Report*, July, 1965, p. 17.

tion might claim to be the true Parliament of the nation. It is here that attempts are made to secure a consensus of opinion. It is through the many and varied links which the Party organization provides that the leaders keep in touch with the grassroots. The Party organization is a delicate mechanism comparable to the system whereby the blood constantly circulates to every part of the human body. Twenty-four hours a day, three hundred and sixty-five days a year (whether the Parliament is sitting or not) messages are passing up and down the veins and arteries of the Party organization, conveying the thoughts and plans of the Government to the men in the back-woods and receiving in return their reactions.

Unlike the Parliament, this mechanism does not require literacy. It does not even demand that all its members should be able to communicate with one another in a single language; it does not require, for its effectiveness, the media of mass communication which can only reach a small proportion of the population but which is vitally necessary to the effective working of the 'Westminster Model'.

Moreover, the African is not yet reconciled to the idea of choosing a representative and allowing him a measure of discretion in judging particular issues. This reluctance to be 'represented' can be recognized in the difficulties with which African trade union leaders have had to contend *vis a vis* their members. The rank and file like to feel that they are participating directly in the negotiations and 'references back' on matters of no great significance are frequently called for. In the political field this danger has largely been overcome through the organization of the Party machine, whereby every member can express his opinion on almost any subject, if he so wishes, even though this may only be to a handful of members at the Party's village branch.

It was a realization of the importance of the Party organization in the new African states which led Julius Nyerere in January, 1962, to resign as Prime Minister of Tanganyika and to devote himself for nearly a year to his responsibilities as Party Leader. It is a realization of this which leads most African nationalist leaders personally to devote a considerable amount of their time to the activities of the Party organization.

It was a realization of this which enabled Sekou-Touré of Guinea to say: 'We have the most advanced democracy in the world. I challenge you to name a more advanced one. Whereas in countries like the USA and the USSR the ruling party is only a fraction of the population, here it is everywhere'.

XVI

Enough has been said, perhaps, to justify the conclusion that representative parliamentary democracy as practised at Westminster cannot be said to have failed in Africa since it has never been established there. Certain outward forms were bequeathed by the departing British but they have not succeeded in attracting and canalizing those elements of democracy which the present generation of Africans inherited from their forebears. Rather has this essentially African approach developed its own institutions, patterns and attitudes, which may well be the most appropriate ones for the Africa of the second half of the twentieth century.

Relationships between the Executive and Parliament, between the Executive and the Civil Service, and even between Parliament and the Civil Service cannot be measured against any yardstick derived from Westminster. The key role of the Party organization which dominates and distorts all these three relationships in Africa has a significance which can hardly be over-estimated. If there is validity in the contention that the real kernel of political power in Africa is in the Party organization and that Parliament is but a husk, then the subjects calling for deeper study are the relationships between the Executive and the Party organization and between the Party organization and the Civil Service. The outward forms may still resemble those of Westminster and Whitehall; but the realities are those of Africa.

Chapter VII

THE SECOND CHAMBER IN PARLIAMENTS OF THE COMMONWEALTH

BY FRANCIS LASCELLES

Although in the Second Chambers of the Commonwealth there is a wide diversity in almost every respect, method of composition, size, powers, the duties they are designed to fulfil and even the names by which they are called, yet they all tend to assume a common pattern, differing from each other in the degree of acquiescence or resistance with which they are prepared to assume a secondary role, a role more easily accepted by those that are nominated than by those that are elected. This secondary role is inherent in Parliamentary democracy on the Westminster model, the essential features of which are that the executive government should be responsible to the lower House and that in that House financial control should rest.

They all naturally bear resemblance to and points of difference from The House of Lords, on which they were mostly modelled. Later in this chapter their position in their respective countries will be compared with the position of The House of Lords in this country.

In some countries, and particularly in the newer African constitutions, the legislatures are unicameral. In these, single chamber government has been adopted for a variety of reasons; in some cases there is a paucity of suitable personnel, and such as there is is required for other purposes; in some, financial considerations loom large and second chambers are regarded as an expensive luxury; in some again, in the enthusiasm for newly-won independence, there has been a determination to impose no potential checks on the march of progress. Nor are the traditional ideas underlying the role of a Second Chamber always accepted. The notion of a grave and dignified body of Senators, aloof from party politics, giving the weight of their experience to matters of State with independence and impartiality and armed with powers for protecting their country against intemperate legislation, has proved unattainable. Other expedients, such as entrenched provisions and bills of fundamental human rights have been preferred to the establishment of a second chamber as the guardian of the constitution and of minorities. Indeed in Africa there is a confusion of thought between the protection of minorities and the encouragement of opposition. Consequently, in some of the newer States, which lack the tradition of parliamentary democracy, single chamber legislatures have been adopted. Of the full members of the Commonwealth, Pakistan, Tanzania, Ghana, Cyprus, Sierra Leone, Uganda, Malta, Malawi, Zambia, Singapore and Gambia have unicameral legislatures.

It was, however, for entirely different reasons, and not from any predeliction for unicameralism, that the second chamber in New Zealand was abolished in 1951, after a chequered existence lasting for one hundred years. The 1852 constitution of New Zealand was a quasifederal one with six provincial legislatures and a general Assembly consisting of two houses. It had been intended that the Upper House should be elected by the Provincial Legislatures, which would have given to it a federal *raison d'être*, but life nomination by the Governor General was substituted. There was no limit to its numbers, it was given concurrent powers, except in finance, with the House of Representatives and there was no provision for settling differences between the two Houses. Even in its early years there were numerous proposals for reforming its composition but the need for reform became urgent in 1891 when a succession of conservative governments gave way to a liberal-labour administration. A term of seven years was then substituted for life membership, but the Council continued to reject a series of government measures. After a constitutional crisis, twelve additional counsellors were created but even so the unbalance was not restored. Appointments to the Council then became a reward for party services, the penalty for opposing the government being non-re-election, and the Council thereafter existed under threat of swamping and became a supine and ineffective body fulfilling no useful purpose. In 1914 an act was passed substituting an elective basis for nomination but the outbreak of war prevented the act from becoming operative and the reform of the Council, which up to then had been a burning question, became engulfed in post war problems. A joint Committee in 1948 failed to produce an acceptable solution and in the following year twenty-six additional members, pledged to abolition and known as the suicide squad, were created and abolition became effective in 1951. The system of nomination, whether for life or for a term of years, had failed in New Zealand. Misconstruing its duties from the start it had travelled in the course of its existence from the extreme limit of obstruction to the extreme limit of subservience. In its latter years it had ceased to initiate legislation and did little revision; on no major matter of policy did it offer any opposition to the wishes of the Government. There was a strong feeling at the time of its abolition that some form of second chamber government should be substituted for it but so far the dangers anticipated from unicameralism have not materialized.

It has usually been maintained as a general principle that a bicameral system is a necessity in a federal constitution in which, if the representative chamber is elected on a population basis, there is a risk that the interests of the smaller constituent states may be submerged. Equal representation from each state in a second chamber should provide a solution to this danger. This theory will therefore be examined in relation to the constitutions of Canada, Australia, India, Nigeria and Malaysia.

In Canada under the Constitution of 1867, the Senate consists of members nominated by the Governor General on the advice, in practice, of the Prime Minister. There is a limit to its numbers, twenty-four from each of the four major divisions of the country, Quebec, Ontario, the Maritime and the Western Provinces and six from Newfoundland. The number may be increased by eight for the purpose of resolving differences between the two Houses but this expedient has never been resorted to, partly because the permitted increase would be insufficient for the purpose and partly because the Senate has conducted its affairs with discretion. Senators must be not less than thirty years of age and possess a property qualification. The powers of the Senate are wide, corresponding approximately to those of the House of Lords before the Parliament Acts. Though undemocratic in its composition, it has therefore an absolute veto in respect of legislation. Ministers who are members of the House of Commons can speak, but not vote, in it, as is the case in most of the Commonwealth legislatures. The intention of life nomination was to enlist a body of statesmen secure in their tenure and consequently able to act without undue regard for party considerations.

The Canadian Senate has not however worked out to fulfil its intended role. The federal aspect of its composition has never been strongly asserted. Nomination on the advice of the Prime Minister has reduced its value as representing provincial interests and indeed these are more firmly safeguarded by the composition of the Cabinet, in the forming of which provincial representation is a major consideration. In fact nominations have been made on a party basis with the resulting inconvenience that when the party complexion of an administration changes, the incoming government finds itself confronted by a Senate composed of the nominees of its predecessor. It has not however behaved obstructively and it contains men of distinction. On the other hand, having no special function to fulfil and suffering in popular esteem from its undemocratic composition, it has become a somewhat lifeless body. There have been movements in favour of its abolition on the grounds that its composition is archaic and that it has failed in its purpose of representing the provinces, but its efficient though unobtrusive conduct of such business as it is allowed to do—and it has frequently complained of not being given more—has postponed serious consideration of its reform, although in 1965 retirement at the age of seventy-five, with certain safeguards for existing senators, was substituted for life tenure.

The provincial legislatures of Canada are unicameral except for Quebec which has a Legislative Council of twenty-four members appointed for life by the Lieutenant-Governor. Steps have recently been taken designed to limit the powers of the Council by reducing its veto on legislation.

The Australian Constitution of 1901 is more modern in its outlook than that of Canada. The Senate, constructed on the USA model of equal representation of states, consists of sixty members, ten from each State, elected directly by the same electorate as that which elects the House of Representatives, but with each State as a single constituency. The age qualification for Senators is twenty-one and the system of election is by proportional representation. Senators are elected for a term of six years, half the numbers from each state retiring every third year. Continuity is not as assured as with the USA Senate since, in the event of a difference between the two Houses, the whole Senate may be dissolved. Its powers are similar to those of the House of Lords before the Parliament Acts but there is an interesting procedure, copied later in India, Kenya and the Bahamas by which the Senate can 'request' amendments to money bills which it cannot amend, and it has claimed that such requests should be agreed to. There is an elaborate procedure for settling intercameral deadlocks which may involve a dissolution of both Houses followed, if disagreement persists, by a Joint Sitting of the two. In the latter case, the views of the House of Representatives, which is twice the size of the Senate, are likely to prevail. This elaborate procedure is the fruit of experience from the already existing state legislatures where intercameral friction had been intense.

The Constitution provides that the number of members in the House of Representatives shall be, as nearly as practicable, twice the number of the Senators. This provision has been under review for some years. Owing to the increase in the population, members of the House of Representatives, who originally represented fifty thousand electors, now represent ninety thousand and all parties appear to agree that their number should be increased, but in view of the necessity of preserving equality of State representation in the Senate and the desirability that the number of Senators retiring each third year should be an uneven one, there are difficulties in arriving at figures that would be workable for the two Houses. Further the Labour Party, who favour the abolition of the Senate, would be opposed to any increase in the number of Senators. It has been proposed therefore that the link laid down in the Constitution between the numbers of the two Houses should be removed so that the lower House could be increased in size without increasing the size of the Senate.

The functions of the Australian Senate, besides the revision of bills and the imposition of a check on ill-considered legislation, were intended to be the safeguarding of state interests against federal encroachment and the protection of the interests of the smaller states whose representation in the House of Representatives might be too small to give them an effective voice. In practice, however, elections to the Senate have been carried out wholly on a party basis. Although at times it has upheld state interests, in the main it has become a party chamber. Possibly the encroachment by the federal government upon matters reserved for the State Legislatures is of decreasing importance in view of the increasing economic integration of the country but the fact remains that it does not fulfil its intended role in this respect. It is criticized on the grounds that, having become a Party Chamber, it is redundant when the Government commands a majority in it and obstructive when it has an opposition majority—a criticism which has been made elsewhere. It does useful work in revision of bills but it may well be that here, as in India, second chambers which command the prestige of popular election would operate more satisfactorily if they could be assigned special functions within particular spheres of administration, preferably of a non-party character, such as might relieve the popular chamber of some of its burden without making any appreciable inroad on its dignity.

The State Legislatures of Australia date from 1855 with the exception of that of Western Australia which dates from 1891. The second chambers, known as Legislative Councils, are mostly elected on a restricted property franchise and are consequently regarded as privileged bodies, acting as guardians of property and unprogressive in their outlook. Intercameral disputes have been frequent and bitter, even though in the main the Councils have exercised their veto only in cases of bills which they consider to be outside the electoral mandate. Agitation for the abolition of these Councils has been motivated by impatience and resentment at restraint rather than by charges of inefficiency, as was the case in New Zealand.

In Queensland and New South Wales the composition of the Legislative Councils was by nomination for life. Friction between the two chambers in Queensland culminated in a claim by the Council to amend money bills. A bill for the abolition of the Council, following the rejection by it of a number of measures, was defeated in a referendum in 1907 but, as a result of the nomination of Senators pledged to abolition, became law in 1922. The Council can only be restored after another referendum.

New South Wales had a nominated Council till 1934. There had been various attempts, owing to intercameral friction, to abolish it, but in 1933 a referendum gave a verdict in favour of reform. Its numbers were then reduced and limited to sixty, to be elected by both Houses sitting as an electoral body and to hold office for twelve years, one-fourth retiring every third year. A government proposal for its abolition was heavily defeated on a referendum in 1961.

In Victoria, the Council consists of thirty-four members, two from each province, elected for a term of six years. There was friction over tacking in 1866 and in 1894 the Council rejected the budget in order to force an election of the Lower House. In the case of differences between the two, resort is had to Free Conferences which often produce a compromise. In the event of prolonged deadlock, the Council can be dissolved.

Southern Australia has a Council of twenty members who must be thirty years of age or more. Relations between the Houses have not been smooth. Free conferences have often been successful in finding a solution to differences but in case of deadlock the Government may dissolve both Houses or appoint nine additional members to the Council. If the deadlock be prolonged there may be a referendum of the electors of one or both Houses.

In Western Australia the property qualification of voters for the Legislative Council has recently been removed as a political gesture. The Labour party is however pledged to its abolition.

The Tasmanian Council has nineteen members elected on a specialized property and educational franchise for a term of six years. It cannot be dissolved. In consequence of perpetual friction over finance, a settlement was reached in 1926 by which it was established that the Council had no power to amend money Bills but had full power over all others, including financial Bills.

It was this history of friction in the State Legislatures that led the framers of the 1901 Commonwealth constitution to impose a careful procedure for solving differences between the two Houses. In fact the procedure of a double dissolution has been only twice resorted to.

In India the federal aspect was considered by the Constituent Assembly of 1947 to be a sufficient reason for a Second Chamber, as its name, the Council of States or Rajya Sabha, would imply. In addition, it was intended to hold dignified debates on important issues and to delay legislation which might be the outcome of passions of the moment. It consists of a maximum of two hundred and fifty members elected indirectly by the State Legislatures on a population basis, a system which does not necessarily provide protection to small states. In addition, twelve members are nominated by the President with special regard to literary, scientific or artistic qualifications. This feature in its composition may have been copied from Eire and it is to be found in the Senates of Ceylon, Nigeria, Malaysia, Kenya, Trinidad and Tobago and the Bahamas. Its powers are similar to those of the House of Lords of today though somewhat wider in that no question of the financial privileges of the other House, the House of the People, can arise. From Australia, as has been mentioned, it has borrowed, though with a rather different procedure, the power of making 'recommendations' to money Bills; from the House of Lords it has borrowed the procedure of 'moving for papers' by which a subject can be ventilated in general debate without the necessity of taking a vote on it. This procedure is well suited for a Second Chamber since a full and free discussion can be held without undue intrusion of party loyalties. Deadlocks between the two Houses are solved by Joint Sittings at which, as in Australia, the Lower Chamber, being double the size of the Upper, would get its way.

The Council of States provides an outlet for many citizens

who have political aspirations; it is useful in assisting the legislative timetable and on occasions produces debates of high quality, but it cannot be said that State interests are any more attended to in it than in the House of the People. The two Houses are distinct neither in the character and social position of their members nor in the work they have to do. Both are elected bodies and the inferior status of the Council of States is bitterly resented by it. There have been quarrels between the two Houses but such quarrels have been over questions of status, procedure or powers in financial matters rather than over policy and so long as both Houses are dominated by the Congress party, this is likely to be so.

The successful adoption of the Westminster model in India has been a remarkable achievement. In the older members of the Commonwealth, Canada, Australia and New Zealand, with a population of British stock, it was natural that parliamentary democracy should be the goal and should be retained on the winning of independence. India on the other hand had had experience of bicameral government only since 1950. Its experience of Parliamentary democracy had been from the point of view of opposition and there was a natural aversion to the adoption of anything that savoured of imperial rule. Its establishment on a reasonably firm basis has been due partly to the long period of peaceful leadership under Mr Nehru, during which the new Constitution could take root, and partly to the dominance of the Congress party which, by democratic means, has given India a virtually one-party Parliament and to that extent has simplified the task of the Government in coping with their new responsibilities.

In such of the Indian States as have bicameral legislatures, proceedings have been even more animated and friction more intense than in the Federal Parliament. The Second Chambers are mostly elected by electoral colleges composed of members of the Legislative Assemblies (the Lower Houses), municipalities, district boards, teachers and graduates of three years' standing. The complaint—common to many Second Chambers but inevitable if they are to be responsible and active bodies—that they are either redundant or obstructive has been made against them. Some of the States which have Second Chambers have attempted to abolish them, others which have no Second Chambers have asked to have one set up.

In recent years two bodies charged with framing constitutions have given careful study to the question of a Second Chamber, both in its general aspects and in its applicability to the territories which they were considering. These are the British Caribbean Closer Association Committee which met in 1948 in pursuance of a resolution of The Montego Bay Conference of the preceding year and the Federation of Malaya Constitutional Commission of 1957. These two bodies came to similar conclusions as to the part a Second Chamber should play but differed to some extent as to how it should be composed. The Commission for Malaya (which has since become Malaysia) recommended indirect election for a majority of the Senate (Dewan Nagara), the remainder to be appointed by the elective monarch on the advice of the Federal Government on the basis of distinction in commerce, culture, literature, science etc., or as representing racial minorities. This recommendation was made in accordance with the principle that the powers of the Senate with regard to legislation should not be equal to those of the House of Representatives but should be revising and delaying powers and that Ministers should be able to continue in office notwithstanding an adverse vote in the Senate. Membership of a State Legislature was not to be disqualification for the Senate on the grounds that useful contacts between the Federal and State Legislatures would be secured and that such a disqualification might make it difficult to find enough members of suitable experience. The Commission state 'We do not envisage the Senate as a body of secondary importance. Our recommendations are made with the intention of enabling the Senate to become an influential forum of debate and discussion and a body which will contribute valuable revision to legislation and which will be able to impose a measure of delay in exceptional cases'. The Commission did not recommend the settlement of differences between the two Houses by a Joint Sitting since they considered it undesirable that the fate of a Bill should depend on the votes of the nominated members, as might then be the case. Accordingly, the Senate was given powers similar to those of the House of Lords. The Senate now consists of sixty members, two elected by the Legislative Assembly of each State and thirty-two appointed members, a variation of the proportions recommended by the Committee. The tenure of a Senator is for six years. The Senate is not subject to dissolution.

The hope that the Senate would not become a body of secondary importance has not been realized. Since the Federal Government command a majority in the State Legislatures, which elect the majority of senators, they are certain to command a majority in the Senate also. Consequently, so long as this state of affairs continues, there is no likelihood of independent action by the Senate. It has become little more than a debating chamber, the value of its debates being enhanced by the contributions of the nominated members. Senators are eligible for re-election at the end of their term of office but it appears that they are disinclined to avail themselves of this privilege, preferring to stand for the House of Representatives rather than remain members of a body which can exercise little influence.

The Caribbean Committee, after examining the advantages of unicameralism on the grounds of saving of expense, saving of delay in legislation and general conformity with modern political trends of thought, came to the conclusion that in a Federal constitution a second chamber was essential; that while a single chamber with numbers proportioned to population would represent the federation as a single unit, it would not reflect the fact that the constituent territories entered into the Federation as equals. They further considered that in any legislature, however constituted, there was a need for some form of revisionary process. As to the composition of the Second Chamber, they decided that the dominant element in the legislature must be an elected body and that if both Houses were elected there would be an obscuration of this dominance since each could claim that it spoke with popular sanction and it would be difficult to place the Second Chamber in a position of definite constitutional subordination. The two Houses should not be constitutionally equal and, to ensure that one did not become a duplication of the other, each should have somewhat different functions and powers. For these reasons, and also with the intention of including experienced persons who might not wish to put themselves forward for election, the committee recommended nomination as the basis of the Second Chamber's composition and, in order to reflect the position of the constituent territories as equal partners, each should have equal representation, members to be nominated for a term of five years and the powers of the Chamber to be limited to a suspensory veto, in the case of non-financial bills, of twelve months. The Federation of the West Indies which was established in 1958 was dissolved, on the secession of Jamaica and of Trinidad and Tobago, in 1962.

In the case of the short-lived Federation of the Rhodesias and Nyasaland, there was a departure from the generally accepted principle that a Second Chamber must be an essential feature of a federal state. The report of the Conference on the Closer Association of the Central African Territories of 1951 stated that in present conditions a bicameral legislature would be inappropriate since it would not be easy to find sufficient representatives to sit on three separate territorial legislatures and a bicameral central legislature. The report recognized that in a federal system with a single chamber legislature it would be undesirable for any one territory to have representation equal to or exceeding that of the other territories combined and the Federal Parliament was constituted in accordance with this principle.

The Senate of the Federation of Nigeria dates from 1959, four years later than the inauguration of the federal constitution. Unlike most federal legislatures, the 1954 constitution provided for a single chamber, the House of Representatives, but in view of the great diversity between the three regions in race, religion and cultural development and also of the vast size and population of Northern Nigeria, which gave to that region a representation in the House greater than that of the other regions combined, the constitution provided that the Council of Ministers should contain three Ministers representative of each region, thus giving equality of representation in the Cabinet to each of the units. The effect of this expedient, by which the federal functions of a second chamber were to be exercised in the Council of Ministers, was that Ministers found themselves acting in a dual capacity and were hampered as Ministers of the federal government by an overriding loyalty to the interests of the regions which they represented. At the review of the constitution which took place in 1957 provisions were agreed to for the establishment of a Second Chamber as an insurance against the domination of the Northern Region and a method of countering strong movements which had sprung up for the creation of new self-governing regions. The Senate was to consist of twelve members from each region (there are now four regions), four members from Lagos and four members nominated by the Federal Government. The regional members are elected by the regional legislatures on the nomination of the regional governments and should be representative not only of the governments but also of opposition and non-party interests. The financial powers of the Senate are limited in the manner of the Parliament Acts. In respect of ordinary legislation it has a suspensory veto of seven months. Members of the Senate must, except for the special members, be forty years old or upwards. The life of the Senate is coterminous with that of the House of Representatives but it can be dissolved on the advice of the Prime Minister. The interests of minority races, which have been the subject of prolonged discussion, are protected by a Bill of fundamental human rights entrenched in the constitution.

In Nigeria, where the size and the population of one of the regions is infinitely greater than those of any of the others, where within each region there are a number of races and religions (the Northern Region being largely Islamic) and where each region has different political parties, the preservation of the unity of the Federation is a matter of extreme importance and may be a matter of extreme delicacy. On the other hand the existence of opposition parties provides a better chance for the principles of parliamentary democracy to take root in Nigeria than elsewhere in Africa and there appears to be a realization among the leading politicians of the importance of preventing disintegration. How far the Senate, which has an undemocratic composition and very limited powers, can be influential in this vital task is a question which will depend on whether it develops as an active and independent body. The regional legislatures are bicameral, the second chambers being Houses of Chiefs, thus enfolding within the structure of the constitution the traditional authority and influence of the Chiefs.[1]

The position of the Chiefs is maintained in the constitutions of various other African territories. In the independence constitution for Basutoland, the Senate will consist of the twenty-two Principal Chiefs or their nominees, the remaining eleven members being nominated by the Paramount Chief. This Senate will have no power to initiate legislation, but will have a delaying power of thirty days in respect of money Bills and ninety days in respect of others. A more limited recognition of the position of Chiefs is noticeable in Zambia where, under the Independence Constitution of 1964, the House of Chiefs is not a part of the legislature but it may discuss Bills and other matters referred to it by the President and submit to him resolutions thereon. Similarly in Bechuanaland, under the constitution proposed in 1964, alongside a Legislative Assembly of thirty-five elected members there is to be a House of Chiefs with the special function of considering draft Bills affecting tribal matters and with the right of making representations to the government on any issue affecting the tribes, while in the unicameral legislature of Gambia the House of Representatives contains fifty-seven elected members and four Head Chiefs elected by the Head Chiefs, and in the island kingdom of Tonga in the Pacific Ocean and in Fiji representatives of the chiefs and nobles elected by their peers form part of the Legislative Assemblies.

With the exception of the Nigerian Senate, it seems that the Second Chambers of the federal states, however constituted, have not exercised, or have been prevented from exercising, any decisive influence either in resisting encroachment by the central government on the powers exercisable by the constituent legislatures or in upholding the interests of the smaller states. The position of subordination, which these Chambers are expected to occupy in relation to the popular House, makes it difficult for them to do justice to the role which they were primarily designed to fulfil, a role which has been further obscured by the ever increasing severity of party discipline. In default of special functions, such as those possessed by the Senate of the United

[1] It is too soon to say whether the constitution of Nigeria is to be changed as a result of the *coup d'état* of January 1966.

States, though not necessarily of such importance, these Second Chambers lack the moral authority necessary to enable them to pull their full weight.

The Second Chambers of the unitary States of the Commonwealth, Ceylon, Kenya, Jamaica and Trinidad and Tobago remain to be considered.

Ceylon has had a Second Chamber only since 1946. The constitution of the island previous to this date had been established by the Donoughmore Commission of 1927 which rejected the suggestion of a Second Chamber. If elected on a communal basis it would be 'a canker in the body politic'. What purpose would be served by endeavouring to abolish communalism in the Lower House and perpetuating it in the Upper? If elected on a functional basis it was likely to perpetuate cleavages in the population which were largely artificial and to obstruct instead of fostering unifying tendencies. Further, as a potential source of friction, it would to some extent neutralize the transfer of responsibility to the elected representatives of the people. The Soulbury Commission, which in 1945 investigated the working of the Donoughmore Constitution, rejected these conclusions and reported in favour of a Second Chamber on traditional lines. It was to be a forum of persons of eminence, comparatively free from party affiliations, capable of exercising an educative influence on the public and constituting a check on extreme legislation. It was believed that these objects would be attained by a method of composition which should secure the inclusion of persons distinguished in their own sphere whose experience might otherwise be lost. Accordingly the Senate consists of fifteen members elected by the House of Representatives and fifteen nominated by the Governor General on advice from the Prime Minister. The members hold their appointments for six years, one-third retiring every second year and are eligible for re-appointment—a method of composition modelled presumably on the Senate of Burma in 1937. The Senate is not subject to dissolution. Its powers are similar to those of the House of Lords in respect of money Bills; other Bills passed by the House of Representatives in two successive sessions may be presented to the Governor General for Royal Assent without the consent of the Senate.

As with other Second Chambers constituted with these aspirations, its purpose has been defeated both by the intrusion of party politics and by its failure to attract eminent persons. The Senate derives however some importance from the presence of the Minister of Justice, who, with one other Minister, must be a member and also from the fact that a recent Prime Minister has been a member. In a constitution which was regarded by a section of the population as 'imposed', the high proportion of nominated members is considered a vulnerable feature. It commands little respect and its future is uncertain.

Of the new African unitary constitutions, Kenya alone is bicameral. A land of many races, it is in fact a close approximation to a federation. There are regional unicameral legislatures with powers in certain spheres. Residual powers are at the centre and the tendency is for the spheres of the regional legislatures to dwindle. The Senate consists of one member elected from each district and one from Nairobi, forty-one in all. Its powers are similar to those of the House of Lords. A Council of State which had been set up as a protection against racial discrimination, on the lines recommended for the Central African Federation by the Monckton Commission, is now abolished, but there are elaborate provisions with prescribed majority requirements (in some cases ninety per cent of the Senate) for constitutional amendment, the alteration of the provisions for fundamental human rights or of the regional structure. Unlike the Commonwealth countries in earlier days, Kenya did not ask for the Westminster model and probably accepted it only with a view to gaining independence. It has never been popular but it may have served a useful purpose in bridging over the period before independence. As in many African countries there is a one-party government. There is therefore no intercameral friction and the Senate does not figure as an important body. Its value lies possibly not so much in upholding district rights as in maintaining equilibrium in tribal rivalries. In her book on the *Tensions of Progress in Kenya,* Susan Wood has written 'The difficulties which a newly established State encounters tend to make for harsh administration of law until its government is strong and stable. Opposition tends to be classed as subversion and an insecure government uses measures which would be classed as ruthless in a stable society. In independent Africa the balance may be difficult to maintain between effective discipline and repressive measures'. It can hardly be expected that in such circumstances a Second Chamber can do much towards maintaining the balance.

Very different traditions prevail in Jamaica and in Trinidad and Tobago which broke away from the West Indies Federation in 1962 after a referendum in Jamaica. Jamaica claims an experience of bicameral government, modelled closely on Westminster, from the year 1664, interrupted only by a period of Crown Colony administration from 1866–1944. In its independence constitution of 1962, the composition of the Senate contains an unusual feature in that, of the twenty-one senators, eight are appointed by the Governor General on the advice of the Leader of the Opposition in the Lower House, the remainder being appointed on the advice of the Prime Minister. The proportion nominated by the Leader of the Opposition is high, especially in view of the fact that a proposal for the amendment of the constitution requires a two-thirds majority. In Trinidad and Tobago, which has a similar constitution, thirteen members in a senate of twenty-four are appointed on the advice of the Prime Minister, four on the advice of the Leader of the Opposition and seven by the Prime Minister after consulting social, religious and economic organizations. In both Senates there is necessarily a government majority and, though they have a suspensory power of seven months in respect of legislation, this has never yet been exercised and there has been no intercameral friction. The Jamaican Senate also has a suspensory power of seven months in respect of statutory instruments. An indication of the subordinate position of these Senates lies in the fact that they can be dissolved on the advice of the Prime Minister. Their strength lies in the tradition behind them and in their strong representation of minority interests.

Of territories which have attained internal self-government but are not fully independent and therefore not full members of the Commonwealth, British Guiana, British Honduras, the Bahama Islands, Barbados and Bermuda have Second Chambers. The three island territories have had a long experience of representative government, Bahamas since 1729, Barbados since 1639 and Bermuda since 1620.

In the Bahamas a new constitution came into force in 1964 with a view to giving the islands a higher degree of responsible government. The life-nominated Legislative Council of eleven members, which had been an active and useful body, was replaced by a Senate of fifteen members appointed by the governor, eight after consultation with the Premier and others whom he might wish to consult, five on the advice of the Premier and two on the advice of the Leader of the Opposition. The Senate has a delaying power of two months in respect of money Bills which it cannot amend, but which it may return to the House of Assembly with a recommendation for amendment, and fifteen months in respect of other Bills including a special category of 'taxation' bills, i.e. Bills imposing income tax, capital gains tax, a capital levy or estate duty. The Speaker's certificate on a money Bill may, if challenged, be referred to the Attorney General.

Bermuda, a small and over-populated island subsisting, like the Bahamas, largely on the tourist, has had a Second Chamber since 1888. The franchise which embraced less than one-seventh of the population was widened in 1963. The Second Chamber, or Legislative Council, consists of three official members, Chief Justice, Colonial Secretary and Attorney General and eight nominated members.

Barbados was granted full internal self-government in 1961. The Legislature includes a Second Chamber, the Legislative Council, consisting of some twenty-one members appointed by the Governor on the advice of the Premier and two on the advice of the Leader of the Opposition. The Council has delaying power of a year.

British Guiana has had a turbulent history resulting from economic upheavals and acute racial animosities. The advance from Crown Colony government to full independence, which seems imminent, has however been very rapid. Following the breakdown and suspension of the 1953 constitution and an interim government with a single nominated chamber, a constitution giving full internal self-government was established in 1961 with a Senate of thirteen members nominated by the governor, eight on the advice of the Premier, three after consulting opposition groups and two at his discretion. Its purpose, as the Report of the Constitutional Conference of 1960 states, was 'to provide the opportunity for persons of wisdom and experience, who might be unwilling to stand for election, to participate in the government of the country. Nevertheless the Senate should be so constituted in membership and powers as not to be in a position to thwart the will of the Legislative Assembly'. The Senate had delaying powers of six months. Demands for full independence led to further discussions for a new constitution and, on the failure of the political parties to come to an agreement, the British Government was invited to settle outstanding issues. Consequently in 1964 the British Guiana (Constitution) Order in Council was made setting up a unicameral legislature to be elected, as a safeguard for minority parties, by proportional representation.[1]

British Honduras has also had a rapid constitutional development and full independence within the Commonwealth, possibly under the name of Belize, seems likely as the result of recent elections. Its economy has been dislocated by a succession of hurricanes and intense resentment, leading to demands for self-government, was occasioned by the devaluation of the currency. There has been a rapid advance from Crown Colony government to internal self-government since this time. A new constitution, established in 1963, provides for a bicameral legislature, the Senate to consist of eight members nominated by the governor, five on the advice of the Premier, two on the advice of the leader of the opposition and one after consultation with various interests. The Senate has no power to initiate or amend financial Bills and its delaying power is restricted to six months.

The Senates of all these territories are composed on similar lines. The leader of the government controls a majority in all

[1] The British Guiana Independence Conference of 1965 prescribed May 26, 1966, as the date on which British Guiana, under the name of Guyana, should become independent. The constitution provided for a unicameral parliament, for which the principle of election by proportional representation is retained, and specially entrenched provisions covering a wide range of fundamental freedoms for all individuals, enforceable by the courts and only alterable after a referendum. There is also provision for an Ombudsman.

of them. Their purpose is to ensure that other interests are represented and to act as a steadying influence.

From this brief review of Second Chambers in the Commonwealth it is apparent that all bear the stamp of the Westminster model, though with divergencies. The limitations on their financial powers are broadly similar but not identical either with it or with each other. While at Westminster the Speaker's certificate on a money bill is final and unchallengeable, in India, Kenya and the Bahamas it can be disputed and referred to judicial authority. The Second Chambers of Australia, India, Kenya and the Bahamas have a power of suggesting amendments to money bills, which they are debarred from amending by the ordinary procedure, a power which the House of Lords does not possess. In Canada and Australia, whose constitutions were formed before the existence of the Parliament Acts, the second chambers have an absolute veto on legislation; the newer constitutions restrict them to a delaying power varying in length, the Bahamas two months (or, if imposing new taxes, fifteen months), the Indian States three months, India six months, Nigeria, Jamaica, Trinidad and Tobago seven months, Malaysia and Kenya thirteen months spread over two sessions. In Ceylon a Bill passed by the House of Representatives in two successive sessions may become law without the consent of the Senate. The Senate of Jamaica has a suspensory power of seven months in respect of delegated legislation. In several constitutions there are provisions for settling deadlocks between the two Houses, usually, as in India and Malaysia and the Nigerian regions, by means of Joint Sittings, an expedient which gives the advantage to the Lower House by reason of its numerical superiority. Australia has a more elaborate provision involving dissolution of both Houses followed, in the case of continued disagreement by a Joint Sitting. Almost everywhere in the Commonwealth Ministers can speak, though not vote, in either House, a practice which has often been suggested at Westminster but against which Westminster has set its face, partly on account of the additional strain it would impose on Ministers and partly because it would deprive junior Ministers representing departments in the Second House of the valuable experience of conducting legislation in that House. The United Kingdom alone has life membership for its second chamber, (Canada, where appointment to the Senate had been for life, having recently imposed an age limit of seventy-five years) and the United Kingdom alone a predominantly hereditary membership. In other countries the tenure of a senator is limited to a term of years, usually six years, though in New South Wales it is twelve years and in Barbados it might be as much as fifteen years. In all cases Senators are eligible for re-election or re-nomination. In Canada and South and Western Australia there is a minimum age qualification of thirty years, in Nigeria forty years. In most of the Commonwealth countries the Second Chambers are not subject to dissolution but in Australia the Senate can be dissolved in certain circumstances and the Senates of Nigeria, Jamaica and Trinidad and Tobago can be dissolved on the advice of the Prime Minister. The principal difference between the Commonwealth Second Chambers lies in and stems from their method of composition; Australia and Kenya directly elected; India and Nigeria indirectly elected, Ceylon and Malaysia part indirectly elected and part nominated; the House of Lords part hereditary and part nominated; Canada, Jamaica, Trinidad and Tobago, the Bahamas, Bermuda and British Guiana wholly nominated. In India, Ceylon, Malaysia, Nigeria, Trinidad, the Bahamas and British Guiana special interests are represented or consulted for a proportion of the nominated members.

In spite of these differences in composition and in powers, the Second Chambers of the Commonwealth are fundamentally based on the Westminster model and yet the House of Lords stands in a wholly different position from any other. The structure of these Second Chambers, embedded in written constitutions, is easy to grasp. This, however, is not the case with the House of Lords. The House of Lords is not a devised body set up for a particular purpose. It is the product of evolution, a part of the structure of a Parliament that has had a continuous tradition of seven hundred years, and it can be properly understood only if it is regarded as having today reached a particular stage in its evolution. In its long history it has changed much, perhaps more in recent years than at any other period. If it were to be examined as what it is and does today, without any reference to its past history or any enquiry as to how it has come about that it is what it is and does what it does, it would indeed seem to be an incomprehensible feature of any constitution. It would be difficult to understand how a body of approximately one thousand members, composed on principles that are regarded as undemocratic and out of harmony with modern ideas, with a predominantly one-sided political outlook, shorn of the great powers it once possessed and with a history in which periods of reaction and obstruction have left memories, could maintain its position in a democratic country; but the force of tradition and the process of evolution, coupled with the occasional stimulus of remedial legislation, have rendered it able to adapt itself to changing circumstances and have moulded it to become, as it works in practice, a business-like assembly capable of carrying out with efficiency the duties required of it today. This characteristic of the House is one which cannot easily be exported into a modern written constitution.

It has been the target for obvious criticism on the grounds of its membership, the method of its composition and its overwhelmingly one-sided political outlook. As regards size, although all its members have a right to attend, only about two hundred and fifty do so regularly, the number varying upwards or downwards according to the nature of the business before the House. The great majority of these are men and women who are well qualified to take part, being persons prominent in most walks of life, many of them former ministers and members of the House of Commons and forming what has been described as a reservoir of informed opinion on any subject. It is to the opinions expressed by these as individuals rather than to the opinion of the House expressed as a corporate body that such influence as it exercises is due.

As regards its composition, a marked effect on the proceedings of the House has resulted from the comparatively recent infusion, consequent upon the passing of the Life Peerages Act, 1958, of a nominated element. The Life peers and peeresses, of whom there are now about 100, take a prominent part in the proceedings of the House and have substantially strengthened the representation of the Labour party. This process is likely to continue and the disparity in numbers between the two principal parties may be expected to become less pronounced. In consequence of the independence of peers from elections, party ties sit lighter in the House of Lords than in the Commons; an adverse vote in the Lords does not entail the fall of the government; debates in the Lords are scantily publicized. These factors make for freedom of expression and of criticism, not always from a strictly party point of view. Still, although the House uses its powers with discretion, Labour governments have felt themselves at a great disadvantage in passing their legislation through the Chamber and have resented being able to do so only through its forbearance.

The House of Lords derives strength from being the Supreme Court of Appeal, a function exercised by the Lords of Appeal, but exercised in the name of the House. It also derives strength from the presence in its ranks of the Archbishops and senior bishops of the Church of England, who constitute an *ex officio* element in its composition. Throughout its history, the Parliamentary system in this country has been geared to the existence of a Second Chamber. Pressure of business in the Commons is so great that a revisionary process is necessary. There have been countless attempts at wholesale reform but all have foundered on the difficulty of rationalising its composition without unduly strengthening its position in relation to the elected Chamber. If judged solely on its performance as a working part of the constitution, it carries out the tasks expected of it with a success that some of its attributes would seem to make improbable.

It seems that the traditional notion of the need in a constitution for a strong second chamber is no longer of general acceptance. Only a second chamber composed on an elective basis would command sufficient authority to enable it to act as a restraining influence upon, or to assert itself against, the Lower House; to claim to be the interpreter of public opinion or have the right to give the country an opportunity for second thoughts. Indeed it is the aim of many governments to secure in their Senates and Legislative Councils, as far as they are able, a majority sympathetic to their own political outlook. Public opinion, it is said, can make itself readily felt through the medium of press, radio and television. Further, some of the functions which used to be regarded as coming within the province of a second chamber, such as the protection of the constitution and the safeguarding of minority rights can, it is claimed, be provided by other means, entrenched provisions, specially entrenched provisions, or Bills of fundamental human rights, which can only be altered by special procedures. In Zambia, for instance, a Bill involving an alteration in the constitution requires the support of two-thirds of all the members of the National Assembly both on second and third readings and its text must have been published in the Gazette thirty days before its first reading, while Bills relating to the code of human rights, the judiciary or the procedure for constitutional amendment require, in addition, the approval of a majority of the total electorate at a referendum. Some constitutions, however, which have bicameral legislatures, Nigeria, Malaysia, Jamaica, and Trinidad and Tobago and others have also similar special procedures for these purposes and in Kenya a ninety per cent majority of all the members of the Senate is required.

Second Chambers tend therefore to be left with the functions of initiating Bills, of debate and of revision. In these they may to some extent relieve the pressure of business on their lower houses, assist the parliamentary time-table and provide a valuable forum for the discussion of public affairs, but this limited and somewhat indeterminate function tends to reduce their status in popular estimation. It is a weakness of the Westminster model, so far as Second Chambers are concerned, that, as exported to countries which lack the tradition of parliamentary democracy, it has provided them with no counterbalancing feature such as would give them the moral authority necessary for carrying out whatever duties may be required of them with greater effect. They would be far more effective if they could be assigned special spheres of responsibility.

Chapter VIII

THE POSSIBILITIES OF THE PRESIDENTIAL SYSTEM IN AFRICA

BY DENIS BROGAN

It can be said of the nineteenth century that its favourite political system and its favourite political export was a variation of English parliamentary government. The export, it is true, was chiefly imitated through French experience and it was the slightly illegitimate child of the Mother of Parliaments, the Chambre des Députés of Louis-Philippe, which was copied, in some degree, all over Europe and in nearly all of the aspiring nations of the rest of the world. Formally, it is true, many Latin American nations imitated the presidential system of the United States; but the United States of Mexico, and the United States of Venezuela and the United States of Brazil (after the fall of the Empire) were very far indeed from their putative model. The only two Latin American countries with a well organized and stable political life, Chile and Uruguay, imitated the British parliamentary system. The attempt to replace it in Chile by the presidential system led to the defeat and suicide of President Balmaceda after one of the most interesting civil wars in modern history.

It is true that when the leaders of the Meiji restoration in Japan provided a constitution for that empire, they copied Prussia and not England. But the Prussian diet was a perverted form of the House of Commons, and there was no question of making the Mikado or any successor of the Shoguns a presidential official of the American type. Outside the Americas, even the formal imitation of the United States constitution was limited to Liberia, and in France, whatever may have been the intentions of the framers of the constitution of 1875, in practice the Third Republic was a very parliamentary government indeed. The prestige of parliamentary government on the British model survived well into this century. For example, the new Irish Free State constitution attempted to break away from the British model, but it failed to do so. The various gadgets and gimmicks in the constitution were ignored, and the Irish imitated the constitutional practice of their oppressors.[1]

The defeat of Germany in the First War encouraged imitations of the political institutions of the victorious powers and, again, imitations took the form of imitating the British constitution. For example, Japan moved from a variation of the Prussian system to an imitation of the British system of parliamentary government. It is true that another type of political organization, destined to a great future, was visible over the horizon, the government of the Soviet Union; but the point on which it is worth while insisting is that none of the new nations adopted the American presidential system.

Today the case is altered. Even in the home of the Mother of Parliaments it is asserted, with a great deal of plausibility, that England herself is moving towards a presidential system of government with the Prime Minister as the equivalent of the President. Whether it is true or not is less important than the fact that it can be said without producing indignant denial and effective refutation. A great many of the new nations outside the Communist zone which have been able to choose their institutions have, in recent times, chosen some form of presidential government rather than any form of parliamentary government.[2] Even France, which was the great imitator of English

---

[1] A very eminent Irishman told two British visitors twenty years ago that although the Irish parliament established by the English was, in many ways, a parody of a parliament and never represented in any real sense the 'mere' Irish, parliamentary habits were in fact observed and imitated and that was one of the few good results of English rule. The political scientist who announced this doctrine was Mr De Valera.

[2] There is an immense literature on the American presidential system, but the four most useful books are: *The Man in the White House*, by Wilfred E. Binkley, 1958; *The President: Office and Powers*, by Edwin S. Corwin, 1957; *Presidential Power*, by Richard E. Neustadt, 1960; *The American Presidency*, by Clinton Rossiter, 2nd edn., 1960.

constitutional practice, has gone forward to—or fallen back on—a presidential system openly imitated from that of the United States. The Fifth Republic, with its direct election of the President, is a denial of the long tradition of imitation of English political methods which the French intellectuals have practised since 1789. President de Gaulle is more an heir or imitator of President Washington or President Lincoln than of Sir Robert Peel or Mr Gladstone!

If one looks at the literature discussing problems of the newly liberated British colonies and the newly liberated French colonies of Africa, after the end of the last war, it is somewhat odd to read so many books based on the belief that the only rational and normal form of political organization which will protect freedom and promote well-being, is the parliamentary form. Traces of this belief that this is the right and normal form of free government can still be found, but whatever the formal structure of government may be, more and more authority is being concentrated in one public official called the President who may be merely a President or, as is more and more common, really be a Dictator.

It is probably true that the attempts at parliamentary government in Egypt were continually thwarted by the 'Palace'; that possibly the WAFD would have made a success of parliamentary government if it had been permitted a free hand; but the fact remains that it was not permitted. Lord Killearn, in the Suez crisis of 1956, did suggest that we should support the WAFD, but he was a voice crying in the wilderness and totally unheard in London and in Cairo. The heir of King Farouk was Colonel Nasser who is possibly also the heir of the Pharaohs or of other personal rulers of Egypt since the Roman conquest. At any rate, parliamentary government has not been a feature of Egyptian political life. The same failure to establish effective parliamentary government has been marked in French Africa. In a sense, this is natural enough; as the French did not make much of a success of parliamentary government in the last years of the Third Republic or at any time in the history of the Fourth Republic, so it is quite natural that the liberated populations should imitate the 'Metropolis' and that the example of General de Gaulle should be followed in Senegal, in the Ivory Coast, in Madagascar.[1]

There can be little doubt that a great deal of the criticism directed against the leaders of the new African states is based on an unconscious assumption that there is something *wrong* in the concentration of power and prestige in a single officer and that it is more or less accidental that in Ghana, in Senegal, in the Ivory Coast, in Tunis, the authority of the state and the prestige of that authority have been concentrated in single individuals. There is, in fact, nothing extraordinary in the decision of the African peoples to choose a form of government which is in itself simple and has the immense prestige of being, on paper, the system of government of the most powerful nation in the world.

The framers of the American Constitution in the Convention of 1787 had in their minds their unfortunate experience with a 'plural' executive, for the 'Continental Congress', the governing body of the United States, had never developed an efficient executive side and it had, with one or two vague efforts at concentration of power, ruled by committees. The results were not satisfactory! It was, therefore, quite natural, especially as General Washington was at hand, to settle for a single executive. Colonial experience, the rule by royal governors, made the idea familiar. (Indeed colonial experience in Africa has made the idea of a single executive familiar both in the former British and the former French colonies.)

The text of the United States Constitution dealing with the presidency starts off with an extremely vague declaration of powers and functions: 'The executive power shall be vested in a President of the United States of America. He shall hold his office during the term of four years'. And the office so vaguely defined could be exercised only after the taking of a special oath: 'I do solemnly swear (or affirm) that I will faithfully

---

[1] The political leaders of the ex-French colonies had, in fact, more experience of parliamentary government than had the British leaders, since many of them had been members of the French National Assembly and acquired, for good or evil, French parliamentary habits. See *Political Parties in French-Speaking West Africa*, by Ruth Schachter Morgenthau, 1964. 'Their experience altered the way in which they thought about political problems, and so differentiated them from their colleagues in Africa, making them a special group apart', p. 120.

execute the office of President of the United States, and will to the best of my ability, preserve, protect, and defend the Constitution of the United States'. Lincoln attached great importance to the fact that the President *alone* took this oath and from this fact developed a theory that he had a general commission to preserve the United States, a kind of variation of the commission given to dictators in the Roman Republic to see that 'no harm befalls the Republic'.

The presidential office in the United States is in form extremely simply defined. The constitution is deliberately vague and it is history over the last 170 years which has created the office now held by President Lyndon Johnson. There is therefore nothing outrageous in the fact that the real powers of Colonel Nasser or Dr Nkrumah cannot be deduced from the formal text of the constitutions of Egypt and Ghana.[1] Nor is there anything surprising in the fact that in the new African countries the office has been built very largely round specific men. All American historians are agreed that the character of the presidency, as vaguely defined in the Constitution, was very much affected by the universal belief that the first president would

[1] The Constitution of the United States of America has only this to say about the powers of the President: 'The President shall be Commander-in-Chief of the army and navy of the United States, and of the militia of the several States, when called into the actual service of the United States; he may require the opinion, in writing, of the principal officer in each of the executive departments, upon any subject relating to the duties of their respective offices, and he shall have power to grant reprieves and pardons for offences against the United States, except in cases of impeachment. He shall have power, by and with the advice and consent of the Senate, to make treaties, provided two-thirds of the Senators present concur; and he shall nominate, and by and with the advice and consent of the Senate, shall appoint ambassadors, other public ministers and consuls, judges of the Supreme Court, and all other officers of the United States, whose appointments are not herein otherwise provided for, and which shall be established by law; but the Congress may by law vest the appointment of such inferior officers, as they think proper, in the President alone, in the courts of law, or in the heads of departments. The President shall have power to fill up all vacancies that may happen during the recess of the Senate, by granting commissions which shall expire at the end of their next session. He shall from time to time give to the Congress information of the state of the Union, and recommend to their consideration such measures as he shall judge necessary and expedient; he may on extraordinary occasions, convene both houses, or either of them, and in case of disagreement between them, with respect to the time of adjournment, he may adjourn them to such time as he shall think proper; he shall receive ambassadors and other public ministers; he shall take care that the laws be faithfully executed, and shall commission all the officers of the United States.'

be General Washington. To him powers were entrusted in vague and general terms which might not have been entrusted to anyone else, and, indeed, if Washington had not been available, it is not certain that the executive of the United States *would* have been concentrated in a single official. More than that, it was in Washington's first term that both by congressional statute and by presidential action the executive government of the United States was given the character which it has never lost of being, above all, the concentration of power in one man elected, although indirectly, by the American people, and that all other executive officers are the nominees and the servants of this chief servant of the American people. There is in American theory and practice no question of *primus inter pares*. The famous story of Lincoln consulting his cabinet and announcing, 'Nos, 7; ayes, 1. The ayes have it' expresses perfectly the spirit of the American Constitution—as it does the practice of the constitutions of Egypt and Ghana, of Senegal and Tunis.

Nor is there anything especially remarkable in the amount of reverence given to the office of leader in an African state. The so-called charismatic character of African leadership has not only got its obvious parallels, especially in the cases of the late and unlamented Stalin, Mussolini and Hitler, but in the degree to which power and representational function even in the cynical country of France are concentrated in the person of General de Gaulle! In the United States the presidency combines, as has often been pointed out, the kind of reverence given to the Crown in Britain and the possibly reluctant respect given to the office of Prime Minister. It is true that this official reverence, which is extremely important and living, is often accompanied in the United States by a degree of personal hostility and personal denigration of a type that would be quite unthinkable in Britain and regarded with disgust even in France. Franklin D. Roosevelt and Harry S. Truman, John Fitzgerald Kennedy and now Lyndon B. Johnson were and are the victims of a kind of scurrility fortunately unknown in Britain and, as far as I can judge, unknown in Africa. But this is the reverse of the medal, an aspect of the appreciation of the immense power and dignity of the office of President of the United States.

Then the rôle of a leader like the Osagyefo of Ghana is again not unknown in the United States. If the President of the United States does not give a lead, for example on the bitter and dangerous question of race relations, no one else can. That President Eisenhower did not give such a lead was one of the most substantial reproaches made against him. In a continent like Africa, in new and largely artificial states whose unity may be purely formal, the temptation to put the burdens of unifying the 'nation' on a leader who is usually the President, is overwhelming and succumbing to it is not a proof of intrinsic vice. The African leader has to do all that an American president has to do—and a lot more. The leader has to 'make his party's policy intelligible to the rank and file, a large proportion of whom are illiterate farmers, fishermen, labourers and market women. He therefore necessarily acquires certain numinous qualities.... His rôle becomes partly that of the Prophet in the more primitive forms of nationalist movement... He may even become the object of hymns, prayers and creeds—"I believe in Kwame Nkrumah" '.[1]

But if it is natural in the circumstances for the new African states to turn to the comparatively simple presidential form rather than the sophisticated and difficult parliamentary form, it does not follow that the imitation is easy or that the institution of the presidency, as known in the United States, is one that can easily be transferred. Notoriously, the Presidents of Latin American states have as a rule been very unlike Presidents of the United States. They have never acquired the prestige and the acceptance of their *Yanqui* prototype. There is no real equivalent in Latin American history for President Washington or President Lincoln, and there is no equivalent in United States history for President Díaz or President Perón. And if this is true of the Latin American states, it is likely to be even more true of the new African states.

Yet there are obvious parallels. Today it is obvious in the new African states, that only those persons who took a conspicuous part in the 'liberation' movements have any chance of entering the new governing class. There is nothing surprising in this. It is only now that Ireland is beginning to have a

[1] Thomas Hodgkin, *Nationalism in Colonial Africa*, 1956, pp. 162-3.

political leadership not created in the 'Troubles'. Martin Van Buren, who became President in 1837, was the first President of the United States not born a British subject—and the first President without direct connections with the American Revolution. There is therefore nothing to be surprised or indignant about in the way in which the leaders of the various liberation movements in Africa have monopolized political power and the quite substantial advantages to be gained from it. The eminent persons in the recently liberated American colonies who were either tepid during the Revolution or actively Loyalist found, with very few exceptions, that they could not have an effective political career in the new republic. Some had, of course, already taken refuge in Canada or in the mother country. Others found, to their annoyance, that they *had* to take refuge in Canada or the mother country or, if they stayed in their native land, accept their effective exclusion from political life. The flight of the Tories to Canada or to Britain was very important for the future of the United States, for it meant that a great many of the naturally conservative elements of the new country played a minor rôle in its history. There was no return of the *émigrés* as there was in France from about 1799. Again there is nothing surprising in the monopolizing of power by the elements most conspicuously opposed to the old colonial system. Whether all the claims to patriotic service in this period are justified or not is a question that, as in Ireland, it is often tactless to ask!

The presidency in the United States was an office which could be competed for only by people with good 'patriotic' records, and a case could be made for the assertion that for a generation after the recognition of American independence, politics on a national scale was a clash between two sections of the old revolutionary party which had been used to call itself the 'Whigs'. But the presidency played an extremely important unifying rôle. The new federation of the United States covered a very great deal of land and covered it with a very thinly distributed population. Almost the only truly national political activity was the election of the President. (After George Washington's first two terms, the elaborate indirect system of election of the President ceased to have any importance. He became the choice of the American people voting *en masse*.) It could be said that then—and perhaps now—the only absolutely indispensable function of the American party system is to organize votes to elect a President, to make sure that in Georgia and in Oregon the same candidates are voted for or against. Indeed, it can be argued very plausibly that the immediate cause of the American Civil War was the breakdown in 1860 of the party system, the inability of the natural majority party, the Democrats, to agree on a candidate. Since then, great sacrifices of principle and acceptance of pretence have been made to hold parties together in order to avoid the dangers to national unity that schisms produce. A third party always meets with a great deal of automatic disapproval which is historically justifiable. And a party which ostentatiously cultivates a violently sectional policy, as Senator Goldwater's Republicans did in 1964, also meets with disapproval. There is a kind of ancestral memory of the risks of a too systematic, a too coherent party system. As far as the new African nations penalize any form of dissent by ostracism, by exile, by imprisonment, they are only exaggerating an American practice. Even the domination of the party system by one party is not a novelty in America, for in American history there have been long periods of control of the federal government by one party which have ended only when that party has itself suffered from external events, like the Great Depression of 1929, which upset the voting patterns.

But—and it is an important but—there always have been at least two parties in the United States, even if the differences between them were almost invisible, as in the so-called 'era of good feelings' after the end of the French revolutionary wars, or have been on strictly traditional points as was the case over a great part of the late nineteenth and early twentieth centuries. Yet the minority party, if it had little hope of effectively controlling the federal government, had always strongholds, unshakable strongholds, in state and city governments. This was true of the Democrats in their long exile from power between 1860 and 1932 (the interruptions of Republic supremacy by Grover Cleveland and Woodrow Wilson did not alter permanently the rôle of the 'majority party'). Since 1932 the Democratic party has been even more the majority party than the Republicans were before that. Yet the Republicans have held very important offices like that of Governor of New York, Senator from New York, Governor of Pennsylvania, Senator from California, Mayor of San Francisco. There never was a time in which *all* Republicans were excluded from all political power. There never was a time in which, even in national politics, the minority party had not a considerable bargaining power. As far as one can judge, this is not true of the new African states where there are no built-in political institutions giving minority parties inexpugnable positions from which they may hope to advance to national control and in which they can, at any rate, rest and recruit themselves! At no time in American history have *all* the jobs *everywhere* been at the disposal of one party machine! And this is in practice very important.

The rôle of the President of the United States as a dispenser of patronage, although not as important as it was, is still important. And although various Presidents like Roosevelt, Kennedy and now Lyndon Johnson have given important posts to Republicans, these have not as a rule carried any intrinsic political power. In the history of the United States after the Civil War, there were plenty of examples of the taking over of extremely profitable as well as dignified political offices by the newly triumphant Republicans and the consequent decline into impotence of the Democrats who had neither power nor profit to offer. An American President, even today, owes a great deal of his practical power to the fact that he can give positions of honour and profit, and possibly by administrative concessions favour whole sections, e.g. in the allocation of great federal programmes; but he has not got anything like the complete monopoly of what we might call the profits of politics, which a successful leader in one of the new African states assumes to be his by right of his leadership. Yet we must notice that there is nothing particularly outrageous in the monopolizing of positions of profit and prestige by the dominant party. 'The spoils system' in American history has an old and not very dignified history, although today it is a shadow of what it was. But there is a danger in the African use of the spoils system which did not and does not affect the American application of it. The 'revolution' in the colonial empires of Britain, France, and Belgium replaced, almost completely, the previous white ruling class. Such members of it as remain are there on sufferance and as employees of the new governments. The new ruling class, as has been suggested, is composed of the leaders of the political parties which struggled, with varying degrees of zeal, for independence. Their experience of actual government before independence was quite limited, more continuous in Ghana than in perhaps any other British colony, and complicated in French Africa both by service in the French National Assembly and by the survival of quasi-representative institutions both in North Africa and in West Africa. But there is no equivalent of the past experience of government which nearly all the leaders of the American Revolution had (e.g. Colonel Washington and Dr Benjamin Franklin). One result has been to block promotion for the increasing number of people who might naturally think that because of their education they are entitled to serve their countries in positions of dignity and profit.[1]

The American spoils system dealt with this problem in a way which was politically justifiable if administratively a nuisance. This was the principle of 'rotation in office'. The victorious President (or Governor) did not only automatically give the jobs to his supporters, but he rotated the jobs among his supporters. Political office was to be 'a joy in widest commonalty spread'. For example, young Abraham Lincoln was allowed only one term in Congress and then was offered an inferior executive job. The President or Governor, not being bound to continue his nominees in office, had means to discipline them and the gratitude which is 'a lively sense of favours to come' held the party together. The growth of a regular civil service in the United States today has greatly diminished the importance of this kind of 'rotation', but it might be a solution for the blocking of promotion and the temptation to violence which marks some African states. It may be undignified to think of the head of a new nation as very largely engaged in rewarding his supporters, but that is in fact what American Presidents have

[1] 'A new generation of secondary school and university graduates, arriving on the scene in ever increasing numbers, is acutely aware that it will not have the opportunities of the present generation to climb rapidly to high positions of power and affluence'. James S. Coleman in 'The Character and Viability of African Political Systems', in W. Goldschmidt, *The United States and Africa*, 1964, p. 54.

been doing for a very long time, and it is perhaps involved in the growth of democratic politics in a society which has lost its traditional aristocracy or traditional ruling class.

There are, however, important difference between the United States and the states of the Union, and the new African states. First of all, the object of the Constitution of the United States is declared to be in the Preamble, to form 'a more perfect Union', and for nearly 200 years this has been done. But all attempts to build up federations in Africa, with the exception of Nigeria, have very quickly broken down. There are several reasons for this which ought to be noted to mark the contrast with the American presidential system.

The thirteen colonies which revolted against the mother country in 1776 were scattered over a very great area, but they had very many social customs in common. They were overwhelmingly English-speaking. Those groups of the population which were not English speaking, e.g. the 'Pennsylvania Dutch' (the German settlers), were comparatively indifferent to politics and were, in any case, subject to constant pressure from politicians to accept the domination of English ways of thought and practice. Benjamin Franklin, for example, was a great believer in enforcing cultural unity in Pennsylvania! Even dissenters from the predominant Protestant culture like the Catholics of Maryland were English-speaking and familiar, from English or Irish experience, with parliamentary government. One of the most formidable centres of rebellious energy in the colonies was provided by the 'Scotch-Irish', more properly called Ulster Presbyterians. They had had a very active training in democratic government through their church organizations and they were spread, by the time of the American Revolution, all over the colonies from north to south.

There was already something like an 'intercolonial culture' in the colonies by 1776 and the word 'American' was already in general use and already was describing a recognizable political and social attitude. The English common law was another source of unity and, as so many observers from Tocqueville on have pointed out, the legal system has been one of the chief sources of the unification of the United States.

This common linguistic, religious, and political inheritance is not visible in Africa. There is a great deal of discussion of Pan-Africanism. There is a great deal of discussion of 'the United States of Africa'. But there is no common language; there is no common historical experience under one imperial power; there is no common religious background; the nearest approach to one being provided by Islam. It is still debatable whether the term Africa effectively covers the Maghreb *and* Africa south of the Sahara.

It is true, as various people have pointed out, notably Mr Colin Legum, that the aeroplane and other modern methods of transport have made the separation of North Africa from Black Africa by the Sahara much less important than it was, but the separation is still a fact. The integration of the transport systems of North America has not, so far, led to the effective assimilation of either Canada or Mexico with the United States.

Négritude is a conception that it is very hard to identify with any particular set of political institutions. It may be that the African, the Negro African, has a far stronger sense of social unity than the white races have. The extended family is a basis for certain types of political action which Europeans and Americans of European descent do not have and do not value. (The American Negro does not seem to have inherited from his African ancestors any such sense of social unity and he is quite as individualistic in his approach to social and political programmes as his white fellow countryman. The Negro family in the United States is, if anything, even weaker than the white family, as the African family structure was destroyed by slavery.) Some of the attempts to create an African unity seem to the outsider highly artificial, for example the great prophet of *Négritude*, President Senghor of Senegal, while he still hoped to create the federation of Mali, described or invented a racial and cultural block to be called 'Negro-Berbers': this was based, apparently, partly on diet; the Negro-Berbers had in common a diet of milk, millet, and yams.[1]

The history of the Ku Klux Klan in America, with its hostility to Negroes, Catholics, and Jews, shows how far the United States is from having achieved a *perfect* union and the outbreaks

[1] See *On African Socialism*, Leopold Sédar Sengor (translated by Mercer Cook), 1964, p. 78.

in Los Angeles and Chicago suggest how far the American Union is from providing a tolerable political and social life for the 10 per cent of its population who are partly African in origin. But yet the degree of unity achieved, partly as a result of the presidential system, is far greater than anything achieved in Africa outside comparatively small states.[1]

This brings one to the problem that is certainly a burning one in Africa, namely the replacement of tribalism by wider loyalties. From one point of view, that of the nation state, it is obviously desirable to replace tribalism with a new nationality or, in fact or in fiction, by the revival of an old one. Let us admit that some of these national traditions recall the famous American college notice: 'This tradition will go into effect next Monday'. Ghana, as a nation, may be something to be made rather than something existing. But the same desire to create a unified national culture which the dominant English-speaking Americans have always displayed and, with a great deal of success have carried into practice, is as reasonable in Africa as it is in America. And there is no doubt that the presidential system, the embodiment of 'We the People of the United States' in one man, has been a very effective force in creating American nationality. The concentration of loyalty on one man is, after all, an old enough tradition and there is nothing surprising in its being cultivated in Africa as the condition of the creation, first of all, of African nations and then, somewhat more remotely, of a United States of Africa. The need was explained and justified in 1962 by one of the most enlightened of African leaders, President Nyerere of Tanganyika,[2] and it is natural that African leaders should be as intolerant of dissent from this objective as European and American leaders have been. Prohibition in the

---

[1] See *African Political Parties*, Thomas Hodgkin, 1961. Mr Hodgkin points out that only three African states have populations of over 20,000,000 (Egypt, Ethiopia, and Nigeria) and that more than half of them have populations of less than 3,000,000. Yet even in these very small states cultural, religious, and linguistic unity may be far to seek.

[2] 'We have to acknowledge that although the people of Tanganyika can understand the idea of law being made by groups, they see leadership and the enforcement of the law as the responsibility of a person with authority, answerable for his actions to the group but not hampered by it in effecting them. Under our proposals, where it is necessary to lead, the President has the powers to lead'. L. Gray Cowan, *The Dilemmas of African Independence*, 1964, p. 10.

United States, for example, was very largely an attempt to coerce the new immigrant groups into an acceptance of American rural Protestant ethics.[1] Some of the decline of the Republican Party is due to its refusal to admit into its community Jews and Catholics, to its identification of itself with the WASPS (i.e. white-Anglo-Saxon-Protestants) and it is for this reason that the election of a Catholic as President in 1960 was gratifying to Jews and Negroes as well as to Catholics.

But there are voices which ought to be listened to which suggest that this kind of artificial unity may not be intrinsically a good thing. First of all, some of the African leaders themselves belong to tribes which are, or think they are, superior in their political and economic qualities to some others. They are African WASPS. Thus, Dr K. A. Busia defends the progressive tribes like the Ashanti, Ibo, Yoruba, Baganda.[2]

In a very sophisticated version of the case for the tribes, Professor W. Arthur Lewis suggests that only by acceptance of the tribal fact and of the clashes of interest and sentiment between groups, can the new African states have a healthy political life. Thus the concentration of power and prestige in an individual is, for Professor Lewis, inherent in the bad colonial past. African leaders 'model themselves on the arrogant and arbitrary pattern set by Governors and District Commissioners, if only because they know no better. . . . A single-party supported by all the tribes is an impossible dream'[3] and it can be met, apparently, only by the suppression of liberty in the Western sense of the term.

Professor Lewis, like Dr Rita Hinden, thinks that the complacency with which Western 'liberal' communities have accepted dictatorial one-party states in Africa, is a new *trahison des clercs*. This kind of government is quite intolerable in Europe, but is quite good enough for Africans! Such is the implication. But it is not merely a matter of tribal loyalties or tribal differences.

A difficulty of any federal system is to get the richer parts of

---

[1] See Andrew Sinclair, *Prohibition*, 1962.
[2] K. A. Busia, *The Challenge of Africa*, 1962, p. 72.
[3] See W. Arthur Lewis, 'Beyond African Dictatorship', in *Encounter*, August 1965, pp. 4–5.

it to subsidize the poorer parts. Thus Gabon and Katanga have been unwilling to share their wealth with their neighbours. Some of the failures of federal governments in French Africa have come from the jealousy of the poorer states and the greed of the richer ones. Mauritania is apparently not willing to share its mineral wealth either with its Islamic neighbours in Morocco or its African neighbours on its southern borders.

This, of course, is no novelty in federal governments even of a parliamentary type. Western Australia, after all, between the wars threatened to secede from the Commonwealth of Australia because of its economic grievances. Various American states, at various times, have convinced themselves that they are the victims of oppressive economic cuts imposed on the federal government by other states or groups of states.[1] A one-party state with authority concentrated in the person of a charismatic leader can, at any rate, postpone some of these tribal grounds of division. But it has proved impossible so far to induce the more prosperous states to make the sacrifice which an effective federalism involves. No preaching of *Négritude* or Pan-Africanism has produced the results produced in the United States not only by the presidential system, but by the judicial system.

But despite the arguments of Professor Lewis, which are impressive, especially on the economic side, the temptation to create a one-party, one-man state is very great. Attempts have been made to avoid this, e.g. in Liberia. Collective leadership has been preached and to some extent practised, but what this means is not quite clear to an outside observer.[2] But assuming

[1] This argument in America sometimes takes a peculiar form. It is said, for example, that the money given in grants by the federal government to the various states is fairy gold, that the money is collected and sent to Washington and then sent back to the states with a heavy overcharge for administrative costs. But this argument ignores the fact that many states are relatively poor and a good many are in fact insolvent. The real grievance, if there is one, is felt by the rich states like New York, Pennsylvania, Massachusetts, California which subsidize the poorer states, especially the poor states of the South which devote so much time to defending States' rights! But in fact the federal programme is a ground of unity if a very expensive method of securing it.

[2] See William Zartmann, *Government and Politics in Northern Africa*, p. 47. At the moment of writing, Colonel Boumedienne has not taken over the title of president used by M. Ben Bella. How far the leadership of the new government in Algeria will remain truly collective is still to be seen.

that for a great part of 'liberated' Africa, a presidential system is essential, what lessons can the Africans draw from the working of that system in the United States, and how far are they applicable to Africa? The attempt of President Tubman of Liberia to bring the indigenous tribes into the Afro-American ruling class may provide an answer to some of these questions, but the experiment has not been going on long and its future is still in doubt.[1]

There are already signs in former French Africa of the possible influence of the armed forces in upsetting the established government in a Latin American fashion (or, if you like, in the way the Fourth Republic was upset in 1958). The future of the Congo is still uncertain and there is the rôle of *its* armed forces. The concentration of power, and the concentration of what it is not much of an exaggeration to call worship in the person of Dr Nkrumah in Ghana, has produced a climate of political opinion which many Africans and others find stifling.[2] And what will be very hard to import into Africa, is the reverence for the electoral process which produces a President of the United States, a reverence which has been a very great source of strength to the American republic. True, the American Civil War was caused formally by the election of Abraham Lincoln to the presidency; but the Southern seceding states did not claim that Lincoln had not been elected; merely that they did not propose to stay in a Union in which he could be elected. The very narrow victory of John F. Kennedy in 1960 was not challenged, despite some protests from indignant Republicans about the electoral methods of Chicago, and, normally speaking, even a bare victor is accepted, however grumblingly, as the embodiment of the American people.[3]

[1] 'The question posed for the future was whether Tubman's presidential system could meet the challenges provoked by his own gradual reforms, or whether some of his younger lieutenants, already attracted by the Ghanaian example, would demand swifter and more radical changes.' John Hatch, *A History of Post-war Africa*, 1965, p. 187.

[2] A recent visitor from Ghana to Nigeria revealed astonishment at the freedom of political conversation in Nigeria as compared with the imposed discretion in Ghana.

[3] The disputed election of 1876 produced the nearest approach to a refusal to accept the results of a formally legal process, but the Democrats who professed to regard President Hayes as a usurper and held that the real president was Governor Tilden of New York were no more serious than English Tory squires drinking to the 'King over the Water'.

As has been said before, the American presidency owed a great deal to the fact that its first incumbent was the national hero George Washington—even more of a national hero than Dr Nkrumah or Mr Kenyatta. But the office that General Washington inaugurated has developed its own autonomy and its own independence. It is an elective monarchy with all the sacredness of a hereditary monarchy. It will be easier to transfer many of the administrative methods (including the spoils system), of the holding by the President of the office of Commander-in-Chief, of the creation of the White House as a kind of political temple, than to inculcate in the peoples of the new African states that reverence for the formal political leadership which made people lament the death of Warren Gamaliel Harding and, even in Dallas, be overwhelmed by the assassination of John F. Kennedy. It must be remembered that although more and more power has accrued to the presidency and although the President embodies, emotionally, the American people, he shares power and prestige with two sets of institutions each with its own form of appeal. Some of the most important changes in American life and law have been due to the initiative of the Supreme Court which has survived so many attacks on its alleged usurpations. And Congress, although it suffers from the concentration of so much federal power in the hands of the President, especially in the field of international relations, has great irreducible powers of legislation, investigation, and finance which the most powerful and popular President must cope with. No President, however powerful and however popular, is as unique a detainer of political power as some of the chiefs of the new African states wish to be and perhaps are. And it is perhaps the fact that the President continually has to deal with other sources of power and other expressions of the whims of the American people, that has kept this great office respected, potent, and flexible. Perhaps an American presidency can be made powerful only in the centre of the political system of a country when it is *not* exalted above all other rival sources of power and is *not* the only embodiment of the national will?

Chapter IX

LEGISLATURES UNDER WRITTEN CONSTITUTIONS

BY S. A. DE SMITH

To Jeremy Bentham the 'opinions of lawyers on a question of legislation' were 'peculiarly liable to be tinged with falsity by the operation of sinister interest'.[1] That he would have viewed without enthusiasm expressions of opinion by lawyers on questions affecting legislatures may be readily assumed. The impression that lawyers, irrespective of the propriety of their motives, are singularly ill-equipped to pass judgment on matters of government is still widespread in Britain. The lawyer tends to emphasize the form rather than the substance of things, to dwell upon procedural niceties at the expense of central issues, to scrutinize institutions when what really matters is the spirit that animates them. And a lawyer, pleading guilty to charges of professional bias, may concede that he lacks any special qualification for writing about the British constitution, the least legalistic of the major systems of government. But the British constitutional lawyer, after years of underemployment as an analyst of the Westminster model, is at last coming into his own. For now he has a plethora of Westminster's export models to inspect with the eye of a frustrated architect; and the student of contemporary politics, while treating his value judgments without reverence, cannot readily dispense with his guidance.

Constitutions drafted by lawyers and interpreted by lawyers

[1] *The Handbook of Political Fallacies* (revised and edited by Harold A. Larrabee), p. 34.

offer a standing invitation to the lawyer to adopt the role of commentator. Today every Member of the Commonwealth except the United Kingdom and New Zealand[1] has a written constitution, in the sense of a basic document or group of documents which define (amongst other things) the structure, functions and interrelationship of the principal organs of government. There are constitutions made in London and autochthonous (or home-made) constitutions; constitutions founded on the Westminster model of parliamentary democracy and constitutions for presidential régimes; constitutions monarchical and republican, federal and unitary, rigid and flexible, short and long. But to classify the constitutions of the Commonwealth in groups is not on the whole very helpful, if only because there is always at least one constitution which obstinately refuses to be fitted into any neat category. Nor, of course, is classification necessarily a key to an understanding of the practice of government. For example, to say that in 1965 Malawi had a Westminster-style constitution and Pakistan a presidential system gave no indication of the part played by parliamentary institutions in the political life of the two countries. Nevertheless, the content of a constitution does usually tell us something about political ideas and political realities in a country, and sometimes it tells us a great deal. Although a comparison of the texts of the Canadian and Australian constitutions may give the erroneous impression that the Australian brand of federalism is less centralized than the Canadian, it will give the correct impression that in both countries the powers of the Federal Parliament are severely circumscribed. From a reading of the Jamaican constitution it becomes clear that parliamentary democracy is practised and that a developed two-party system exists. Ghana's republican constitution proclaims the pre-eminence of the President in political life. The constitution of Malta recognizes the dominant position of the Roman Catholic Church in the life of the island. The conception, substantive content and ultimate breakdown of the constitution of Cyprus all reflect the passionate communalism of Greeks and

[1] The New Zealand Constitution Act, 1852, incorporated the rudiments of a written constitution, but it has been extensively amended and its provisions are no longer specially entrenched.

Turks which has undermined all efforts to construct a cohesive political society. The asymmetrical federal features of Malaysia and Uganda testify to the political importance of Sabah, Sarawak (and, till its forced secession, Singapore) and the Kingdom of Buganda. Some of the peculiarities, and indeed the very name, of Tanzania's Interim Constitution of 1965, are explicable only by reference to the difficulties involved in integrating the Afro-Shirazi Party, the single party of Zanzibar, with the Tanganyika African National Union.[1]

A constitution, then, will normally mirror significant political facts; and in so far as it is respected it is likely to exert a significant influence over political behaviour. If it fails to accord with political realities or political needs it may be adapted, amended or superseded. Adaptation may be possible if the constitution leaves gaps which can be filled in by ordinary legislation or if conventions and usages can be evolved to modify the strict letter of the law. But recent Commonwealth constitutions have been detailed and leave few gaps, and in any event the political ethos in developing countries is generally unfavourable to that cautious empiricism which characterized the constitutional history of Britain and the older Dominions. In an atmosphere of breathless impatience constitutional problems will receive more abrupt answers.

Constitutional difficulties may be removed, and new rules and institutions introduced, by formal amendment if it is politically practicable and expedient to bring the machinery for altering the constitution into operation. For example, the first Act passed by the Parliament of Malawi was one to amend the constitution so as to make it fully flexible and to enable Dr Banda to deal peremptorily with his opponents inside his own party. In Ghana President Nkrumah commanded sufficient support in 1964 to procure the swift adoption of amendments converting the country into a one-party state and rendering superior judges dismissible in his discretion. In Kenya, following the voluntary dissolution of KADU, the opposition party, a series of amendments was passed introducing a presidential system and whittling

---

[1] The constitution of TANU is set out in a Schedule to the Interim Constitution of Tanzania.

away the entrenched position of the regions; presumably the Government decided that to proceed by stages was preferable to ushering in a new constitutional order by a single comprehensive measure. At a more modest level, the Indian constitution has been amended several times in order to nullify the effect of unpalatable judicial decisions on its interpretation. In Canada and Australia, on the other hand, party alignments and regional pressures have made it extremely difficult for the Federal Governments to secure even minor constitutional amendments designed to circumvent inconvenient judicial rulings on the distribution of powers.

Supersession of a constitution may take place if those who wield (or aspire to wield) political power find its restraints intolerable. In 1958 President Mirza, faced with a clamorous and obstructive Assembly, abrogated Pakistan's constitution of 1956, only to be superseded himself three weeks later by General Ayub Khan. In 1962 President Ayub Khan enacted a new constitution, calculated to emphasize the primacy of the executive branch of government. In Cyprus the constitution precluded any major legislative or executive decision from being taken without the concurrence of the representatives of the Turkish community. When that concurrence was withheld, after persistent inter-communal friction had led to open conflagration, the Greek majority proceeded to carry on the government of the island in its own way, notwithstanding the constitution.[1] In Zanzibar the short-lived constitution and the largely unrepresentative régime that it buttressed were destroyed by an old-fashioned revolution. Constitutions that will not bend are likely to break or be broken, unless there is general agreement that the preservation of an unserviceable instrument is better than summary disposal. Seldom will one find so devoted a veneration of constitutionalism.

However, the fact that a constitution is discarded does not necessarily imply that it has given rise to insupportable difficulties. Within three years after having become independent,

---

[1] In *Attorney-General of the Republic* v. *Mustafa Ibrahim of Kyrenia* (1964) 3 *Judgments of the Supreme Court* 1, it was held that ostensibly unconstitutional legislation was validly enacted by virtue of the implied constitutional doctrine of necessity.

Ghana, Tanganyika and Nigeria had adopted new constitutions; but there is nothing to show that the original constitutions (or, in Ghana and Nigeria, the original constitutions as amended) were unworkable. The original constitutions were simply thought to be inappropriate for the needs of the time. Each of these countries wanted to become a republic, but the constitution provided that the Queen was to be head of state, with a Governor-General as her representative. The constitution, moreover, was contained in an Order made by Her Majesty in Council. To adopt a home-made constitution at the same time as becoming a republic was the obvious course to follow. But in Ghana and Tanganyika there were other reasons for adopting a new constitution. Strong government had been possible under the original Westminster-style constitution, but the leaders of the ruling party wanted a constitution that would facilitate still stronger government, a constitution in which the effective head of government would also be head of state and would stand apart from the legislature. And in Ghana there was an intense urge to instil into the basic constitutional instrument an ideological content by consecrating Nkrumahism, instating the people as a collective entity and affirming Ghana's attachment to the ideals of pan-Africanism.

The generalization that the purpose of a constitution is to limit the powers of government is, therefore, far too wide; indeed, on the contemporary African scene it is largely irrelevant. A constitution may be designed as an accelerator rather than a brake. It may be used as a means of declaiming and propagating political ideas and aims. Even so, the constitution will define the competence of the legislative and executive organs of government and in defining that competence will usually restrict it. Under the unwritten constitution of the United Kingdom, Parliament is sovereign inasmuch as it can pass any Act whatsoever on any subject whatsoever; and a simple majority vote in both houses, followed by the royal assent, always suffices. Among Commonwealth countries with written constitutions, only Malawi and Singapore have Parliaments so free from restraint.[1] All the other constitutions

[1] The statement in the text refers to the position at the end of 1965. Under the unwritten constitution of New Zealand, parliament is as unrestricted as the United Kingdom parliament.

include provisions which cannot be changed except by a special amending procedure. If a measure inconsistent with the constitution has been enacted without compliance with this procedure (which may prescribe a special majority in the legislature, or submission to the electorate at a referendum, or a variety of complicated variants) it may be pronounced invalid by the courts. Under federal constitutions, which assign exclusive fields of competence to the centre and the units, and under constitutions which incorporate justiciable guarantees of fundamental human rights (as do the large majority of recent Commonwealth constitutions), judicial review of the constitutionality of legislation may become a factor of some importance, given a political climate in which the judges are permitted to do their work without impediment.[1] Judicial review is, of course, a major factor in constitutional affairs in Canada and Australia; it has helped to sustain the principles of constitutionalism in India and also in the unitary State of Ceylon; it is still a matter of some account even in Pakistan and Cyprus; it will probably exert a marginal influence over constitutional development in the countries of the Caribbean; it has not yet made any appreciable impact in the new African States, where the wielders of political power will seldom be willing to accept from the courts rebuffs which they would never countenance from adversaries.

Hence the constitution is likely to limit the area of legislative competence, or at least to regulate the ways in which the legislature is to exercise its powers.[2] This is not to say that these restrictions will make the business of government more difficult in practice. In a single-party state, or a state in which one party is overwhelmingly dominant, obstacles may be lightly brushed aside; they may, indeed, have been devised in the confident expectation that they will not effectively obstruct a government's legislative programme.

The constitution will also contain other provisions about the

[1] For the constitutional position of the Judiciary in new Commonwealth countries see E. C. S. Wade at Chapter X, *post*; de Smith, *The New Commonwealth and its Constitutions*, pp. 137–143, 293.

[2] For the proposition that a legislature may be sovereign although the constitution regulates the manner in which it is to exercise its powers, see *Bribery Commissioner* v. *Ranasinghe* [1965] A.C. 172, at pp. 197–198.

legislature and its relationship with the executive branch of government. Legislative-executive relations call for separate treatment. They reveal, as we shall see, some differences in constitutional structure between the Westminster-style systems, on the one hand, and most of the presidential systems, on the other. But there are no clearly identifiable distinctions between the two classes of systems with regard to those constitutional provisions which deal with the legislatures themselves. When a new state moves over to presidentialism its Government may be influenced by a desire to make a demonstrative repudiation of tutelage to Westminster, but the constitutional rules relating to its Parliament will almost certainly remain strongly reminiscent of the earlier model. And the earlier model will not have been an exact replica of Westminster.

The constitution will provide for annual (or bi-annual) sessions of Parliament. It will define the composition of the legislature, but not always in detail, and may have something to say about the manner in which it is to be selected. If there are two houses it will lay down the legislative relationships between them, specifying the procedure to be observed if conflict arises over a Bill; this procedure may prescribe a joint sitting, but is more commonly based on the provisions of the Parliament Act, 1949, which ensures the ultimate supremacy of the lower house. Since the *raison d'être* of an upper house is usually to give special representation to regional, traditional or other minority interests,[1] its composition is likely to be defined with precision in entrenched sections of the constitution. In order to maintain flexibility the constitution may leave the composition of the lower house (or the House of Representatives or National Assembly in a unicameral system) to be determined by ordinary legislation or by the results of periodical constituency delimitations, but where it has been thought important to give specific guarantees of representation (for example, to chiefs in Sierra Leone and The Gambia, to women in Pakistan and to the Turkish community in Cyprus), explicit provision will be made in the constitution.

The basic qualifications and disqualifications for election or

---

[1] On second chambers see generally F. Lascelles, Chapter VII *ante*; K. C. Wheare, *Legislatures*, Chap. VIII; de Smith, *op. cit.*, pp. 121-8.

WRITTEN CONSTITUTIONS 215

appointment to membership of the legislature may be set out; so, too, may be the circumstances in which a seat will become vacant. Here deviations from the Westminster pattern are manifold. Under most of the modern constitutions only citizens of the country are eligible for election; it is not enough for a candidate to be a citizen of another Commonwealth country. A member's seat may become vacant if he absents himself without leave from the sittings of the legislature. In Ghana, where party and state are now one, every candidate for membership of the National Assembly must be a member of the Convention People's Party, and public officers are no longer disqualified. A member's seat is vacated if an order is made placing him under preventive detention. In Tanzania also all elected members must be members of the bicephalous national party. If more than two candidates present themselves as candidates for a constituency seat in Tanganyika, the number must be reduced to two before the election by a prescribed vetting procedure involving the participation of the Annual District Conference and the National Executive Committee of TANU. No Commonwealth constitution explicitly confers on the electors a right to revoke their member's mandate, but the constitution of Malawi now renders tenure somewhat precarious by providing that a member is to lose his seat if, having been elected as a candidate of a political party, he subsequently ceases to be a member of that party or to represent that party. He is deemed to have ceased to represent the party if the Speaker is satisfied that the executive committee of the constituency party has so resolved. It may be assumed that local committees can be induced to pass such resolutions if the party leadership expresses its will on the matter. In Trinidad and Tobago, where twenty senators are appointed on the advice of the Prime Minister and four on the advice of the Leader of the Opposition, a senator may be removed on the initiative of the person who advised the original appointment. In Pakistan a member of the National Assembly loses his seat if he has been so imprudent as to give notice of his intention to move a resolution for the impeachemnt of the President and the resolution subsequently fails to obtain the support of half of the Assembly's membership.

The details of electoral law will be regulated by ordinary

legislation, but many of the constitutions expressly provide for universal suffrage, the secret ballot and single-member constituencies. In Malta the single transferable vote system of proportional representation is constitutionally entrenched. So, too, are the systems of indirect election to the National Assembly adopted in Pakistan and, for the Kingdom of Buganda, in Uganda. Compulsory voting is prescribed in Australia by legislation; elections to the Commonwealth House of Representatives are conducted in accordance with the alternative vote system and to the Senate by proportional representation.

It has become usual for the constitution to vest the power to delimit constituencies in an independent electoral commission. This body may also be entrusted (as in Nigeria) with the supervision of the registration of voters and the conduct of elections—matters which in the United Kingdom are left to central and local government authorities. Attempts have been made to ensure the political detachment of those who discharge these various duties. In The Gambia, for instance, the members of the Constituency Boundaries Commission are appointed on the advice of the Judicial Service Commission, and are removable only for proved inability or misbehaviour in pursuance of the recommendations of a judicial tribunal of inquiry. In Jamaica a different course has been followed. There delimitation is primarily a matter for a standing committee of the House of Representatives, with the Speaker as chairman; the constitution provides that of the six other members three shall be appointed by the Prime Minister and three by the Leader of the Opposition.

In the large majority of Commonwealth countries, new and old, the Speaker is a party nominee and is not expected to display that total detachment from partisan considerations which the Speaker's office has recently acquired in the United Kingdom. Degrees of political commitment vary; in some countries the Speaker has achieved a large measure of political neutrality; in the Western Region of Nigeria in 1962 the Speaker of the House of Assembly put his name to a letter requesting the Governor to remove the Premier. Under some constitutions his security of tenure is protected by the requirement that he shall not be removed except on the motion of two-thirds of the members of the house. In a bicameral system his function of certifying a Bill as a Money Bill (and so attenuating the delaying powers of the upper house) is potentially controversial; Kenya's independence constitution, and the constitution of the Bahama Islands, therefore provided that if a dispute arose over the propriety of giving such a certificate the question should ultimately be determinable elsewhere—by the Supreme Court in Kenya and by the Attorney-General (who is a non-political public officer) in the Bahamas. Again, whereas in the United Kingdom any doubt as to the identity of the Leader of the Opposition is resolved by the Speaker, in Jamaica, Trinidad and Malta the occupant of that office is designated by the Governor-General acting in his discretion. In Pakistan the Speaker has larger responsibilities. He may summon a meeting of the National Assembly at the request of one-third of its members, and he is thereafter empowered to prorogue it; and he is required to 'make such arrangements as are necessary to ensure that the members of the Assembly understand the function of the Assembly as an organ of the State and of [sic] their own responsibilities as members.'[1]

Apart from the peculiar case of Cyprus, the constitutions deal only cursorily with the internal organization and procedure of the legislature. There may be provision for taking the oath of allegiance, official languages, the quorum, the method of voting and the appointment of official staff. (In Cyprus it is provided that there shall be four Greek and two Turkish clerks of the house appointed from among the members by the Greek President of the house and the Turkish Vice-President of the house respectively, and that votes in the house shall be counted and recorded by a Greek and a Turkish clerk acting jointly.) In India and Malaysia the constitutions forbid any parliamentary criticism of a judge except on a substantive motion. The constitutions now always preclude a legislative house from proceeding upon a Bill or motion which will impose taxation of a charge upon the public revenue in the absence of the executive's approval. In bicameral systems Ministers may be given the right of audience in both houses. For the rest, parliamentary procedure is left to be laid down by standing orders (except in

[1] 1962 constitution, art. 112.

Tanzania, where the Constitution now names six standing committees which must be established in the National Assembly). Standing orders are normally founded on those of the United Kingdom House of Commons, with a less sophisticated committee system. And in most of the newer states the government in office has already established a more comprehensive dominance over the legislature than any United Kingdom Government has achieved in peace-time. As in the United Kingdom, the government has the sole initiative in financial matters. It may employ its majority so as to appropriate the whole of parliamentary time. It will fix the duration of sessions. Almost all Bills will be government Bills. The parts played by private members and the official opposition (if one exists) in the parliamentary process may vary in efficacy, but unless a government gets into grave internal difficulties it is unlikely to experience any serious problem in implementing its will through the medium of the legislature.

Everywhere in the Commonwealth parliamentary privilege is geared closely to the rules evolved at Westminster. Even if the Speaker has shed the ceremonial trappings of the Speaker of the House of Commons, a copy of Erskine May will rest at his elbow. It has become exceptional for the constitution itself to deal expressly with matters relating to privilege, except perhaps by guaranteeing members freedom of speech in Parliament and giving the courts jurisdiction to determine questions involving the right to membership. Up to a few years ago, however, it was quite common for a constitution to state (notwithstanding the possible taint of 'terminal colonialism') that the privileges of the Parliament were to be those of the United Kingdom House of Commons except in so far as the Parliament otherwise provided. But this kind of formula did not necessarily remove difficulties. In a recent advisory opinion (which evoked strong criticism from members of the Union Parliament) the Indian Supreme Court held that Indian legislatures, unlike the House of Commons, lacked an inherent power to oust the jurisdiction of the courts by committing outsiders to prison for contempt on a general warrant without cause stated; that the power to commit for contempt was subject to the guarantees of fundamental rights set out in the constitution; and that it was not a contempt for a person so committed or his lawyer to petition the courts for release on an application for *habeas corpus* or for the judges to entertain such an application.[1] The best solution seems to be the enactment of legislation spelling out the different kinds of breaches of privilege and contempts and specifying the manner in which they are to be adjudged and the penalties that may be imposed. In Nigeria twenty-one forms of contempt, punishable by the courts after proceedings have been instituted by the Attorney-General, have been listed by statute.[2]

Canada and Australia preceded the United Kingdom in making legal provision for the payment of a salary to the Leader of the Opposition, but not until 1962 was this office built into the framework of any Commonwealth constitution. In that year it was referred to in the constitutions of Jamaica, Trinidad and Uganda, and since then it has appeared in Malta and some of the Caribbean and Atlantic territories. In Malta the Leader of the Opposition must be consulted before appointments are made to the Electoral Commission, the Public Service Commission and the Broadcasting Authority. In Jamaica, Trinidad, Barbados, the Bahamas and British Honduras some members of the upper house are appointed on his advice. His constitutional role in Jamaica is important, for eight out of the twenty-one senators are appointed on his advice; and if eight senators withhold support from a government Bill for the amendment of an entrenched section of the constitution, the amendment must be put to the electorate voting at a referendum where a special majority must be obtained. As we have observed, he also appoints three members of the committee that delimits constituencies. In addition, a number of the Governor-General's functions (e.g. the appointment of the Chief Justice and of members of the service commissions) are expressed to be made 'on the recommendation of the Prime Minister after consultation with the Leader of the Opposition.' To ensure fair play, a set procedure must be observed: the Prime Minister consults the Leader of the Opposition and then submits his recommendation; the Governor-General informs the Leader of the Opposition of the recom-

---

[1] Opinion of the Supreme Court of India on Special Reference No. 1 of 1964.
[2] B. O. Nwabueze, *Constitutional Law of the Nigerian Republic*, pp. 222–225. See also F. A. R. Bennion, *Constitutional Law of Ghana*, pp. 326–332.

mendation and if he concurs in it the Governor-General is to act in conformity with it; but if he does not concur in it the Governor-General must refer it back to the Prime Minister, and the advice then rendered by the Prime Minister must be followed. No comparable situation can be found in the constitutional law or political practice of the new African states. There the status of the Leader of the Opposition, if recognized at all, is apt to be evanescent; occupants of the office have tended to find their way either to the government benches or into detention or exile. Disinclination to accept the legitimacy of organized political dissent is more pronounced in the presidential systems, but it is also present in countries with Westminster-style constitutions. A basic presupposition of parliamentary democracy can be destroyed while the constitution still speaks with a Westminster accent.

When we turn to the relationship between the executive and the legislature, we find that the conventional rules evolved in Britain are substantially reproduced, with some modifications, in the texts of all the most recent Westminster-style constitutions. Neither the head of state nor the Queen's local representative is the executive head of government; the executive head of government is a Prime Minister who presides over a Cabinet composed of Ministers appointed and removable on his advice; the Cabinet is a parliamentary body inasmuch as Ministers must be members of the legislature; Ministers are collectively responsible to the legislature (or to its lower house, if it is bicameral); the lower house of the legislature may be dissolved on the Prime Minister's advice.[1] None of these features is present in the American presidential system. Nor is any of them present in the constitution of Cyprus. Most of them are absent from the constitutions of Pakistan, Ghana, Tanzania and Zambia; but these presidential régimes seek to avoid the dangers of conflict between executive and legislature which are inherent in the American system by continuing to draw on the Westminster rules for certain purposes.

One of the Prime Minister's most potent political weapons

[1] In Nigeria, Jamaica, Trinidad and (in certain circumstances) the Commonwealth of Australia the Senate is also subject to simultaneous dissolution on the Prime Minister's advice.

is his power to choose the most convenient time for advising a dissolution of Parliament. If his party commands an overall majority in the house he can be reasonably certain that his advice will be accepted. That the head of state retains a residual discretionary power to refuse a dissolution in exceptional circumstances is recognized by the provision now to be found in several of the newer Westminster-style constitutions that the Governor-General (or President) may reject the Prime Minister's advice if he considers that the government can be carried on without a dissolution and that a dissolution would not be in the interests of the country. As far as is known, the residual power to refuse a dissolution has been exercised only once in a new Commonwealth country; it was exercised by the Governor of the Western Region of Nigeria, who was removed from office shortly afterwards.[1] In Jamaica, Trinidad, Uganda and the Eastern Region of Nigeria, the Governor-General, President or Governor has no power to reject the Prime Minister's or Premier's advice. Except in Cyprus (where the House of Representatives may be dissolved only in pursuance of its own resolution) the presidential constitutions vest the discretionary power of dissolution directly in the head of state. In Pakistan a general election is followed shortly afterwards by a separate presidential election. In Zambia and Kenya, elections to the office of President are geared directly to general elections; for the election of the President is based on the previously declared preferences of candidates at the general election.[2] These constitutional devices do not guarantee that the legislature will always be in step with the President; they do, however, reduce the likelihood of disharmony, even in a multi-party system.

The modern Westminster-style constitutions make it clear that the Governor-General (or non-executive President) cannot refuse to assent to a Bill except on ministerial advice. But an executive President who is a not member of the legislature must

---

[1] On the advice of Chief Akintola, the Regional Premier, to whom he had refused a dissolution and whom he had then purported to dismiss. See p. 223, *post*.

[2] This method of electing a President is founded on the method first adopted in the republican constitutions of Ghana (1960) and Tanganyika (1962). In 1965, however, both Ghana and Tanzania replaced this method by procedures under which a single candidate would be presented for election under the auspices of the Party.

have a personal discretionary power to withhold his assent, in view of the possibility that the legislature may pass Bills to which he objects. In the United States the President's veto may be overridden by two-thirds' majorities in Congress. Most of the Commonwealth presidential systems, on the other hand, fortify the President's position by subordinating the powers of the legislature. In Ghana he has the unchallengeable right to refuse assent to the whole or any part of a Bill; in Tanzania and Zambia a Bill to which assent has been refused may be re-submitted to him if supported by two-thirds of the members of the Assembly, but he may elect to dissolve Parliament instead of assenting to the Bill; in Pakistan the President may choose to submit such a Bill to a referendum of the electoral college. The President is thus given the opportunity of putting a truculent legislature in its place. In Kenya, however, the President has no power to refuse his assent to a Bill that has been duly passed.

Presidential constitutions often incorporate versions of the doctrine of separation of powers. In Pakistan and Cyprus, as in the United States, the doctrine is understood to require a non-parliamentary executive; not only the President but also his Ministers must stand apart from the legislature. In the African presidential systems, however, Ministers must be chosen from among members of the legislature and must remain members of the legislature after appointment to office. An important link is thereby created between the executive and legislature; and indeed some of these constitutions have contrived to achieve the best of both worlds, for except in Kenya the Cabinet is not collectively responsible to the legislature. (The position in Kenya is unique: not only is the Cabinet collectively responsible to Parliament, but the President is also required to be an elected member of the House of Representatives.) A rule that Ministers must be chosen from the membership of the legislature (unless Parliament is dissolved at the time) appears in most of the Westminster-style constitutions as well. In the United Kingdom the conventional rule is less stringent: a Minister need not be a member of either house at the date of his appointment, but he is expected to resign if he does not obtain a seat within a reasonable period of time. Some constitutions substantially reproduce the United Kingdom rule by allowing a seatless Minister a specified period of grace—three months in the Commonwealth of Australia, four months in Ceylon and the Federation of Nigeria, six months in India. In Malawi up to three Ministers who are not members of the legislature may be appointed. In view of the dearth of prospective ministerial talent on the back benches of many legislative bodies, it is perhaps surprising that devices of this kind have not been resorted to more frequently.

The constitutions now state expressly that Ministers are to be appointed and removable on the Prime Minister's advice (or by the executive President). The Prime Minister himself is to be appointed by the Governor-General (or the non-executive President) in his discretion (except in Uganda, where the President is bound by a detailed code of rules) and is to be that member of the lower house who appears likely (or who appears 'best able') to command the support of a majority of members. In Ceylon this rule is not set out; the functions of the Governor-General are to be exercised 'as far as may be' in accordance with the conventions applicable to the corresponding functions of the monarch in the United Kingdom. The vagueness of that formula made it possible to appoint Mrs Bandaranaike as Prime Minister in 1960 although she was not a member of either house at the time.

Provision may also be made for the circumstances in which a Prime Minister may be dismissed—a matter that is not clearly regulated by convention in the United Kingdom. The possible disadvantages of spelling out such rules in a constitution were illustrated by the events in Western Nigeria in 1962. A majority of members of the House of Assembly petitioned the Governor to remove the Premier; the Governor, who was empowered by the constitution to dismiss a Premier if it appeared to him that the Premier no longer commanded the support of a majority of members of the House of Assembly, proceeded to dismiss him. The Governor's act raised a justiciable issue; the Federal Supreme Court held that the Governor had acted unlawfully, but they were overruled on appeal by the Judicial Committee of the Privy Council.[1] The effect of this decision was immediately nullified by a retroactive amendment

[1] *Adegbenro* v. *Akintola* [1963] A.C. 614.

of the regional constitution, and under the federal and regional constitutions of 1963 the President and Governors were divested of power to dismiss a Prime Minister or Premier.[1]

Some of the constitutions have established a close interrelationship between the Governor-General's power to dismiss a Prime Minister, his power to impose a dissolution of Parliament, and the principle of collective responsibility. In The Gambia, for example, if the House of Representatives passes a resolution of no confidence in the Government and the Prime Minister does not within three days either resign or advise a dissolution, the Governor-General may, on his own initiative, dissolve Parliament or remove the Prime Minister from office. Kenya stands unique among the Commonwealth's presidential systems in that Parliament is automatically dissolved if the President neither resigns nor dissolves in these circumstances. By these means a specific sanction is supplied to redress a fundamental breach of the principle of collective responsibility. Attempts to define the principle in more general terms have not been wholly successful. The constitution often lays it down that the Cabinet shall be collectively responsible to Parliament for 'all things done by or under the authority of any Minister in the execution of his office'. On the face of it, this would appear to lead to the absurd conclusion that the Cabinet is debarred from disclaiming responsibility for gross blunders committed by Ministers in the course of their duties, unless it can be argued that a gross blunder cannot be committed by a Minister 'in the execution of his office'.

In any event, where the principles of ministerial responsibility prevail and there is more than one party represented in the legislature, the government is obliged to treat the legislature seriously. Some of the proponents of presidential régimes in Africa today assert that one major disadvantage of a West-

[1] The temporary resolution of the constitutional crisis in Western Nigeria did nothing to restore political stability to the Region. In October 1965, the victory of Chief Akintola's governing party in an improperly conducted general election led to widespread and prolonged violence. The sequel was the military *coup d'état* of January 1966, in which Chief Akintola was assassinated and the whole country was placed under the rule of the army commander. References made in the text of this chapter to constitutional arrangements in Nigeria relate to the position before the *coup d'état*.

minster-style constitution is the amount of time that Ministers have to devote to their work in the legislature, participating in its proceedings and placating its members. If, it is said, Ministers knew that the legislature was powerless to overthrow a government they could apply themselves more single-mindedly to their primary executive tasks. To this extent demands for presidentialism imply that legislative bodies are important (if only potentially) and that their importance ought to be diminished. And President Ayub Khan, in introducing his 1962 constitution, made it abundantly clear that it was his intention to stabilize the executive by freeing it from the threat of dominance by the legislature.

Exasperation at the behaviour of legislatures has, of course, a long and respectable history. Legislatures are lauded as the voice of the people and berated because they fail to behave in a manner worthy of deity. Members of fixed executive bodies have been dismayed by the unco-operative conduct of intractable assemblies; public confidence has been shaken by the frequency with which legislatures have overturned removable governments; moralists have expressed disgust at the antics of corruptible careerists, and soldiers have stepped in to restore the reign of virtue. But, as the experience of Pakistan has indicated, in the modern world a legislature cannot be dispensed with for long. A critical and obstructive assembly is, on the whole, a lesser political evil than no legislature at all. So, indeed, is a compliant, single-party assembly of faithful acolytes. We are all democrats now, and in a one-party state it would be difficult for the government to claim that it was democratically based unless it was sustained by an elected legislature. Elections may be no more than a ritual demonstration of public loyalty to the party and its leader; the legislature may be in practice little more than a ceremonial part of the constitution, and its proceedings may be regarded primarily as a means whereby the party can show itself off to the world; but the existence of a formally representative legislature helps to allay self-doubt and to endow a régime with the trappings of legitimacy.

It is obvious, however, that in a state where only one party is allowed to exist, or in a state where the pressure towards conformity is such that only one party can hope to exist as a going concern, the role of the legislature is bound to differ radically from that of the House of Commons in the British constitution. In Ghana the constitution now recognizes that the role of the legislature is indeed of a different order. Since 1964 Parliament has been designated as 'the corporate representative of the People'; the 'powers of the State derive from the people'; and in 'conformity with the interests, welfare and aspirations of the People . . . there shall be one national party which shall be the vanguard of the People. . . .'[1] There can be no opposition, no political alternative government, though it is still possible for members to voice particular grievances of their constituents and to embarrass Ministers in public. In Tanzania the lack of interest generated by parliamentary proceedings—in 1962 the Tanganyikan National Assembly passed the republican constitution and fourteen consequential measures without debate in a single morning, and in 1963 it sat for only 31 days, passing 73 Bills—aroused the concern of TANU's leaders; a presidential commission admitted in April 1965 that debates had tended to be 'lifeless and superficial' whereas discussions in the secret sessions of the party's National Executive had been frank and animated.[2] But to encourage constructive criticism of administration while penalizing destructive opposition to government policy is manifestly an elusive art. For power to criticize ultimately implies power to discredit and destroy.[3]

It may be conceded that a single-party legislature may serve practical purposes other than those of a law-making machine and of a platform for issuing government announcements. In Malawi Dr Banda successfully used the legislature as a public forum in which to denounce his opponents within his own Cabinet. And a seat in the legislature provides devoted or restive party supporters with a place of profit and some dignity. (In

[1] In the republican constitution of 1960 the people appeared in lower case; in the 1964 amendments they ascended to capital status.

[2] Report of the Presidential Commission on the Establishment of a Democratic One Party State (Dar es Salaam, 1965), para. 58.

[3] In such a political context the provision of non-parliamentary machinery for the redress of grievances may be particularly valuable. The working of the Permanent Commission of Enquiry, set up under the Tanzanian Constitution of 1965 to act as a collective Ombudsman with power to investigate alleged abuses of authority by Ministers and public and party officials, will be observed with great interest.

developing countries elected members of the legislature are often of modest social status and financial means, and their salaries as part-time legislators may be substantially larger than any earnings they could command in any alternative full-time occupation.) The power of a government to offer patronage through the medium of a legislature may be still more significant in a country where there is a shifting two-party or multi-party system. Floor-crossing to the government benches may be encouraged by the inducement of appointment to ministerial office, which only members of the legislature may hold. In the Western Region of Nigeria, where the political situation was particularly fluid early in 1965, every occupant of a seat on the government side of the House of Assembly was an office holder.[1] The fact that there is a floor to be crossed does at least show that the place of the legislature in political life is of some importance. But persistent floor-crossing, be it prompted by ideological or other considerations, may lead to a situation of endemic governmental instability, if members are willing and able to cross to opposition benches. Such a situation arose in Pakistan, and it has been only narrowly averted in Ceylon. A state of affairs in which the government is neither too strong for there to be a meaningful interplay between executive and legislature nor too unsure of its parliamentary backing to be able to rule with assurance is not easily attained. It has been largely attained by India, despite (or perhaps because of) the continuous preponderance of the Congress Party, despite the presence of deep social, economic, religious, linguistic, regional and ideological rifts within the body politic, and despite mass illiteracy and grinding poverty. But in India a commitment to the principles and institutions of parliamentary democracy has been widely diffused among the political elite; and political pluralism, like social pluralism, has been accepted as a fact of life. In many new Commonwealth countries attitudes such as these have yet to take root and may never be given the opportunity of taking root. And it is probably still too early to estimate how deeply they have taken root even in India.

[1] See Nnamdi Azikiwe, 'Essentials for Nigerian Survival' (1965) 43 *Foreign Affairs* 447 at p. 450. By the end of 1965 the situation was not only fluid but combustible.

The lawyer has drifted from jurisprudence into politics; and in politics it is easier to reach an end than to come to conclusions. We have seen that the written constitutions of the Commonwealth cannot easily be fitted into familiar pigeonholes. Westminster's export models do not intimately resemble the original on which they are based, and in many points of detail they are dissimilar from one another. The presidential constitutions do not form a distinct genus; there are wide differences between Ghana and Kenya, Zambia and Cyprus, Pakistan and Tanzania; most of them have inherited a legacy from Westminster, and none of them would be viewed in Washington as an associate member of the American constitutional species. The part played by the legislature in political life may be influenced by the form and structure of the constitution, and this influence is likely to be substantial once the constitution has become the most firmly established feature of the political scene. But until the constitution has asserted its dominance, the significance of the legislature must be conditioned mainly by such factors as the personality and opinions of a national leader, the attitude of the governing party towards organized dissent, the strength of communalism, and the pressures exerted on the style and tempo of political activity by external dangers, by the thrust towards economic development and by the stimulation of and resistance to social change. In the long run the constitutional lawyer may receive due homage, but in many new states it will be a very long run.

Chapter X

PARLIAMENT AND THE COURTS

BY E. C. S. WADE

In *Parliament: A Survey* to which this volume is the successor there was a chapter, 'The Courts and the Constitution', contributed by the present writer. A book dealing with Parliament considered in the light of its reproduction in new Commonwealth States calls for a division of the subject-matter to ensure that the part of the courts in the interpretation of written constitutions receives separate treatment. What remains then for discussion within the United Kingdom constitution? The independence of the judges in the exercise of their functions alike from Parliament and the Executive is an obvious topic, although in view of the ambiguity which obscures an exact interpretation of the famous clause in the Act of Settlement, Commonwealth States are more interested in alternative ways of securing their independence, e.g. appointment by a Judicial Services Commission and removal subject to judicial investigation.

The relationship between Parliament and the higher Judiciary will be discussed first. The Act of Settlement provided that judges' commissions should be made during good behaviour 'but upon the address of both Houses of Parliament it may be lawful to remove them'. This wording suggests that Parliament intended to provide that, while a judge should hold office during good behaviour, Parliament itself should enjoy an unqualified power of removal. The equivalent provisions of the Supreme Court of Judicature Act 1925 substitute for 'but' the words 'subject to' a power of removal on an address presented to the Queen by both Houses. It would seem that there was no intention to alter the effect of the Act of Settlement by this wording and therefore it is theoretically possible for a judge to be dismissed not only for misconduct but for any other reason which may induce both Houses of Parliament to pass the necessary address to the Sovereign. It is, however, extremely unlikely that Parliament would be willing to pass an address from any motive other than to remove from the bench a judge who had been guilty of misconduct. It was formerly the case that offices held during good behaviour could be determined by the processes of *scire facias*, criminal information or impeachment. An address to the Crown for the removal of a judge must originate in the House of Commons. The procedure is judicial and the judge is entitled to be heard. There is only one instance of the removal of a judge being carried out by this method since it was introduced by the Act of Settlement, namely a judge in Ireland in 1830. In 1924 a motion for the removal of a King's Bench judge was tabled in the House of Commons; it was withdrawn without being debated.

There is little likelihood of an authoritative interpretation of these provisions. The effect of the wording of the Act of Settlement may well have been that a judge could be removed by other means for misconduct, but that both Houses of Parliament could secure a judge's dismissal for any cause including misconduct. So long as the House of Lords retains in substance its present composition and powers there is little chance of a challenge to the independence of the judiciary by the address method. But the danger might occur if the House of Lords ceased to be a part of the legislature or even if it was deprived by statute of its right to address a request to the Sovereign to dismiss a judge. A uni-cameral legislature would enable the Executive to use the machinery of removal after an address for political purposes. Even to suggest such a possibility may be dangerous, however remote the likelihood of its occurrence. But it should be borne in mind that if the House of Lords lost its powers, the demand for an alteration in the law relating to judicial independence might be insistent. Before discussing alternative safeguards it is to be noted that the protection of the Act of Settlement does not extend to county court judges, recorders or chairmen of quarter sessions, stipendiary or lay magistrates. Yet the tradition of non-interference by the

Executive and by Parliament with the administration is as strong as in the case of the higher courts and these judicial officers enjoy for all practical purposes the immunities of their brethren in the superior courts.

To advocate a Judicial Services Commission with executive powers would be superfluous today in the case of the newer Commonwealth States where the device has been adopted. The functions of such a Commission are to give binding advice on appointments to High Court judgeships (normally excepting the Chief Justice who is himself a member of the Commission) and to control the staffing of inferior courts, including the appointment, promotion and dismissal of the judges. These functions are, of course, all performed in England and Wales by the Lord Chancellor. Their transfer to a counterpart of the Civil Service Commission would not necessarily change the intimate connection between the appointing authority and the Bar, if the Commission contained, as it normally does overseas, a strong judicial element. Indeed if solicitors became eligible for judgeships, the change in judicial patronage would be desirable, since Lord Chancellors can have but little knowledge of the qualities of leading members of that profession, at all events outside those practising in the Metropolis. This is, however, a reform which would not change the relationship between the courts and Parliament, as would the amendment of the provisions of the Act of Settlement and the Judicature Acts relating to security of tenure and to removal.

On a literal interpretation the judges are not independent of a Parliament which by addresses in each House can request the Crown to dismiss them on the proposal of the Government of the day with its command of a majority in the Commons and maybe in the Lords. Even if the absence of the Party Whip may be assumed on votes on motions for removal, the votes might reflect government policy. Under a uni-cameral system the present procedure would be even more undesirable. An alternative is suggested by the new method of safeguarding judicial tenure which was introduced in two Commonwealth federal constitutions in 1957 (Malaya and the West Indies). The principle is that a judge should be removed only on the recommendation of a body experienced in the judicial process. The analogy with a variety of professional disciplinary bodies is obvious. In the United Kingdom the Judicial Committee of the Privy Council is already experienced in its appellate capacity in judging cases of professional misconduct. The only ground for removal, in addition to misconduct, should be inability to perform the functions of a judge whether due to physical or mental infirmities. The resulting decision would take the form of advice to the Queen, as in the case of appeals to the Privy Council. Effect would be given to the advice by formal Order in Council. This procedure removes the issue from the influence of both Parliament and the Executive. The knowledge that infirmity could be invoked as a ground of removal would suffice to hasten the resignation of a judge whose faculties decreased before attaining the statutory retiring age.

There remain three other main topics. Two of them relate to the supremacy of Parliament—(a) the power to override the courts by retrospective legislation and (b) the exclusion from the jurisdiction of the courts of areas reserved by Parliament for its own judgment, particularly in relation to privilege and internal procedure. It does not need a reproduction in a written constitution of the principle of parliamentary sovereignty to cover these topics, but a statement of the constitutional position in the United Kingdom may help to a decision whether or not the power to legislate with retrospective form should be written into a constitution or the exclusion of the jurisdiction of the ordinary courts narrowed or widened. The unsatisfied demands of both Parliament and the courts in relation to parliamentary privilege is of particular relevance. The third topic is the judicial control of legislative powers which have been delegated to the Executive by Parliament. This is so closely linked with the judicial control of executive powers that it can more appropriately be discussed in a book on Government or Administrative Law than under the title of Parliament. The common law world was slow to recognize public law as a separate field and it has been largely through development of exceptional remedies that the courts have exercised jurisdiction over those areas of discretionary power which are capable of adjudication by forms of judicial control.

Before examining the topics of retrospective legislation and exclusion of jurisdiction in some detail, it may help to consider the relationship between the two institutions, Parliament and the High Court of Justice. The High Court, like the High Court of Parliament, claims jurisdiction as a superior court, but this does not mean that one House acting alone can claim to change the law. It does result in an unresolved conflict, as will be seen, when the House of Commons in particular exercises its power to commit for contempt—a power which strictly is that of the High Court of Parliament as a whole. So far as the law relating to either House of Parliament is concerned, the High Court of Justice has, quite apart from conflicts with the House of Commons over privilege claims, declined to accept as binding law a resolution which the latter passed to accelerate the collection of income tax in advance of the annual Finance Act. This issue was promptly resolved in favour of the House of Commons by a statute which gave legal effect, limited as to both duration and contents, to such resolutions for the future; *Bowles v. Bank of England* [1913]; Provisional Collection of Taxes Act, 1913. Bowles, himself a back-bench member of Parliament, thus succeeded in frustrating the assumption by a department of government that administrative convenience could justify in law the action of the House of Commons in approving the tax in advance of the enactment in due form of a statute by Parliament as a whole. The Act when passed did not invalidate any past action which had succeeded in the courts. Thus the High Court can, if its jurisdiction is invoked, ensure that each House of Parliament observes its own forms for enacting new law, though it cannot challenge any change of those forms which Parliament as a whole may make by statute. Even so, it would seem that each House acting independently can change its internal processes for the examination of Bills without let or hindrance from the other House or from the courts. The existing five stages through which a Bill has to pass,—first reading, second reading, committee, report and third reading—are not immutable processes, though the reluctance to introduce any changes of substance has long been the attitude of the House of Commons to recommendations even of its own Committee on Procedure.

Both members and officers of each House are subject to judicial processes. Such minor privileges as exist today are based on the importance of giving priority to attending to parliamentary business. A sub-pœna to compel attendance as a witness in courts of justice probably cannot be enforced in either civil or criminal causes while Parliament is in session. The ancient privilege of freedom from arrest for a period of forty days before to forty days after a meeting of Parliament has remained unaltered through the centuries which have seen successively the ages of stage-coach, railway, motor car and aeroplane in place of travel on foot or horseback; but it has ceased to be of any practical importance since imprisonment for civil debt (except where a court is satisfied as to capacity to pay) was abolished a century ago. The peer who successfully resisted committal for failing to hand over chattels to his wife under a court order is probably the only member of Parliament to benefit from this privilege in recent years. It has no application to criminal prosecutions or to detention under war-time statutory regulations.

Retrospective legislation

It is accepted that the courts can only interpret and may not question the validity of an Act of Parliament. The Law Reports can offer no case which denies this, even if they show little positive evidence in support. The recent controversy about the intention of Parliament in conferring immunity by the Trade Disputes Act 1906 arose out of a House of Lords decision (*Rookes v. Barnard*) which sought only to interpret the letter of the law enacted nearly 60 years earlier—not to deny the power of Parliament to grant immunity, but to pinpoint its failure to do so by the terms of the statute. This process does not deny the successful litigant the benefits, nor his opponent the burdens, resulting from the action, however unexpected the result of the case from the point of view of the legislators. The sequel, the Trade Disputes Act, 1965, does not challenge the interpretation by the courts, but seeks to fulfil the intention of the Parliament of 1906. This is the accepted way of using the supremacy of Parliament to change the law when the courts have given final judgment.

But the courts will not give retrospective force to new laws enacted by Parliament unless they are compelled so to do by express words or by necessary implication from the statute. This is the resistance put up by the courts against making void or penalizing what was lawful when done. They will assume that Parliament intends by changing the law in order to reverse a decision of the courts that the change shall operate for the future and not to make illegal what was lawful at the time of the transaction. That the courts may be forced to accept the retrospective change was shown by the legislation arising out of the dismissal by the Government of the claim (which had been upheld in the House of Lords in its appellate capacity) of the Burmah Oil Company. The War Damage Act 1965, like the Trade Disputes Act, purported to alter the law for the future, but, unlike the latter Act, also expressly denied to the Company and all other claimants, the right to claim damages for destruction of their property by the military in seeking to deny such properties to the enemy who threatened occupation in time of war.

Exclusion of the courts
This is not the place to discuss the details of the privileges claimed by either House, but it is important, as was seen in *Bowles* v. *Bank of England,* and in the early nineteenth century conflicts over the publication of parliamentary papers which contained defamatory references to an individual, to distinguish the supremacy of Parliament as a whole (the Queen, Lords and Commons) from the claim of either House to legislate by resolution or to adjudicate upon privilege to the exclusion of the courts. There is no machinery for Parliament as a whole to adjudicate a privilege claim. Accordingly each House exercises this jurisdiction. It is not surprising that the House of Commons has been reluctant to limit its powers to adjudge a claim to the violation of an accepted privilege. Yet the courts deny its capacity to judge the scope and extent of privilege. The possibility of conflict with the courts has been reduced since 1884 when in *Bradlaugh* v. *Gossett* the High Court held that it had no jurisdiction over the exercise of privileges which related to the internal proceedings of the House of Commons.

Though, in theory, there is deadlock on the question of

jurisdiction, there is agreement that privilege as part of the existing law cannot be created or enlarged by declaration of one House alone, even by resolution passed by a formal vote. This was really settled as far back as the Parliamentary Papers Act 1840. What is, or is not, a new or extended privilege is, therefore, capable of determination by the courts. Such process has long since recognized absolute control by each House over its internal proceedings and that punishment by committal for contempt is accepted by the courts. The door is left open for possible conflict, because if the case of committal is disclosed it may show a breach of the law which the courts can examine.

There is one area of unresolved conflict. Where a privilege has been defined by statute, it is for the courts to interpret the Act, even if it purports to exclude their jurisdiction. We need look no further than the well-known Article in the Bill of Rights—that the freedom of speech and debates or proceedings in Parliament ought not to be impeached or questioned in any court or place out of Parliament. The threat to sue a member of Parliament for repetition outside of a defamatory speech on the floor of the House is a real one. What is a proceeding in Parliament? Even the House of Commons is in such doubt that it rejected in 1957 by a narrow majority on a free vote the recommendation of its Committee of Privileges that a letter written by a member to a Minister about a matter within the latter's responsibilities to the House for the conduct of a nationalized industry was a proceeding within the meaning of the Bill of Rights. The letter referred to a 'scandal which should be instantly rectified'. If shown to be untrue to the satisfaction of a jury in a libel action, this allegation might have exposed the member to substantial damages (apart from a successful plea in the courts that the words were written in the course of duty without malice and thus privileged in law, irrespective of the place of publication). If the Committee of Privileges' view is the correct one, it might equally have been reached by the courts. Since the House of Commons (and not the Committee) decides, the possibility of conflict with the courts remains unresolved. The wider the responsibility of Ministers, the greater the chance of conflicts with private rights and so of a renewal of the old battles with the House of Commons over jurisdiction. We may be on the threshold of changes in parliamentary procedure. For long there have been advocates for a proposal to attach small committees of members, selected for their special qualifications, to advise departmental Ministers. Conflicts between members of such a committee and their Minister would be protected from legal action if reproduced on the floor of the House as proceedings in Parliament. How far beyond this would abuse uttered by either of the parties be tolerated by the courts?

That the case of exclusion of the courts, i.e. immunity from legal process, should extend beyond formal proceedings in the Chamber, was inevitable, once *Bradlaugh* v. *Gossett* had decided that each House enjoyed exclusive control over its internal affairs. The best-known illustration of this is to be found in the successful challenge made by Sir Alan Herbert in 1934 to the non-application of the Licensing Acts to the refreshment bars in the Commons. The High Court held that the complaints of non-observance of statutory hours in those bars were matters where the House was entitled to act collectively within the area of its internal affairs.

The uncertain boundary between Parliament and the courts was in evidence when in 1954 the Court of Appeal expressed the view that Parliament had not contemplated that the House of Commons (Redistribution of Seats) Act 1949 and the statutory rules made under that Act gave the courts power to determine whether a Boundary Commission had followed the right line or not. Yet the case was decided by the court upholding the action of the Commission as endorsed by the Home Secretary in the form of a draft Orders in Council, for redefining constituency boundaries. To challenge the validity of statutory Orders is certainly within the competence of the courts and the Court of Appeal accepted jurisdiction by deciding the validity of what the Commission had done. In effect it rejected a claim that delegated legislative power had been exercised *ultra vires* by the Boundary Commission. This case (*Harper* v. *Home Secretary*) may be evidence of the reluctance of the courts to clash with the Commons, but the issue was really one of the validity of delegated legislation. No court has ever regarded this as beyond its competence, nor has Parliament claimed that such legislation is binding on the courts, if made *ultra vires*. It must, however, be admitted that the procedure for a challenge of a draft statutory instrument issued by a Minister of the Crown presents difficulties which probably limit a court's competence to the issue of a declaration of validity or *ultra vires*; if the latter, enforcement would be by political, not legal measures.

Of the topics discussed the relationship between Parliament and the higher judiciary is the one where a possible solution is at hand in the form of removing patronage from the Executive to a Judicial Services Commission and discipline from the Act of Settlement safeguards to a judicial investigation at top level, without bringing in the House of Lords in its capacity as an Appellate Court. Retrospective legislation is a more difficult topic. Merely to prohibit in a written constitution its enactment by the legislature is not sufficient. There are occasions when the arguments in favour of its enactment may be overriding and therefore the ban has to be subject to qualifications. The obvious example is a state of emergency, the loop-hole through which so many constitutional guarantees may be avoided by hard-pressed governments. Defining the boundaries between parliamentary privilege and the jurisdiction of the courts is necessarily impracticable so long as a Commonwealth legislature under a written constitution is content to base its privileges on those of the House of Commons. This in practice means Erskine May's Treatise, coupled with a measure of judicial restraint. But the definition of areas of exclusion from the courts' jurisdiction is not an impossible task for the draftsman. Indeed the Parliament Act 1911 provides an example which has never been challenged. Section 3 (certification of Money Bills) provides that 'any certificate of the Speaker of the House of Commons shall be conclusive for all purposes and shall not be questioned in any court of law'. What can determine the powers of the House of Commons in their relationship with the Lords could with reasonable restraint be used by the legislature to prevent other conflicts with the courts without encroachment on the field of individual liberty of person or speech.

Interpretation of statutes

(1) *Parliamentary supremacy*. Battles still rage furiously over

the issue of the sovereignty or supremacy of the Parliament at Westminster. Can a particular Parliament enact unrepealable legislation? Can Parliament be compelled to observe a particular manner and form when exercising the legislative function? These are questions which fall to be discussed under written constitutions where the validity of legislation can be challenged in the courts. What is constitutional thus becomes a question of what is legal. In the United Kingdom the courts can declare invalid on the grounds of an excess of power (*ultra vires*), the exercise of legislative power when it has been delegated by Parliament to the Queen in Council; to Ministers by name or to other organs of the administration (the Executive). The validity of an Act of Parliament cannot be successfully challenged by the judicial process. The questions posed above are thus academic, so far as the courts of the United Kingdom are concerned.

There are illustrations in plenty of the repeal or amendment of earlier statutes of great constitutional importance by later Acts. These range from the Act of Settlement to the succession of Acts which prolonged the life of Parliament during the two world wars. Few of these statutes are expressed to be immutable, but some like the Act of Settlement have been so regarded constitutionally, but not as a matter of law. The one substantial doubt lies in those Acts, of which the Statute of Westminster 1931 is the best illustration, where Parliament limits its own sphere of jurisdiction by requiring an extraneous consent to the process of enactment. Can statutes so enacted be reversed by a later Act without that consent? The effect of a repeal of the provision (s. 4.) of the Statute of Westminster which declares that no Act of the Parliament of the United Kingdom shall apply to a Dominion (as therein defined) 'unless it is expressly declared in that Act that that Dominion has requested and consented to the enactment thereof' would be twofold. The courts of the Dominion, or other Commonwealth State to which a similar provision now applies, would disregard the enactment as not being part of the law of the country concerned. The courts of the United Kingdom would be most unlikely to be called upon to adjudicate at all. If they were, e.g. in an appellate capacity in the now limited sphere of jurisdiction of the Judicial Committee of the Privy Council, they would have to recognize the validity of the repeal as a matter of English law. Truly, to quote Lord Sankey's judgment of thirty years ago 'This is theory and has no relation to realities'. It does not follow that the judgment would be enforceable in the State from which the appeal lay. The independence of the former Dominions as well as of other territories which used to fall within the jurisdiction of the supremacy of Parliament at Westminster is nowadays fully recognized as a matter of public international law and of less interest in English constitutional law.

Another example is offered by the Ireland Act 1949. Section 1 (2) provides that 'in no event will Northern Ireland or any part thereof cease to be part of His Majesty's dominions and of the United Kingdom without the consent of the Parliament of Northern Ireland'. Such consent purports to restrict the United Kingdom Parliament, as well as its Government, from reaching agreement with the Republic of Ireland for the cession of even a tiny fraction of the territory of Northern Ireland unless an external consent is given. Could a Government which had failed to reach agreement with Northern Ireland over the cession go to Parliament with a Bill amending Section 1(2) by dispensing with the consent of the Parliament of that country? Or if an ordinary Bill was passed at Westminster, could a challenge in the courts be met by the plea of the implied repeal of the sub-section by the later Act? Happily the unexpected now seems not improbable and the Republic and Northern Ireland are at last politically on speaking terms. So the Prime Minister of the latter would presumably control a majority in his Parliament if the need for such legislation should ever arise. But a court would otherwise be faced with the argument that the later Act did not comply with the manner and form of enactment laid down in the Act of 1949 and that therefore all Northern Ireland remained in law part of the United Kingdom. It would be open to a court to interpret the later Act as repealing s. 1 (2) of the Ireland Act 1949 by necessary intendment. The alternative would be to recognize that there can be a legal limitation on the supremacy of Parliament based on a requirement of compliance with the manner and form of legislating laid down by an earlier

Parliament. Unless the House of Lords changes its judicial 'spots', the probability is that the first answer would be given. But Dicey's exposition on the sovereignty of Parliament recognized that a sovereign power can divest itself of authority by transferring sovereignty to another person or body of persons.

(2) *How far a literal interpretation?* The topic of interpretation of statutes is not one that usually leaves the courts in prolonged conflict with Parliament in the United Kingdom, for the reason that Parliament has the power to prevail in the event of deadlock by passing amending legislation to bring judicial interpretation into line with legislative intent. We have seen what happened in 1964–5 as a result of an unexpected interpretation by the House of Lords in its judicial capacity, of the Trades Disputes Act 1906. Sixty years after its enactment Parliament gave to a section of the Act the meaning intended by its promoters by reversing (but not retrospectively) the judicial interpretation of the wording of the section. It must be confessed that, apart from cases like the above, the battles of judicial giants over the manner of interpretation do not excite much interest outside the legal profession. The public is vaguely aware that Parliament can redress grievances disclosed by litigation whether they are caused by legislative or judicial obscurity or changing social conditions.

The processes of legislation and adjudication operate in quite different situations. This must be borne in mind in criticizing the somewhat elaborate rules worked out by the judges for interpreting the intentions of Parliament. Legislation is designed to deal with future situations and is couched in general terms. Adjudication relates to what has already occurred in individual cases. But the result of adjudication by a higher court is that Parliament's intention is what the judges think was meant by the wording of a general enactment in its application to a particular context. The judicial doctrine of *stare decisis* makes this interpretation of general application for the future. The doctrine was developed incidentally a good deal later than the acceptance by the judges of the supremacy of Parliament in the seventeenth century. So the law is what the judges say it is rather than what the legislators may have intended. The interpretation of how Parliament has exercised its powers of enactment in any given case is what prevails as law, however remote from the actual intention of Parliament may seem the meaning given to the enacted word. The adoption, wherever possible, of the rule of literal interpretation is intended to harmonize the intention of the legislature with the process of adjudication.

It is not only a question of disagreement between legislators and judges. The wording of a statute may have been left deliberately in such general terms that ambiguity is inevitable and perhaps intentional for political reasons prevailing at the time of enactment. Opposition in Parliament may be soothed by ministerial undertakings that only certain categories of acts will in practice be brought within the operation of general prohibition. Yet the courts may be later called upon to apply a literal interpretation which cannot be tempered by reference to such undertakings and so penalize other acts which are shown to be within the words of the statutory prohibition. The doctrine of binding precedent ensures that the intention of the Parliament which passed the statute is defeated to the extent that the operation of the prohibition is extended. In most cases the ambiguity or conflict is not apparent, at all events until a borderline case is brought to court.

The prevailing view of the House of Lords, despite the strong dissent of the present Master of the Rolls (Lord Denning), is that the courts may not usurp the legislative function under cover of exercising the interpretative role. All that a court of law can do with an Act of Parliament is to apply it. The gaps and even the lack of sense disclosed by an analysis of the words used by the draftsman cannot be remedied by the judges, but must await new legislation however damaging the result to a litigant. The courts have, however, worked out a number of rules for interpretation not all of which are restrictive. In this way they retain some discretion in the application of statute law. Thus it was at one time said that there was a presumption against it being the intention of Parliament to change the common law, except by express and unequivocal language. When the claim of lawyers that the common law meant the whole body of the law, enacted and unenacted, had to be abandoned as the price of the alliance with Parliament against the Crown, it was difficult to maintain even in an attenuated form that an Act should be construed so as not to change the common law more than seemed unavoidable. Even in the sphere of statutory encroachment on personal liberty, little remains today of this presumption. Even so, courts in the twentieth century have declined to assume that it was the intention of a statute to bar access by an individual to the courts, or to confiscate private property without compensation. Statutes involving encroachment on individual rights are apt to be frowned on by judges: equally Parliament is reluctant to sanction them. The presumption against giving retrospective effect to legislation designed to penalize conduct which was lawful at the time of its happening is an example of this, as is the stricter interpretation of penal statutes in general.

The literal interpretation of the language of a statute may produce results which seem to conflict with the intentions of Parliament because of restrictions which the judges have laid down. They have denied themselves access to all outside sources which might assist in the elucidation of a statute's intention. This restriction covers both proceedings in Parliament on the passage of the Bill and official publications such as White Papers, recommendations of Royal Commissions or Select Committees which could be aids to an explanation of the purpose of the legislation.

Another difficulty which the courts nowadays face in their task of ascertaining the intention of Parliament has been created by the form of much legislation. Modern statutes, however prolix the language may appear to the laymen, including most of those responsible for their enactment, are drafted in less detail than their predecessors and as often as not require for their application to individual cases a further process of elaboration by statutory instruments. This delegation of the power to make statute law cannot be challenged in the courts, but the resulting instruments must fall within the limits laid down by the enabling Act, e.g. the power to legislate is normally restricted to narrowly defined limits. An excess of the exercise of power will be held by the courts to be *ultra vires* the Minister or other authority to whom it has been delegated by Parliament. This makes more unrealistic the judicial decision based on what Parliament intended to be enacted under the power to enact delegated legislation. Nor is it uncommon for the delegated power to be exercised by further delegation to a subordinate officer or authority, though express power for this must be given by the enabling Act itself, so as to exclude the presumption, *delegatus non delegare potest*. Thus a dispute may fall to be determined at three removes from the original provision enacted by Parliament. In such circumstances the rule of literal interpretation of statutory intent may be difficult to apply. There can be little doubt that the object of much modern legislation could be more accurately ascertained if the judges were allowed to be informed of its context and background which are not usually learned from the actual text to the construction of which their attention may alone be directed. It may be objected that this would result in judicial legislation and imperil the independence of the judges by enlarging their function. The doctrine of *stare decisis* in its present rigid form supports this, though it would still secure uniform interpretation. Judges are constantly emphasising that the policy of a statute is not their business. But the policy of the legislature can demand more than literal interpretation of its enacted word, if it is to be effective. After all, words and even whole sentences are sometimes capable of more than one meaning. At present to determine that meaning only the enactment can be examined; even its preamble is, in theory, excluded. Would it really imperil the independence of the judges if they were allowed to examine the background material which is available to all but themselves in the form of parliamentary papers and reports? They are already entrusted with wide discretions, in criminal cases as to the nature and extent of punishment, in civil matters in relation to the administration of estates and trusts and the welfare of children. The present position has led to the invention by successive generations of judges of a medley of artificial rules, some of them difficult, if not impossible, to reconcile with others. Parliament would still retain its supremacy by its capacity to pass amending legislation, but the occasions for this might be reduced if the judges were somewhat freer to inform themselves of the real intention of Parliament.

The author wishes to acknowledge his indebtedness to the writings of Professor S. A. de Smith and Sir Kenneth Roberts-Wray, especially on the question of

Parliament's part in the machinery of removal of the judges of the superior courts. (See *inter alia*—de Smith, *The New Commonwealth and its Constitutions*; Roberts-Wray, *Changing Law in Developing Countries*, Chap. 4.)

For the reader who seeks fuller information on the subjects of legislation and statutory interpretation Chapters 4 & 5 of *Jurisprudence* by R. W. M. Dias offer a concise and stimulating discussion.

Chapter XI

PARLIAMENTS IN SMALL TERRITORIES

BY HILARY BLOOD

Until recent years the term 'Small', or more usually 'Smaller' Territories was used to describe British dependencies which were regarded as unlikely, because of geographical, economic or social limitations, to be able to assume the burdens of sovereignty. *A fortiori* their parliaments would never be sovereign, and *pro tanto* would fall short of the British parliamentary system. Somaliland and Cyprus saw the first exceptions made to this broad generalization. Jamaica, Trinidad and, more recently, the Gambia, in becoming sovereign, have made it clear that the old criteria no longer apply. Although a territory may be tiny—e.g. Malta; unable to balance its recurrent expenditure budget—the Gambia; or short of the necessary educated manpower to provide political leaders as well as senior civil servants—certain Caribbean islands; it can still aim at independence and expect to achieve a parliament with sovereign status. In considering the chances of the British parliamentary system being followed by the parliaments in the small territories it is, therefore, necessary to specify the particular countries to be had in mind. Grouped geographically by areas they are as follows: in the Caribbean British Honduras; the Virgin Islands; Jamaica; the island groups once known as the Windward and the Leeward Islands; Barbados; Trinidad; British Guiana: in the Indian Ocean Mauritius and the Seychelles: in the Atlantic the Bahamas; Bermuda; St Helena; the Falkland Islands: in the Pacific Fiji; the Solomon Islands; the Gilbert and Ellis Islands: in the Far East Hong Kong: in tropical Africa the Gambia; Malawi.

It would take too long to examine in detail the constitution, nature and functioning of the parliament of each of these territories and on this basis to try to forecast the future; nor indeed for the purposes of this volume is it necessary to do so. A reasonable general picture of the subject can, I believe, be obtained by concentrating attention on the Caribbean islands, where parliaments function generally on lines very similar to those in the United Kingdom, on Mauritius where the accent is laid on a semi-permanent coalition form of government, and on one or two other countries where local conditions override the general rules and make the territories *sui generis*.

First a few general observations to provide the necessary background against which the question posed must be considered.

A word of warning is necessary regarding the phrase 'British parliamentary system'. It suggests that our method of government in this country is an orderly, tidy, inorganic system, fixed and settled, like the planetary system or the metric system. In the absence of a written constitution this is not the case. The model whose export we are considering has vague specifications and sketchy blue prints. It is a method rather than a system, and a method that is constantly being adapted to meet modern needs and to provide appropriate instruments for very varied political craftsmen. And it is organic, it lives, and grows, and develops, sometimes in undesirable directions. More than ten years ago Mr G. M. Young pointed out[1] the continuing growth in power of the executive branch with a corresponding diminution in the power of parliament. This process is still going on. The much enhanced position[2] of the Prime Minister is another recent development. It is therefore necessary to get back to some basic principles and to consider how far in small countries these principles have been adopted and are likely to continue. I take such basic principles of the British parliamentary system to be—universal suffrage, an executive responsible to parliament, the right to free speech and to oppose, and the separation of the

[1] *Parliament, a Survey*, p. 273.
[2] For the contrary view see *Parliamentary Affairs*, Vol. XVIII, No. 2, p. 167.

powers of the judiciary and the executive. These principles, as followed and interpreted by the parliament of Great Britain sitting at Westminster, are the exportable commodity with which this volume is concerned.

Among the strains to which parliaments in the large Commonwealth countries are subjected is that of tribal rivalry leading to the danger of partition. This danger may be met, as for example in Ghana, by the gradual creation of a one party government, the party and the state being visualized as an entity to provide a measure of protection. How far the basic principles referred to above are affected by this development is not the concern of this chapter. Small countries, on the other hand, are not subject to this pressure and a party system once established—provided it is not, as, e.g. in the case of Cyprus, based entirely on racial distinction—is not likely to be abandoned. Indeed, it has no need to be abandoned since the danger of partition and the need to combat it does not arise. It is true that in some small countries racial or religious differences may have a centrifugal effect. Mauritius, which is considered in detail below, is an example of such disruptive influences: indeed only in the Falkland Islands, with a static population of between two thousand and three thousand souls, are the inhabitants all of European, and mostly of United Kingdom descent, with a common, i.e. Christian religion. But small scale racial or religious divergence however acutely felt, cannot compare with the massive power of tribal eruption—the one can be contained, the other in the end cannot. It is therefore unnecessary to take into account in small countries the effect of mass movements on the local version of the British parliamentary system, nor need its final shape be influenced thereby.

All small territories, however much they may like the English parliamentary system and however well suited it may seem to be to their needs, are at a disadvantage just because of their smallness. It must be admitted that the 'Westminster Model' is not better adapted to the administrative needs of small territories than is a powerful racing car to their road systems. Either can be used for local purposes but not without inconvenience, and sometimes danger, and always with unnecessary expenditure.

The equivalent of the sovereign and, in certain places, two houses of parliament is a burden greater than a population numbered only in hundreds, perhaps in tens, of thousands or less can politically and economically carry. And this political set-up puts an almost unbearable strain on the available local manpower. It is not perhaps generally realized how very limited are the reservoirs of trained and mentally adequately equipped persons—men or women—from which can be drawn senior civil servants of permanent secretary grade, and from which are thrown up political leaders. It is not so long since one graduate a year was regarded as a normal addition to the ranks of those holding post-matriculation qualifications. An interesting example of how thinly the ground is covered is to be found in an island where, on the establishment of a full ministerial system, the local librarian became one of the new senior secretaries. And in any event there is a tendency for the best equipped men not to enter the civil service, they can earn more, much more, elsewhere; until higher education is widespread the ranks of responsible politicians can only be increased at the cost of the ranks of the civil service and *vice versa*.

Further, the relationships between the legislature and the executive are bedevilled by the fact that everyone knows too much about everyone else. One of the reasons for the success in this country of our system of government is anonymity. Votes are anonymous: members of parliament do not start out with an intimate mutual knowledge of their fellows: ministers and their senior civil servants frequently know nothing of each other apart from their official relationships: the loyalty of the civil service is to its political masters as politicians not as individual people. Examples of anonymity may be multiplied indefinitely. It is not so in a small territory. The source from which senior civil servants, qualified professional men and skilled technicians may be drawn is, as has been pointed out, a trickle. In one family of six brothers in a small territory, one is overseas: the remaining five provide a minister; the head of a technical department; the head master of the leading government boys' school; a senior member of the secretariat; and a non-government lawyer practising at the local bar. In such circumstances there is but little of the saving grace of anonymity. Family confusion may well arise when the headmaster's proposals for an extension to his school are translated into formal plans by the technical department, commented on adversely at secretary level, approved by the minister, but opposed by the lawyer whose client does not wish to part with the necessary land.

Clearly a method of administration more akin to the local government set-up in this country would have been more suitable for the small territories. Even if history imprisoned the Caribbean countries within the framework of the Westminster model we should have found something more suitable and less onerous than the crown colony system for use elsewhere.

And yet, as we shall see, it is in the Caribbean islands that the chances of the British parliamentary system being followed are at their highest.

Finally a word on the relationship between parliamentary procedure at Westminster and in the small territories, in particular the complication which has arisen as a result of the practice of having the Governor as President, or Chairman, of the Legislative body.

Lord Campion has said[1] that the procedure of the House of Commons consists of two components—the traditional component, the 'practice of the House' or the 'ancient practice', and the Standing Orders. The traditional component is a living thing which has grown and developed, nurtured by, and enshrined in, precedent. It may be likened to the Common Law. The Standing Orders are imposed, the statute law of the house; they are 'shears pruning the overgrowth of leaves and branches' where the 'ancient practice' tends to get out of hand and choke the work which the House has to do. They have two primary objects; first to give the government rights to control the order of business and the use of the time of the house; and, secondly, to prevent government business being held up by 'strategic obstruction' because, in the end, a government must be able to govern.

The Caribbean territories, with the Bahamas and Bermuda, have the longest history of parliamentary government, approximating to the British system, but their 'ancient practice' only goes back approximately half as far as does that of West-

---

[1] *Parliament, A Survey*, p. 141.

minster. Elsewhere a hundred years or less is the span during which British parliamentary procedure has had a chance to take root in small countries.

The young life of this plant—and it may well be a plant which will only flourish in the political climate of Great Britain, tended by the husbandry of the British people—has been adversely influenced in two ways. Those who were trying to reproduce in tropical countries parliamentary procedure on the lines of that at Westminster were left to do this work, almost entirely on their own, with but little guidance other than their own knowledge of what happened in this country. This knowledge may have been reasonably extensive, as in the case of the Atlantic and Caribbean settlements where members of one of the Houses were among the settlers. More usually the knowledge of parliamentary procedure in the United Kingdom was based on an expatriate officer's reading of the daily newspapers when on leave, and perhaps an occasional visit to the House of Commons. It was only in the nineteen-twenties that, at a Colonial Conference, an attempt was made to draw up standing orders for colonial legislatures based on a simplification of the House of Commons standing orders, and it is remarkable that the application of 'the shears' was considered of importance, before the ancient practice, save in the West Indies, had time to take firm root and grow. If, for the sake of uniformity some parliamentary code were required, surely it would have been possible to produce something live and creative, e.g. a child's edition of Erskine May. The wonder really is that the procedural side of our parliamentary system has survived overseas in recognizable form at all.

The second adverse influence was the continued presence of the governor in the chair of the legislative body. Obviously someone had to be initially in the chair who had some knowledge of parliamentary procedure, however slight, and sufficient skill as a chairman to get business done and decisions taken. But the governor was kept far too long in the ridiculous position of trying to be an impartial chairman while, frequently, his policies were being roundly attacked and his officers abused. There were few territories where some local dignitary, not of course necessarily a member of the legislature, could not have been found at an early stage of political development to take the chair. In fairness it must be remembered that it was often the legislative bodies themselves who tried to insist on retaining the governor, much against his will. 'Governor baiting' was a well-known sport.

To help in assessing the likelihood of the British parliamentary system being followed in small territories it is helpful to review the stages by which this system has been adopted in these areas, and also the extent to which the system has been developed or already modified. There is, in some quarters, an idea that the crown colony system historically came first and was, or is, by degrees developed into the method of responsible government which prevails at Westminster. This idea is of course incorrect. The earliest settlements in the American mainland and in the Caribbean and Atlantic islands—small territories *par excellence*—came under a representative, though not a responsible, system of government from their earliest days. A Governor, sometimes a royal governor, sometimes a company governor, representing the king, a nominated Legislative Council somewhat resembling the House of Lords, and an elected House of Assembly corresponding to the House of Commons.

No other system of colonial government was seriously considered for territories great or small before the American revolt. Crown Colony government, i.e. government by a Governor with the assistance of a Council selected by him—the system was in force long before the name was in common use in the Colonial Office—probably began in Senegambia, and by accident.

In 1765 Parliament had under consideration a report by the Board of Trade on the British position in West Africa.[1] It recommended *inter alia* that the areas newly acquired from France as a result of an expedition sent to the Senegal by Prime Minister Pitt in 1758, extending from the Senegal river to the Gambia river, should be vested in His Majesty 'for the more effectual protection and encouragement of the trade to Africa'. An act to give effect to this recommendation was passed thus divesting the Company of Merchants trading to Africa of its authority over the Senegal and Gambia region.

The Act made no provision for the government of the area.

[1] See Dr Eveline Martin, *The British West African Settlements*.

This was done by an Order-in-Council, dated November 1, 1765, which declared the territory lying between Cape Rouge and Cape Blanco to be the 'province of Senegambia' under the immediate authority and direction of His Majesty. The province was to have a civil and a military establishment; and the organic documents consisted of the Order, which set up a constitutional framework, together with a commission to the governor and his instructions which contained the practical details. The constitution was modelled on that type obtaining in the American Colonies 'as far as difference of circumstances will permit'. There was to be a Governor and a Council, part *ex-officio* and part nominated, over which, by various devices, the governor had control. This is almost precisely what, some fifty years later, became known as the crown colony system of government. But, in the case of Senegambia, if the American Colonies system had been fully adopted as was envisaged in the Order, there would also have been an elected body—a House of Assembly or the like. Why was this branch of the legislature missing?

The operative words were 'as far as difference of circumstances will permit'. And the circumstances in America and in Senegambia were entirely different. There were so few Europeans in the African territory, and the local inhabitants were so backward, that the creation of an elected body was impossible. Thus the first crown colony was created by accident, not by design.

But in any event some such system would have had to be invented to provide for the administration of 'Colonies of conquest or cession' which were acquired around the beginning of the nineteenth century as a result of the French and other European wars. In such cases the Royal Prerogative allowed the application of whatever form of government was thought by the Sovereign's advisers to be most suitable for the individual territory. In practice the constitutional set-up already existing was, as a rule, continued until there was time and money to make a change: and, when made, the change was to government by a governor and council. Thus on the one hand the policies of the Metropolitan government could be locally imposed, and on the other, excessive autonomy, or at any rate the appearance thereof, could be avoided. This system was also adopted, either by bringing local pressure to bear or by the over-ruling power of the Metropolitan parliament, where a territory with representative government got itself into trouble, financial or political, with Westminster. This happened in the case of a number of the Caribbean Islands after slavery was abolished.

With complete control by the Imperial Parliament thus imposed, two courses for the political development of the Colonies, were open to Great Britain: to regard the Crown Colony system as the embryo of eventual self-government on Westminster lines, a goal to be reached by slow and well graduated advances, or to think out some other system. It is understandable that, in the contemporary circumstances, the first alternative should have been followed: and the impetus in that direction was strengthened by the desire of colonial territories to develop on British lines. Great Britain was a world power. It was itself a comparatively 'small territory'. A form of government under which it had become great might be the path leading to greatness for others. Any attempt by the metropolitan power to invent some other constitutional set up was regarded as an attempt to work off an inferior political status on a subject people. There may have been political leaders who looked far enough ahead to see that, having obtained sovereignty by this course, they could later mould their constitutions to a form which they considered more suitable to their own circumstances. Dr Nkrumah with his 'first the political kingdom' was perhaps one of these. But it is most unlikely that any politician in the small territories looked so far ahead. If proof is required that this view was taken by colonial territories it will be found in the case of the Donoughmore constitution in Ceylon which, in the nineteen thirties, attempted to introduce into that island a new kind of colonial constitution based on the London County Council. This was a failure, and Ceylon, at its own instigation, went back to the Westminster model. At the moment, as will be described later, a modification of the model is operating in Mauritius which has a Council of Government based on an all-party coalition. But what the end product will be remains to be seen.

The Crown Colony system once imposed, the small territories

set to work to develop and modify their form of government to bring it more and more into line with Westminster. In this they were helped and encouraged by the Colonial Office, though the speed of political progress was strictly controlled from London, and, as is now apparent, insufficient was done to educate and train local *personnel* to fill the greatly increased numbers of responsible posts which self-government would eventually require to be filled by local people. By contrast with the larger territories, particularly in Africa whose 'British' period has been relatively short, less than a century at the most, the era of constitutional development in many small territories has been prolonged. British political and constitutional philosophy has taken a greater hold, tribal difficulties, as we have seen, do not arise, and the identification of party with state is not required as a counter-measure to centrifugal forces. Generally speaking, therefore, the climate seems favourable for a continued following of the British parliamentary system in the small territories.

We can now examine the actual situation in certain countries in more detail.

The Caribbean territories, with the Bahamas and Bermuda in the Atlantic, are the best, and so far the most successful examples, of the adoption of the British parliamentary system in small territories. This is, for two reasons, not surprising. As has already been noted the pattern of the early transatlantic settlements frequently included a leader or chief settler who had first-hand knowledge—personal or through a near member of his family—of our system. More humble settlers were often the leaders' servants—domestic, garden, or skilled artisans. In any event all early English immigrants to the West had lived under our system. It was, therefore, to be expected that English forms of government, both local and central, would be reproduced in the new world. And it was so. A few years after the first English settlers reached Barbados—early in the seventeenth century—a vestry system on Tudor lines was established: a few years later the government of the country consisted of a governor and two houses of the legislature. This was a normal development to be expected in the circumstances in which emigration to the west had taken place.

But there was an interesting second stage. When white labour was abandoned as uneconomic, and slave labour was introduced to deal with the extensive field work involved in the newly introduced sugar industry, the new West African immigrants were poured from the start into an English mould. The English way of life was what they saw their masters follow: it was no doubt the way of life they would wish to follow if the opportunity ever came. No tribal life was possible, particularly since, for safety, slaves from the same tribe were always mustered in separate gangs—thus incidentally making a knowledge of English necessary if they were to communicate with each other; tribal customs might be practised occasionally—and indeed until not many years ago still were—but the only 'way of life', the only culture, was English. Again, it is therefore not surprising that as and when the freed slaves, or their descendants, were able to take part in the government of their countries the British method should be a natural way of setting about the job. It is true that as the crown colony system was gradually modified, or, in the colonies with representative government, as the franchise was widened, politics became more a matter of following an individual leader than of creating and fostering a party. But, with the arrival of the internally self-governing stage, when the supposed need to unite to 'throw off the British Yoke' no longer exists, when in fact Great Britain has sometimes all too readily shed her responsibilities for politically immature countries, a party system does develop. Jamaica, with the Manley party and the Bustamante party, and the mutual exchange of power between the two at a series of general elections, is a good example. And other islands are not far behind. Party politics was a slow growth in Trinidad, but the success which has attended Dr Williams' able organization of his party, now in power, will no doubt create a commensurate reaction among his opponents leading to the formation of a powerful opposition party offering an alternative government. The smaller islands show signs that they will, in all probability, follow suit.

It is now time to look at some of the variants which are developing or may be expected to develop.

Mauritius was taken from France in 1810 to prevent its use

by the French navy as a base from which to attack British merchant fleets sailing between the Cape and India. As a colony of conquest the Royal Prerogative applied and the contemporary form of government was continued until Crown Colony government was imposed. But political evolution was very slow. Some small development took place but there was no major constitutional change during the sixty years prior to 1947—the formative years for most colonies. In practice political power in Mauritius was, until that year, largely in European hands: the white population provided the electorate, most of the elected members and many senior civil servants, while the governor and many of his chief advisers were from Great Britain.

Then came a sudden and, politically, a somewhat indigestible change. Indian immigrant labour, imported for the sugar estates when slavery ended, had by immigration and by natural increase become racially the largest section of the population. When what was virtually universal suffrage was introduced in 1947 this predominance of the East Indian in the population was reflected in the membership of the legislature. It is so reflected today: Hindus hold twenty out of forty seats; the 'General Population'[1] fourteen; Muslims five, and Chinese one. Political power had been taken from the hands of the well-to-do white and put into the hands of the poor non-white, with the balance tilted in favour of the descendants of Indian immigrants whose forebears had arrived on the Island at most a hundred years earlier. The governor retained reserve powers for use as a last resort, but had to manage a legislative council in which the white, French by extraction, nominated members were disgruntled because they had lost their political power, the Indians had a growing sense of importance, and a strong nationalistic and racial upsurge, and the descendants of the ex-slaves were torn between aligning themselves with the European members, their co-religionists, to avoid being submerged by the Hindu, and joining up with the Indian to wring every possible concession out of the European, be he nominated member or the governor himself.

[1] General Population is the expression used in Mauritius to cover Europeans and the descendants of released African slaves. The latter are known as the 'coloured people'.

This political advance called for considerable assimilation. The change should of course have come over a period of years and not in one heavy mouthful, and preparation for the successful operation of this advanced form of Crown Colony government had to be made after it came into existence and not before. The major problem was to turn people who thought entirely in terms of their own particular section of the community—Indians, Africans and Europeans—into citizens of Mauritius, people who thought not in terms of a section of the community but in terms of their island.

It became clear that the rift between the sections of the community had been exaggerated by the increase in elected members and the decrease in the governor's powers. Fear that their occidental way of life might be swamped by the oriental majority was a very real influence in the white approach to politics, just as was the Indian and 'coloured' determination to work off old scores on the European minority. Thus any party alignment in the legislature tended to be of a racial nature. Either the gaps between the sections of the community had to be so firmly and generously bridged that mutual representation became possible, and this must at best be a long process, or an attempt must be made to bring the various sections of the community into the government of the country on a co-operative basis, in other words a permanent, or at least semi-permanent, coalition. The latter method of approach has been adopted and is reflected in the modifications to the constitution introduced since 1947. The 1964 constitution provides for a Legislative Assembly consisting of a Speaker, the Chief Secretary *ex-officio*, forty elected and not more than fifteen nominated non-official members. The old Executive Council has become a Council of Ministers on whose advice the governor normally acts. But this Council is not, as the executive governing body of a country normally would be, a one-party body—the majority party body—it includes representatives of other parties or elements, which have accepted the invitation to join the government and the principle of collective responsibility. Thus the premier has no formal authority to insist on excluding from the government members of parties other than his own if they are willing to serve and to be collectively responsible. In practice the participation of other parties—as distinct from individuals—in a coalition government would hardly be feasible unless the premier agreed.

Mauritius, therefore, at present is an example of an advanced embryonic form of the British parliamentary system substantially modified to meet the needs of a country in which communal differences are still acute. As things are, some sort of guarantee to the main sections of the community that they will be adequately represented in the body which governs the country appears to be essential, and to this extent the British system is not followed. When Mauritius becomes internally fully self-governing it will be for Mauritians themselves to decide whether, or to what extent, this artificial arrangement must be continued. My guess would be that some special arrangements will be necessary until the occidental fear of the oriental has been shown by experience and in practice to be unfounded. Heaven forbid that it should become permanent: that would be a confession of failure, an acknowledgment of the existence of a racially divided state which cannot find a nationally unifying principle. There can be no ultimate diversification of interests in Mauritius. But the fact remains that the basic principles of the British system—universal suffrage; responsibility of ministers to the legislature; separation of the executive and judicial power; the right to free speech; and to oppose—are generally accepted and seem likely to prevail.

In passing it may be observed that racial and religious conditions in British Guiana and in Fiji present difficulties in some ways similar to those in Mauritius. It may be that in these two small countries—if British Guiana may for convenience here be so classified—a coalition on lines now obtaining in Mauritius is the solution at least as a short term operation, and may help to perpetuate the existence of our parliamentary system on the mainland of South America and in the Pacific.

There are two small countries—one a mainland territory, one an island—which deserve particular attention—the Gambia and Hong Kong. The Gambia is the most artificial of nation states. Its very existence arose from the abandonment of the Senegambia to which reference has already been made. Its boundaries were drawn, by arrangement with France, with a ruler and a pair of compasses to enclose an area some seven or eight miles back from the Gambia river to the north and to the south. Great Britain thus found herself responsible for an area which was administratively difficult and economically non-viable. The ground-nut is the only exportable agricultural crop which Gambian farmers can produce on the light soil to which the mangrove swamps in the river bed give way. This crop, which just covered the country's expenditure in earlier crown colony days, cannot meet the cost of very reasonable demands for higher education, more extensive medical care, and the other social needs of a modern state—quite apart from the capital costs of 'infrastructure' development. It has therefore been necessary for the British Treasury to make annual grants in aid to balance the budget.

Since the country reached the full internal self-government stage in 1962 the minds of the Colonial Office and of Gambian political leaders have turned to the consideration of what looks obvious to anyone who studies the map—some kind of fusion with the Senegal from which country the Gambia was excised. Now, as an independent territory since February 1965, this question becomes vital and can be discussed with the Senegal government on equal terms. Agreements have been reached between the two countries covering defence and foreign affairs; but the problem is whether some political and/or financial arrangement can be made to the mutual advantage of both.

The Gambia has become sovereign, following very closely the Westminster model, though there is only one house of parliament. Otherwise what has been described as the 'Mark XXI' model is true to form, a Monarchy within the Commonwealth, with the Queen—in this case the Queen of the Gambia—as the executive power, represented locally by a Governor-General acting constitutionally in accordance with the advice of a Gambian cabinet headed by a prime minister. So far well and good; and were it not for the economic problem the Westminster model might well survive. The country is too small for tribal difficulties seriously to influence politics and the British tradition of parliamentary democracy is strong and widely held.

On this basis it is hard to see how any political fusion with the

Senegal is possible. The differences between the political outlook of an ex-French and of an ex-British colony are fundamental: and while perhaps up-river, where the arbitrary boundary line runs on occasion through the middle of a village, constitutional differences are at a discount, the same is certainly not the case at the western end of the river: in particular St Mary's island, with Bathurst the capital, is as British in background as is Freetown further down the coast.

Even a customs union would present great difficulties and could hardly in itself greatly ease the Gambia's economic problem.

Looking again at the map any big scale development would seem to involve the extended use of the river for irrigation, for power, and as a waterway: a joint operation by the two governments would be required to achieve such a plan. Whether such a large scale operation[1] would be feasible without some form of political union is a matter of speculation. Alternatively, if no large scale development is possible the British Treasury may tire of financing the Gambia and Gambian politicians may throw their hands in and agree to political fusion with Senegal.

In the context of this paper the point is that the chances of the British parliamentary system being followed in the Gambia, are in principle, high, but may well be affected by the economics of the country.

He would be a brave man who put any money on the chances of the British parliamentary system being followed in Hong Kong. Originally a by-blow of the 'Opium Wars'—a barren rock ceded to the United Kingdom in 1841 for the simple purpose of providing the security and freedom from arbitrary interference necessary for successful trade with China—Hong Kong has become the largest trading centre of the Far East, a place where fortunes are made, a world's market place rather than a colony. Our parliamentary system has in fact never been developed. The colony was created for economic reasons and economics rather than politics are of paramount importance. All that the local Chinese—ninety-nine per cent of the population—

[1] Two F.A.O. specialists have reported to the Governments of the Gambia and the Senegal on 'Integrated Agricultural Development in the Gambia River Basin'.

ask for is the maintenance of peace and order while they get on with their work of money making.

There has been little progress in forming self-governing institutions since the crown colony system was imposed on this unique functionally minded territory. The government has been stable: there has been freedom from internal political upheaval.

No one can look beyond 1997 when the lease of the mainland area, ten times the size of the colony proper, falls in. It may suit China to come to some sort of arrangement which would allow Hong Kong to carry on more or less as it is—making money and serving as a window through which China and the free world can catch glimpses of each other. I would hazard a guess that such an arrangement would be more feasible if the present method of government is still in force. The idea of Hong Kong as an independent state, its sovereign parliament negotiating with China, need not be pursued. In short the Colony is an exception in more ways than one to the general rule of constitutional development on British parliamentary lines.

To sum up: from this very general survey of British parliamentary practice in small countries the following facts emerge. Whatever may be the case in large countries the Westminster model has so far been successfully perpetuated in many of the island territories. There are two main reasons for this success: the system is not subjected to the strains imposed upon it by tribal interrelationships as in the African countries, and thus does not have to create a monolithic constitutional block as in the African view, a method of protection for the politically developing state. To such a necessity small countries are not required to succumb. Secondly, the British system, particularly in the western islands, is a long established method of government and has become part of the normal way of life. There are, however, certain small countries where special circumstances obtain, e.g. Mauritius, where a comparatively minor modification appropriate to local needs has been found: in others again future developments, particularly financial, may call for major modifications—the Gambia; or in which the functional development of the colony is locally considered of more importance than its political constitutional development—Hong Kong—

and an elementary form of crown colony government is appropriate and generally acceptable.

Broadly speaking, the answer to the question posed is that, so far as small countries are concerned, the chances of the British parliamentary system being followed are good.

INDEX

Aden, party system in, 133
African Commonwealth countries
and one-party rule, 37, 90–1, 96, 162; democracy v. tribal rule in, 80–90; the franchise, 87; party system in, 120–31; primitive background as bar to development of 'Westminster model', 147; and 'conventions', 152; Cabinet system in, 151–2; problems of the Executive following independence, 154–65; Co-operative Movement and trade unions, 156; demands for complete replica of the 'Westminster model', 159; influence of tribal background on new states, 160–2; importance of party organizations in, 163–5; relationship between Civil Service, Executive and Parliament, 150 ff.; position of minorities in 148–9, 167, 198; unicameral system in, 166–7; presidential system in, 191–207 *passim; See also* entries for individual countries
Amery, L. S., and Commonwealth Parliamentary Association, 75
Asia and the 'Westminster model', 146–7
Australia
and Dominion status, 14–15; representative government introduced, 25–6; Commonwealth status, 27; as a federation, 81; MPs and State Government, 82; MPs' salaries and allowances, 86–7; proportion of full-time members, 87; the franchise, 87–8; party system, 107–8, 133; and the 'Westminster model', 145; the Senate, 170–2; bi-cameral system, 170–3, 185; powers of Federal Parliament, 209; the constitution, 213, 219

Bahamas
'representative' system in, 24; unpaid MPs, 86; and the Second Chamber, 173, 185; constitution, 217, 219; parliamentary system, 255

Banda, Hastings (Malawi), 130–1, 210
Barbados
representative government, 24, 183; Legislature, 183; constitution, 219
Basutoland
party system in, 131; position of the Chiefs in, 179
Bechuanaland
party system in, 131; position of the Chiefs in, 179
Bennett, R. B. (Canada), 104
Bentham, Jeremy, and the drafting of laws, 51–3 *passim*, 57
Bermuda
representative government in, 24; parliamentary government, 255
bi-cameral legislatures, 27, 31, 33, 37: *see also* House of Lords; Second Chamber
Bills, procedure for passing, 100–1
Blackburn, Lord, on drafting of laws, 52
'Brains Trust', the (in lectures on UK parliamentary procedure), 77
British Guiana
party system in, 131–2, 138; new constitution of, 183–4; parliamentary government, 259
British Honduras, new constitution of, 184, 219
British South Africa Company, 26
Brougham, Lord, 42–4 *passim*; on drafting of laws, 52
Burma, constitution of, 33

Cabinet system
functions of, under colonial government, 14, 36; the Legislature and, 92; African models, 150–2; and principle of collective responsibility, 151–3; problems of, in new nation-states, 154–7
Canada
and Dominion status, 14–15; protection of French interests in, 21–2; Crown Colony rule, 22; early changes in constitution, 25–6;

federation, 27, 81, 83; Uniformity of Legislation, 49–50; standing of Central and State governments, 82–3; position of MPs, 83–4; allowances, 85–6; rights and privileges, 94; the franchise, 88; party system, 104–6, 133; and 'Westminster model', 145; and the Second Chamber, 168–9, 185; the Cabinet, 169; unicameralism in provincial legislatures, 169; the constitution, 213, 219

Cape of Good Hope, British acquisition of, 22

career politicians, increase in, 84, 86, 92

Caribbean states
 'conventions' in, 151; and bi-cameralism, 175, 176–7; parliamentary government in, 250, 254, 255: see also entries for individual states

Central government and State government, relations between, 81–2

Ceylon
 British acquisition of, 22; party system, 118–20, 137, 138; Second Chamber, 173; bi-cameralism, 180–1, 185; the constitution, 213, 223

Chalmers, Sir Mackenzie, and drafting of laws, 45, 47, 51

Chiefs' position under new African constitutions, 178–9

Chile and the British parliamentary system, 190

Civil Service
 under 'old colonial' system, 14; and 'conventions', 150–1; and post-Independence problems in new nation-states, 151–60; relationship of, with the Executive and Parliament in Commonwealth countries, 142–65; growth of, in USA, 200

colonies of settlement, 21

Commonwealth, the British
 and British parliamentary system, 37; course in legislative drafting for legal officers, 48; procedural links with Westminster, 59 ff., 102; exchange of clerks with British House of Commons, 69–71; MPs' remuneration, allowances, rights and privileges, 85, 93–4; election of MPs, 89; and Government Bills, 218; see also African Commonwealth countries and entries for individual countries and areas

Commonwealth Parliamentary Association, 75–8

Constitutions
 of 'old colonial' system, 13 ff., 21; changes in, 25–6; doctrine of necessity in discarding, 211; unwritten constitution of UK, 212; written constitutions, 208–28: see also under entries for individual countries

'conventions' and the Ministerial system, 150–3

Co-operative Movement in Commonwealth countries, 156, 162–3

Coulson, Walter, and drafting of laws, 40–1, 44

courts, exclusion of the, 235

Crown Colony government, 14, 22, 252, 254, 258; and the slave trade, 22–3; reasons for change to, 24–5; changes in, 36–7; and drafting of laws, 47–8

Cyprus
 unicameral system in, 167; causes of disunity in, 209–10; constitution, 211, 217, 221, 222

defence expenditure: colonies' resentment of, in peace time, 20

delegated legislation, dangers of, 100

democracy, African countries and, 80

detention without trial (Ghana), 95–6

dictatorship in overseas governments, 81

Diefenbaker, J. G. (Canada), 104

'Dominion' status: meaning of term, 14–15

Durham, Lord, on colonial government, 20, 26

East India Company, 29–30

Emancipation Act (1933), 23

English common law, role of, in unification of USA, 201

Ethiopia: admission to UNO, 143

INDEX

Executive, the
    functions of, under 'old colonial' system, 13; and the Legislature, 92–3; 214–15, 220 ff.; relationship with Civil Service and Parliament, 150 ff.; African problem of, 154–7

Falkland Islands, 22

federal parliaments, 27; in India, 31–2; and constitutions, 81; MPs and, 82–3

Federation of the Rhodesias and Nyasaland, 177–8

Fiji, 31, 259

finance, control of, 20, 167, 218

France
    control of dictatorial powers in, 90; and the presidential system, 191–3, 195

franchise, the
    under 'old colonial' system, 13; slaves and, 24; in UK and Commonwealth countries, 87–8

Frazer, Peter (New Zealand), 109

freedom from arrest, as privilege of MPs, 92–3

Gambia
    unicameral system in, 167, 179; constitution, 216; and Senegal, 259–61: *see also* Senegambia

Gandhi, Mrs Indira, 116

Gandhi, Mahatma, 112, 114

Ghana, 37; MPs' remuneration, privileges and rights, 85, 94; detention without trial in, 95–6; one-party government, 96, 125, 210; dismissal of judges, 95, 96, 210; private members' Bills, 99–100; failure of party system, 138; unicameral system, 167; constitution, 95, 212, 215, 226: *see also* Gold Coast

Gold Coast, 123–5: *see also* Ghana

governors
    functions and rights of, under 'old colonial' system, 13–14, 20; Assemblies clash with, 20; negative powers of, 21; in Crown Colonies, 22; as guardians of British humanitarian principles, 25

Grenada, constitution of, and export taxes, 21

Guyana: proposed new name for British Guiana, 184 *n*

Holland, Sidney G. (New Zealand), 109

Holyoake, Keith J. (New Zealand), 109

'home rule' in 'old colonial' system, 14

Hong Kong, 259, 261, 262

House of Lords
    and codes of Standing Orders, 68; as 'Westminster model' for Second Chamber in Commonwealth countries, 186–8: *see also* Second Chamber

Houses of Assembly, in 'old colonial' system, 13–14, 20

Imperial Act (1892), 30

India
    early British rule in, 29–31; as a republic, 32; and federation, 31–2; and Model Bills, 48; procedural links with Westminster, 69; Government of India Acts (1919 and 1935), 31, 33; and presidential constitution, 81; the franchise and the electorate, 97; party system, 110–16, 136; demands for 'Westminster model', 159 *n*; the Senate and finance, 170; success of bicameral government, 173–5, 185; judges' immunity from criticism, 217; constitution, 211, 213, 223; privilege of legislatures, 218; parliamentary government, 257

Indonesia, 210

'internal self-government' in 'old colonial' system, 14

Irish Free State
    and Dominion status, 15; constitution on the British model, 191

Jamaica, 17, 18, 20; as a colony of settlement, 21; contests British attitude to slave trade, 23; party system, 131; and the 'Westminster model', 145; secession from West Indies Federation, 177; and the Second Chamber, 185; constitution, 216, 217, 219; parliamentary government, 256

Jagan, Cheddi (British Guiana), 132

Japan as copyist of other countries' constitutions, 190, 191
Jersey (Channel Islands), 77, 86
Jinnah, Mohammed Ali (Pakistan), 114, 115
judges
  dismissal of, in Ghana, 95, 96; immunity from criticism in India and Malaysia, 217
jury system, 89

Kaunda, Kenneth (Zambia), 130, 136
Kenya
  party system in, 125-7; as a one-party state, 136, 186; problem of the Executive and civil servants, 155; and the Second Chamber, 173, 185; bi-cameralism, 181-2, 185; presidential system, and presidential elections, 210-11, 221; constitution, 217, 222, 224
Kenyatta, Jomo (Kenya), 125, 126
King, William L. Mackenzie (Canada), 104
Ku Klux Klan (USA), 202-3

Latin America, presidential system in, 190
laws, history and revision of the drafting of, 38-58
Leader of the Opposition, status of the, 219-20
Legislature, the
  in 'old colonial' system, 14; dangers of delegated legislation, 100; method of, 100-1; similarities between Britain and Commonwealth countries, 102; constitutional provisions for, 214 ff.; and the Executive, 92-3, 214-15, 220 ff.
Liberia
  presidential system in, 191; attempts to avoid one-party government in, 205; experiment in uniting tribes and ruling class, 206
Life peerages (UK), 187-8
Lyons, J. A. (Australia), 107

Macaulay, Lord, on drafting of laws, 51
Malawi
  party system in, 130-1; as a future one-party state, 131; unicameral system, 167; constitution, 210, 212, 215
Malaya
  party system in, 133; Federation's Constitutional Commission (1957), 175-6: *see also* Malaysia
Malaysia
  and the Second Chamber, 173, 175-6, 185; judges' immunity from criticism in, 217: *see also* Malaya
Malta
  unicameral system in, 167; and Roman Catholic Church, 209; constitution, 216, 217, 219
Massey, William Ferguson (New Zealand), 109
Matrimonial Causes Act (1937), importance of the, 99
Mauritius
  British acquisition of, 22; party system in, 133; parliamentary government in, 256-7, 259, 262
May, Erskine, on parliamentary procedure, 60, 92, 100, 218, 228, 251
Mboya, Tom (Kenya), 125
members of parliament
  comparisons of position of, in Britain and overseas, 81; remuneration, prizes and perquisites, 84-5; increased work and hours of, in Britain, 86-7; qualifications and election of, 88-9; rights and privileges, of 91-3: *see also* Private Members' Bills; Questions
Menzies, Robert G. (Australia), 107, 108
Merchant Shipping Act (1854), 41
minorities in Commonwealth countries
  British attitude to, 145; precarious position of, in Africa, 148-9; protection of, 167, 198
Model Bills: *see* Uniformity of Legislation

nation-states, newly-founded
  problems following independence in, 143 ff.; in Africa, 154-65
necessity, doctrine of: in discarding of constitutions, 211
Négritude, 202

Nehru, Jawaharlal (India), 114, 115, 174
Nehru, Pandit Motilal (India), 112
New Zealand
    Dominion status, 14–15; representative government in, 25; responsible government in, 26; the franchise, 88; MPs' remuneration, rights and privileges, 85, 94; self-government granted to, 108; party system, 108–10; and the 'Westminster model', 145; abolition of the Second Chamber, 167–8
Newfoundland
    status of, 14–15; responsible government in, 26; and federation, 27
Nigeria, 37; as a federation, 81; legislature's privileges and immunities, 93–4; party system, 120–2; bi-cameral system, 173, 185; under new Federation, 177–9; position of Chiefs in, 179; constitution, 37 *n*, 216, 219–21, 223
Nkrumah, Kwame (Ghana), 96, 123, 124: *see also* Ghana; Gold Coast
North America, early British colonies in, 13
Northern Ireland, 240
Northern Rhodesia, party system in, 130: *see also* Zambia
Nova Scotia
    representative government in, 25; and responsible government, 26
Nyasaland: *see* Malawi
Nyerere, Julius (Tanzania), 91, 128, 129, 164

'official members' of Legislative Council, 14
'old colonial' system
    meaning of, 13; constitutions under, 13 ff.: *see also under* entries for individual countries
Old Dominions, 25–9; constitutional development in, 36–7; 'conventions' in, 151
one-party rule, 78, 81, 137, 213; in Africa, 37, 90–1, 96, 162; election of MPs under, 89
overseas parliaments
    procedural links with Westminster, 59–61; problems of adapting legislation to Westminster pattern, 61 ff.; the franchise, 87–8

Pakistan
    constitution, 33, 211, 215, 216, 217, 221, 222; party system, 116–18, 138; unicameral legislature, 167
Parliament
    relationship with Civil Service and the Executive, 150 ff.; and the courts, 229–45; British system and small territories, 246–63
party system
    in British constitution 103 ff.; in Commonwealth countries, 104–41; importance of, to party organization in Africa, 163–5: *see also under* entries for individual countries
Peel, Sir Robert, and revision of drafting of laws, 44
presidential system, 78, 81; in Africa, 191–209 *passim*; Egypt, 192; France, 191–3 *passim*, 195; Latin America, 190; USA, 190, 193–207 *passim*
prisons in Crown Colonies, 23–4
Private Bills, 50, 51 *n*
Private Members' Bills, 50, 91, 99–100
professionalism in parliament: *see* career politicians
Public Service Commissions (Africa), 158

Quebec Act (1774), 21–2
Questions, Members'
    procedure, 74–5; as safeguard of liberty, 97–8

'representative government' and 'old colonial' system, 13–14, 24–5
'responsible government' in 'old colonial' system, 14, 15; failure of, 24; colonies' demands for, 26
retrospective legislation, 234–5
Rhodesia, party system in, 130: *see also* Southern Rhodesia

St Helena, 22
St Kitts, election system in, 24
St Lucia, British acquisition of, 22

Second Chamber, the
   attitude to establishment of, in Commonwealth parliaments, 166 ff.; and the House of Lords, 186–8; weakness of system as an export, 189
Senegal
   British acquisition of, 22; and Gambia, 259–61: *see also* Senegambia
Senegambia, as first Crown Colony, 22 n, 252, 253: *see also* Gambia; Senegal
separation of powers, 247–8
Seychelles, British acquisition of, 22
Sierra Leone, unicameral system in, 167
Singapore
   party system in, 133; unicameral system in, 167; constitution, 212
slaves
   and the franchise, 13, 24; colonies contest with British government over, 22–3
small territories, parliaments in, 246–63
Smith, Ian (Rhodesia), 130
South Africa
   and Dominion status, 14–15; representative government introduced in, 25; responsible government in, 26; establishment of Union of, 27
Southern Rhodesia, 26, 27: *see also* Rhodesia
sovereign's rights under 'old colonial' system, 13–14
Standing Orders, Westminster and Commonwealth procedures under, 60 ff., 217–18
State Government and Central Government, relations between, 81–2
Statute Law Committee, 46–7
Statute Law Revision Acts, 45
Statutes, interpretation of, 238–45
Stephen, Sir James Fitzjames, as critic of law-drafting, 41–2, 47, 55
Swaziland, party system in, 131
Symonds, John Addington, and revision in drafting of laws, 41–2, 43, 46, 51, 53

Tanganyika
   as one-party state, 91, 129; party system in, 128–9, 136; the Executive in, 155: *see also* Tanzania
Tanzania, 129; unicameral system in, 167; and Standing Committees in National Assembly, 218; constitution, 210, 215, 222, 226: *see also* Tanganyika; Zanzibar
Thring, Henry (later Lord), on draftting of laws, 38–42, 44, 46, 51, 53, 56–8 *passim*
Tobago: *see* Trinidad and Tobago
trade, colonies resentment of restrictions in, 20
trade unions in Africa, 156
tribal system, 149–50, 160–1
Trinidad and Tobago
   British acquisition of, 22; registration of slaves in, 23; party system in, 131; and the 'Westminster model', 145; and the Second Chamber, 173, 185; secession from West Indies Federation, 177; constitution, 215, 217, 219

Uganda
   party system in, 127–8; unicameral system in, 167; constitution, 219
unicameral system in Commonwealth legislatures, 166–8, 177: *see also* Second Chamber; *and under* entries for individual countries
Uniformity of Legislation, in USA and the Commonwealth, 48–50
United Kingdom
   parliament as model for overseas territories, 59–79; powers of front bench *v.* back bench, 84; the Franchise, 87; and the electorate, 89; party system, 134, 137, 139; unwritten constitution of, 212
Uruguay and British parliamentary system, 190
USA
   and uniformity of legislation, 48–9, 50; and drafting of laws, 54–5; differences between UK and USA on civil liberties, 98–9; party system, 198–9; presidential system, 190, 193–207 *passim*; no party-monopoly of important offices in,

199; role of English common law in unification of, 201; increase in civil servants, 200

West Indies
under 'old colonial' system, 13–15; Prisons Act (1838), 23; party system in, 131; and the 'Westminster model', 146; Federation of, 177: *see also* entries for individual countries

Westminster, Statute of (1931) and Dominion status, 14–15

'Westminster model', the
development of, 142–5; as an 'export' to Commonwealth countries, 145 ff.; and the Second Chamber, 185–6; Commonwealth parliamentary privilege geared to, 218: *see also under* entries for individual countries

Zambia, 37; unicameral system in, 167; constitution, 189, 222; presidential elections, 221: *see also* Northern Rhodesia

Zanzibar
union with Tanganyika, 91, 128–9, 210; revolution in, 211

For Product Safety Concerns and Information please contact our EU
representative GPSR@taylorandfrancis.com
Taylor & Francis Verlag GmbH, Kaufingerstraße 24, 80331 München, Germany

www.ingramcontent.com/pod-product-compliance
Lightning Source LLC
Chambersburg PA
CBHW061438300426
44114CB00014B/1736